BENJAMIN B. WOLMAN, author of this book, is Dean of Faculty and Director of Research at the Institute of Applied Psychoanalysis and Professor of Psychology in the Graduate Division, Long Island University. He has practiced psychoanalysis and psychotherapy since 1939. Dr. Wolman is the author of many books, among them *Contemporary Theories and Systems in Psychology* and *Mental Disorders*. He has edited such volumes as *Handbook of Clinical Psychology,* and is associate editor of *American Imago* magazine. He is the author of over one hundred scientific papers and articles.

THE UNCONSCIOUS MIND

The Meaning of Freudian Psychology

THE UNCONSCIOUS MIND
The Meaning of Freudian Psychology

BENJAMIN B. WOLMAN

A SPECTRUM BOOK

Prentice-Hall, Inc., *Englewood Cliffs, N. J.*

Preface

The aim of this book is to give a thorough, systematic, lucid, and objective description of the theory and technique of psychoanalysis as developed by Freud and his disciples.

The literature on Freud can be divided into three categories:

1. Source materials, such as Freud's own writings and personal letters.
2. Biographies written either by disciples and admirers or by adversaries.
3. Summaries and elaborations of Freud's ideas, teachings, and techniques.

The reader who wants to learn what Freud actually did and said during his lifetime (1856-1939) may face considerable difficulties despite the abundance of printed material. Of course, there are the seventeen volumes of the German edition of Freud's works, and many monographs and collective volumes in English (the English Standard Edition is almost complete). There are the three biographical volumes by Jones, and volumes of letters and biographies. Several summaries and elaborations of psychoanalysis were written by Fenichel, Glover, Hendrick, Kubie, and others, who interpreted Freud in the light of their own studies.

This volume is designed to portray the authentic teachings of Freud. It is a volume devoted to Sigmund Freud and psychoanalysis as created, taught, and practiced by him and his loyal disciples. Neither praise nor criticism can do justice to the house Freud built. The reader himself must enter the house and view its architecture and beauty.

This book is planned as a *guide* to psychoanalysis. It opens the gates of the house Freud built to the visitor, inviting him to see this intellectual masterpiece.

The Unconscious Mind is written for the millions who are interested in psychoanalysis. Knowledge of psychoanalysis will broaden the horizons of educated readers and deepen their understanding of human nature. They will find in psychoanalysis an indispensable intellectual tool, a prerequisite for appreciation of certain aspects of contemporary culture, something to read and think about.

In the presentation of the material I have tried to combine scientific precision with a simple language. Technical terms are kept at a minimum. The book is written both as a textbook and as a guide for the intelligent nonprofessional reader. It may serve as a text in university courses in psychology, psychiatry, social work, contemporary civilization, and cultural history.

The book is composed of two parts. The first part deals with psychoanalysis as a psychological theory, the last chapter describing Freud's disciples. The second part delves into the details of psychoanalytic treatment technique; again, the last chapter describes the post-Freudian modifications.

BENJAMIN B. WOLMAN

Contents

PART TWO   The Practice of Psychoanalysis

12   The Early Technique   161

13   Interpretation and Insight   167

14   Transference: The Therapeutic Neurosis   175

15   Resistance: The Fight Against Being Cured   182

16   Working Through and the Final Phase   190

17   Variations and Modifications   195

18   The Psychoanalyst and His Training   215

     References   224

     Index   233

THE UNCONSCIOUS MIND

The Meaning of Freudian Psychology

PART ONE
The Theory of Psychoanalysis

1

Dreams and the Unconscious

Joseph, son of Jacob, the interpreter of the dreams of Pharao, king of the Egyptians, did not dream that thirty-five centuries later another Jew, Sigmund, son of Jacob (Freud) would invent a method of interpreting the dreams of all men, kings and beggars alike.

The art of dream interpretation is probably as old as human dreams, but dreaming is older than humanity. Recent studies proved that even animals dream during the so-called REM (rapid eye movement) periods (Snyder). Experimental research largely confirmed Freud's findings (*Ibid.*). But in 1900, when Freud published the monograph *Traumdeutung* ("The Interpretation of Dreams"), his ideas came as a revelation to some and a shock to others. Only six hundred copies of the book were printed, and it took eight years for the first edition to be sold. Ten years later the book won some recognition and the second edition came out. The first edition brought Freud $209 in income, but during his lifetime there were seven other editions and eight translations.

Although today Freud's theory of dreams and the unconscious is almost generally accepted, at the turn of the century the situation was entirely different. Psychology was a young and pompous science that pretended to know more than it actually did. In the second half of the nineteenth century psychology finally broke away from philosophy. Though the pioneers of modern psychology such as Wundt, Ebbinghaus, Külpe, and Titchener had received philosophical training, they themselves and their disciples were anxious to move their academic

3

chairs from philosophy departments into the halls of science, close to chemistry, physics, and biology. The first psychological laboratory opened by Wundt in Leipzig in 1879, combined experimental method with introspection, that is, observation of one's own feelings and thoughts. The reasons for introspection were self-evident to psychologists at that time, for they believed that all mental processes were "given in an inner experience" and as such, accessible only to the individual who experienced them: "Only the worrying person knows his worries," and "Only the thinking one knows the content of his thoughts."

The unconscious, prior to Freud, was an ill-defined metaphysical concept. Several authors used the term in a variety of connotations, but no one really understood it. To Freud the unconscious was not an abstract term or a logical category. The unconscious was a matter of fact, a "province" of the human mind, and an undeniable part of human experience. It was quite a while, however, before the idea that some mental processes are unconscious began to appear in psychology textbooks.

At the crossroads of centuries, the notion of the unconscious was believed to be a self-contradictory concept. Since psychology was then considered to be the science of the conscious, a psychology that dealt with the unconscious did not make sense at all. Mental processes were, by definition, processes that took place in one's awareness or conscious or consciousness (these three terms are used in this book interchangeably); physical processes could be observed from without, psychological ones being perceivable only from within. There was, therefore, no room in science for something that could be assessed neither by external indications nor by introspection. Of course, psychologists knew of dreams, slips of tongue, and strange cases of forgetting and losses of memory, but they could not understand these processes and preferred to write them off as "unscientific." Split personality phenomena, discontinuities in memory, and one's awareness of himself have been known since ancient times, but they were believed to belong to the domain of magic and the supranatural.

Ultimately psychology was forced to recognize the fact that even unusual phenomena of the human mind could not be dismissed and left to charlatans. When Anton Mesmer purported to demonstrate his theories of "animal magnetism" and "magnetic fluid," official medical science censured him and rightly so. A special committee appointed by the French *Academie des Sciences* and the Faculty of Medicine in Paris concluded that since "the magnetic fluid could not be noticed by any of our senses therefore, such fluid does not exist" (Zilboorg and Henry, p. 245). Mesmer spoke of a "magnetic fluid" that allegedly fills the entire universe. A proper balance of this fluid in the human organism was supposed to bring good health. Mesmer maintained that he was restoring this magnetic equilibrium by touching his patients.

Of course, no such form of magnetism exists, but a British surgeon, James Braid, accepted the idea of influencing people's minds in a manner patterned after Mesmer. This new method was called *hypnotism*. In 1864, the French physician Liebeault wrote a book about the influence of "moral factors" upon the human body and described his treatment methods based on hypnotism. In 1882, the neurologist Jean Martin Charcot reported to the French *Academie des Sciences* far-reaching changes induced in hysterical patients, under hypnosis.

Freud became acquainted with the hypnotic treatment of hysterics at the Salpêtrière clinic in 1885. Charcot produced and removed hysterical symptoms by hypnotic suggestion. Charcot believed that psychogenic disturbances are a byproduct of organic factors possibly related to heredity.

More or less at the same time, Pierre Janet in France developed a new theory of mental disorder. Although Janet linked mental disorder to heredity and, like the Italian scientist, Cesare Lombroso, saw in mental disease some "degeneration," his theory dealt with a nonorganic "automatism" that he called "unconscious."

In 1889 Freud went to the Nancy-School and witnessed experiments in hypnotism conducted by H. M. Bernheim. The hypnotized subjects experienced hallucinations, but could not recall them when they woke up. When Bernheim urged the subjects, assuring them that they could recall, the subjects actually recalled everything.

Bernheim's experiments convinced Freud that people may not "know" what they *actually* know. Certain parts of one's mental life are concealed and not accessible to the consciousness. Bernheim's work proved that people are not always aware of what they are doing and quite often they are capable of making unconscious decisions. The traditional theory of will and willpower was finally discredited, and the rationality of human behavior put under a question mark.

Hypnotism opened the door for the study of the unconscious mind.

THE UNCONSCIOUS

The idea of the unconscious or unconsciousness was not a new idea. Prior to Freud, philosophers and thinkers wrote about the unconscious, and many of them antedated Freud in the discovery of unconscious mental life (Whyte, 1960). But academic psychologists in Freud's times (and even today) frowned on the idea of studying invisible phenomena, and doubted their existence.

Freud refused to accept the idea that what is inaccessible to our means of observation does not exist. In his search into the unobservable areas, Freud followed in the footsteps of all great discoverers, such as Newton, Darwin and Pasteur. The fact that we haven't had direct contact with something, and we don't know how to find it, does not necessarily mean that what is unknown to us does not exist. America existed before Columbus, the earth rotated before Copernicus, and germs existed before Pasteur. Recent Soviet studies in interoceptive conditioning proved beyond doubt that people may perceive and react without ever being aware of it (Bykov; Wolman, 1964a), but it was Freud who discovered the unconscious phenomena and incorporated them in his scientific system.

Freud's main contribution to the idea of the unconscious relates to a *topographic* concept of the human mind, and to the evidence that he adduced. According to Freud, the unconscious is not merely a way people have of experiencing mental phenomena, but sort of a province or layer of the human mind. Freud suggested the division of the mind into three strata, the lowest being the unconscious (Ucs), the middle, the preconscious (Pcs), and the upper, the conscious (Cs).

Freud never accepted his own findings uncritically and was fully aware of the hypothetical nature of his ideas. With regard to one area, however, he was absolutely sure that he dealt with indisputably empirical facts. This area was the unconscious. Freud believed that the unconscious is not a hypothesis but a fact, a fact that can be proven.

Freud produced five kinds of evidence: amnesias and split personality, dream interpretation, psychopathology of daily life, symptom-formation, and the processes of resistance and transference in psycho-analytic treatment.

But before discussing the five proofs of Freud's concept of the unconscious, let us follow Freud's explanation of the concept itself. This part of Freud's theory is called *topography,* for it deals with the layers of the human mind (Freud, 1900; 1901; 1911; 1915b).

According to Freud, even neonates perceive and react to pain and pleasure. Though these sensations and responses are believed to leave memory traces, they are unconscious. The unconscious, viewed as a layer, stores past memories. The memories of early childhood experiences are inaccessible except in dreams, in hypnosis, and psycho-analytic treatment that brings the unconscious to the surface. Many childhood wishes are unrealizable, yet they do survive in the unconscious. Stimuli coming from within and without are dimly perceived by the infant's mind, but they are unconscious and uncommunicable. It is impossible to observe directly the deep and preverbal layers of the human mind; what Freud discovered was an indirect access to the unconscious. Freud studied the *observable* phenomena of dreams, free association, slips of tongue, and the symptoms of mental disorder, and traced therefrom the hidden forces of the great mental province of the unconscious.

In accordance with the homeostatic principle, Freud believed that the infant's mind avoids overstimulation. Falling asleep leads, as it were, to a disconnecting of the outer world. The infant wakes up under pressure of disturbing stimuli such as hunger, bowel or bladder discomforts, pain, loud noises, and so on. As soon as the infant can get rid of the stimuli, he shuts out the outer world and falls asleep again.

In the waking state, the infant hallucinates rather than perceives, dreams rather than sees. But the external stimuli do not permit the perpetuation of the equilibrium of relief and sleep. Tension-provoking stimuli force themselves upon the infant and make him perceive them. The infant has no alternative but to cope with them and try to master them. This is probably the origin of the realistic perception of the outer world. This is also the way that the conscious gradually emerges out of the unconscious. Tension and frustration lead to the development of the conscious perception of reality.

The development of the conscious depends on the infant's ability to utilize his past memories. Then memory accumulates, as it were, on the "surface" of the unconscious; it is more accessible than the deeper layers of the unconscious, and it may become conscious. This part of the unconscious that easily turns conscious is called the preconscious.

The unconscious is therefore divided into two parts, the preconscious (Pcs) and the unconscious proper (Ucs). The preconscious processes may become conscious either spontaneously or by a conscious effort. They are like conveniently stored goods: while not on display, they are easily accessible. Conscious is actually conscious for a short while only, and can easily submerge into preconscious and unconscious. The preconscious can become conscious "without any activity on our part." It is temporarily unconscious. One could say that the preconscious is what is *in* our mind but not right then *on* our mind. Freud put it as follows:

> Thus there are two kinds of unconscious, which have not yet been distinguished by psychologists. Both of them are unconscious in the sense used by psychology; but in our sense one of them, which we term the Ucs, is also *inadmissible to consciousness,* while we term the other Pcs because its excitations—after observing certain rules, it is true, and perhaps only after passing a fresh censorship, though nonetheless without regard to the Ucs—are able to reach consciousness (1900, pp. 614-615).

Usually people are aware of only a small fraction of their mental processes at a given time. The content of conscious or consciousness is a product of a selective process. What is unconscious may become preconscious and eventually conscious; only a part, however, ever becomes conscious. Some impulses and perceptions may become preconscious or conscious for a while and then be pushed down into the unconscious.

Dynamics of the Unconscious

Following in J. F. Herbart's footsteps, Freud ascribed to the conscious and unconscious dynamic properties (Wolman, 1967b). The unconscious energy is free floating, unbound, moving on without a definite goal. The unconscious, *primary* energy does not serve survival, for its actions are not reality-directed.

The conscious, *secondary* energy is bound, goal-directed, and geared toward the purpose of self-protection and survival. In the preconscious, primary and secondary processes mingle. Some analysts believe that the creative inspiration of writers, artists, and scientists starts in the preconscious (cf. Kris, 1950).

In Freud's words:

All that I insist upon is the idea that the activity of the *first* system is directed towards securing the *free discharge* of the quantities of excitation, while the *second* system, by means of the cathexes emanating from it, succeeds in *inhibiting* this discharge and in transforming the cathexis into a quiescent one, no doubt with a simultaneous raising of its potential. . . . The second system succeeds in retaining the major part of its cathexes of energy in a state of quiescence and in employing only a small part on displacement. . . . When once the second system has concluded its exploratory thought-activity, it releases the inhibition and damming-up of the excitations and allows them to discharge themselves in movement. . . . The second system cathects memories in such a way that there is an inhibition of their discharge, including, therefore, an inhibition of discharge (comparable to that of a motor innervation) in the direction of the development of unpleasure. . . . It would be an unnecessary expenditure of energy if [the second system] sent out large quantities of cathexis along the various paths of thought and thus caused them to drain away to no useful purpose and diminish the quantity available for altering the external world (1900, pp. 599-601).

In Herbart's system, perceptions (*Vorstellungen*) were the indivisible elements of mental life. These elements, however, were viewed by Herbart both as units of energy and as psychological concepts of perception. Thus, in Herbart's system, a "brighter"—a more precise—perception "pushes" itself up in the consciousness as if the perception were a physical dynamic unit.

Something similar to Herbart's *Vorstellungen* was conveyed in Freud's early work. In his "Project for a Scientific Psychology," primary processes indicate the urge for an immediate action, come what may (Freud, 1954). When an infant wants something, he must get it right away. This urgency was called by Freud the "pleasure principle." Pleasure in this context is rather a poor translation of the German *Lust;* the pleasure principle should be called, rather, the principle of lust, of urge (cf. Freud, 1887-1902; Holt, 1962; Pribram 1962).

Very much on Herbartian lines, Freud made the need for an immediate gratification isomorphic, if not identical, with the need for a physical discharge of energy. As will be explained below in connection with the interpretation of dreams, Freud's primary processes are full of symbolization, condensation, displacement, and fusion in their *meaning*. At the same time, the primary, that is, the unconscious processes are characterized by a high tension of unbound energy that presses for immediate discharge. The conceptual irrational content of primary processes was fused by Freud with their dynamic property— their action parallels that of a bursting volcano.

The conscious, secondary processes are conceptually, rational, goal-directed, logical and reality-oriented. Mature and normal individuals perceive things as they are and comprehend them in a rational way. All these are secondary processes. On the dynamic side, the secondary processes reflect quiescent energy, controlled action, and delay in the discharge of energy dictated by survival considerations. The ability of delaying, controlling, and anticipating future results was called by Freud the "reality principle." Both the pleasure and the reality principles will be explained in detail in connection with the id and ego theories (Freud, 1915b; Hartmann, 1939).

In the later development of his psychological theory, Freud transferred the dynamic concepts of energy to libido and its destructive counterpart, located in the id; and the control apparatus was conceptualized as ego and superego. Some psychoanalytic thinkers question the necessity of the topographic "provinces" (Arlow and Brenner, 1964; Gill, 1963). Freud himself viewed the terms conscious, preconscious, and unconscious not as dynamic forces in personality, but, as the "mental provinces." They are "topographic" concepts indicating the "depth" of the mental processes. The surface processes that we are aware of are conscious; what we are unaware of, but what we may easily become aware of is preconscious; what we cannot become aware of without the unraveling efforts of free associations, or hypnotic or psychoanalytic procedures (or what we cannot become aware of at all) is unconscious.

Most unconscious processes were never conscious, but some of them became conscious for a while and were pushed back. Some are thrown back before they ever reach the conscious.

Some unconscious processes are always unconscious; some appear temporarily on the conscious surface. Freud distinguished between the conscious rejection of an impulse, often called suppression, and repression proper. In suppression, the energy put at the disposal of the impulse that is seeking to "convert itself into action" has been withdrawn; the impulse has lost the load of energy attached to it and has become, as it were, powerless. It survives in our mind as a mere memory.

Repression is a "vehement effort" that has been exerted to prevent a given mental process from penetrating into the conscious as a result of which the process has remained unconscious. Repression is an act by which a mental act is either prevented from entering into preconscious and forced back into unconscious; the term also describes an act by which a mental system belonging to preconscious is thrown into unconscious. Repression is a concept that combines "topography" and "dynamics."

Amnesia and Split Personality

The fact of forgetting can be explained in Pavlovian terms as extinction; whatever has been conditioned may become unconditioned unless it is reinforced (Pavlov, pp. 55 ff.). But how can one explain the fact of complete loss of memory that includes well-known and otherwise well-remembered facts? How can one account for the strange cases of forgetting one's own name, address, and occupation in a shell-shock traumatic neurosis?

When the loss of memory disrupts the continuity of awareness of oneself, one becomes a so-called "split personality." Freud described a case of hysterical dissociation from oneself; other authors registered this peculiar symptom in schizophrenic, epileptic, and other patients.

The most intriguing aspect of amnesia is, however, not the loss of memory, but its recovery. Where did the hidden memories go and how could they reappear after a substantial lapse of time? Since memories of the past can come back, apparently they are not completely lost. Most adults have long forgotten their early childhood; yet they recall it under hypnosis and in psychoanalysis. Sometimes people experience spontaneous recalls of past events.

Where had the lost memory hidden? Freud's answer was simple: in the unconscious. The unconscious is not a hypothesis; it is a fact. The recall of forgotten material shows that what was forgotten was not completely lost, but just stored away. The name of this storage house is the unconscious. When one loses his identity and regains it, whether spontaneously or in hypnotic or psychoanalytic treatment, his dissociation is unconscious; his past experiences are buried there and are brought to the surface in the process of regaining of self-awareness.

Often people forget significant events and recall inconsequential childhood occurrences. In the process of psychoanalytic treatment it becomes evident that irrelevant memories substitute for some really significant impressions, whose direct reproduction is prevented. Unimportant events are recalled not because of their own contents, but because of their association with important but repressed thoughts; thus they should be called "concealing memories."

Sometimes these concealing memories belong to the first years of childhood, while the thoughts represented by them that remain unconscious may belong to a later period of life. Freud called this phenomenon retroactive or regressive displacement. Often an irrelevant impression from earliest childhood is associated with an even earlier experience that cannot be recalled. In such a case the concealing memories are called encroaching or interposing memories. Finally, the concealing memories may be connected by simple temporary contiguity with the impression they try to conceal. This type of concealing memory is called the contemporaneous or contiguous. In all these cases, what was concealed was concealed in the layer (or province) of the unconscious.

Dreams

Dreaming is the main area in which the unconscious manifests itself and thus becomes accessible to research. Dreams occur in sleep, and sleep was viewed by Freud as a turning away from the outside world. Our relationship with the world which we entered so unwillingly at birth seems to be endurable only with intermission,

> hence we withdraw again periodically into the condition prior to our entrance into the world; that is to say, into intra-uterine existence. At any rate, we try to bring about quite similar conditions—warmth, darkness and absence of stimulus—characteristic of that state. Some of us still roll ourselves tightly up into a ball resembling the intra-uterine position.
>
> [A dream] may be coherent, smoothly composed, like a literary work, or unintelligibly confused, almost like a delirium; it may have

absurd elements, or jokes and apparently brilliant inferences; it may seem clear and well defined to the dreamer, or it may be dim and indefinite; the pictures in it may have the full sensuous force of a perception, or they may be as shadowy and vague as a mist . . . (Freud, 1932, pp. 79, 20).

One may wake up from a dream full of hope and joy, the heart beating faster expecting good things to come. One may wake up in a confused and perplexed mood, full of doubts, anxieties, and worries. One may fear to raise his head after a dream of crime, death, and horror. One may wake up in a desperate scream dreaming about a Frankenstein monster. One may not wish to get up after a dream that has made one feel guilty.

With rare exceptions even highly unpleasant dreams do not wake us up. Dreaming seems to protect sleep.

Dreams are a reaction of the mind to external or internal stimuli that act upon the organism in sleep. In dreams the individual attributes objective reality to the imagery that forms the material of his dreams. "A dream, then, is a psychosis with all the absurdities, delusions and illusions of a psychosis," said Freud.

Sleep is a willed and temporary withdrawal from the external world and a regression to the state of mind that preceded the development of the conscious. Dreaming is a compromise between the inner or outer disturbance of sleep and the desire to sleep. The sleeper "dreams away," as it were, the disturbance and continues to sleep. Dreams usually reflect wishes stemming from the unconscious; these wishes are repressed demands for instinctual gratification. Often these demands contain residues of the day's activities in the waking state, and are related to a decision that has to be made or to a conflict to be resolved. The dreams of one night usually represent one continuous context and each of them is a logical part of the total story.

These unconscious demands are pressures coming up against the conscious part of personality, the part that represses the unconscious wishes. In "The Interpretation of Dreams," the conscious acted as a *censor,* preventing the unconscious from becoming conscious. "The censorship between the Ucs and the Pcs, the assumption of whose existence is positively forced upon us by dreams, deserves to be recognized and respected as the watchman of our mental health" (1900, p. 567). An additional censorship is established between the Pcs and the Cs: "The transition from a preconscious to a conscious cathexis is marked by a censorship similar to that between the Ucs and the Pcs" (*Ibid.,* p. 617).

In 1912 Freud classified some of his ideas on the nature of the unconscious. He wrote: "The term *unconscious,* which was used in the purely descriptive sense before, now comes to imply something more. It designates not only latent ideas in general, but especially ideas with a certain dynamic character, ideas keeping apart from consciousness in spite of their intensity and activity" (Freud, 1912c, p. 262). And further on: "Every psychical act begins as an unconscious one, and it may either remain so or go on developing into consciousness, according as it meets with resistance or not" (*Ibid.,* p. 269).

But already in 1915, Freud realized that the censoring force is not necessarily conscious, and that the repressing force may be itself unconscious. He wrote:

> The reason for all these difficulties is that the attribute of being conscious . . . is in no way suited to serve as a criterion for the differentiation of systems. . . . [Thus] not only the psychically repressed . . . remains alien to the consciousness, but also something . . . that forms the strongest functional antithesis to the repressed (Freud, 1915b, pp. 192-193; see also, Gill).

In "The Interpretation of Dreams" Freud assumed that the unconscious was the dynamic force of hidden desires, while the conscious censored such wishes and worked to prevent them from coming true. A dream is a compromise: through dream-work, the unconscious, forbidden wish becomes disguised and is, as such, allowed to appear as a manifest dream. The censoring force repressed the forbidden wish, and the only way the wish could come through was in dreams, errors, and neurotic symptoms. When an individual presented himself for psychoanalysis, he was expected to cooperate in the removal of repressions. After all that was what he had come for.

However, Freud soon discovered that all patients displayed *resistance* (to be discussed later). Obviously resistance was a continuation of repression; moreover, the patient could not willfully break his resistance. Equally obviously, the censoring force that caused repression and resistance was *unconscious.*

At a later stage of his work (1923), Freud transferred the censorship to the ego (see Chapter Five). He stated clearly that resistance "in the ego itself which is also unconscious . . . behaves exactly like the repressed" (1923b, p. 171). The ego controls the unconscious impulses. In dreams the ego holds in check the forbidden wishes "by what appears to be an act of compliance: it meets the demand with what is in the circumstances the innocent fulfillment of a wish and thus disposes of the demand. This replacement of a demand by the fulfillment of a wish remains the essential function of dream-work" (Freud, 1938, p. 55).

The unconscious wish was called by Freud *latent dream thoughts*. The story reported by the dreamer, that is, the dream itself, was called *manifest dream content*. Freud wrote about a physician who was supposed to be in a hospital very early. The physician was tired and he dreamed that he was in the hospital as a patient who does not have to get up early in the morning. This was the manifest dream. The latent thought was the wish not to go to the hospital. The sleep was protected by means of the *dream-work* that transformed the unconscious wish into the manifest dream content of being already in the hospital as a patient.

Dreams reflect hidden wishes that cannot be accepted in the conscious, waking state. Every dream is an attempt to protect sleep and "to put aside a disturbance of sleep by means of a wish-fulfillment." This wish-fulfillment of a repressed impulse is toned down because the path to motor discharge is closed in the sleep. The repressed impulse that presses toward motor discharge has "to content itself with an hallucinatory satisfaction." The latent dream thoughts are therefore turned into a collection of sensory images and visual scenes. This transformation of a wish into a dream is called dream-work (Freud, 1932, p. 32).

Wish-fulfillment

Through the analysis of his own dreams, Freud arrived at the conclusion that wish-fulfillment is the essence of a dream. Freud dreamt the dream reported below in July 1895. At that time he had been treating a friend of his, Irma, for somatic symptoms related to anxiety hysteria. The treatment had been temporarily discontinued for the summer, Irma having been reluctant to accept Freud's interpretation. The day preceding the dream Freud asked a friend, Otto, how Irma was doing. "She is better, but not quite well," Otto replied. Freud sensed a note of reproach. The same evening, in an apparent effort to justify himself, Freud prepared the case history of Irma to present to Dr. M., a mutual friend. At night Freud dreamt the following dream:

A great hall—a number of guests, whom we are receiving—among them Irma, whom I immediately take aside, as though to answer her letter, and to reproach her for not yet accepting my "solution." I say to her: "If you still have pains, it is really only your own fault." . . . She answers: "If you only knew what pains I have now in the throat, stomach, and abdomen—I am choked by them!" I am startled, and look at her. She looks pale and puffy. I think that after all I must be overlooking some organic affection. I take her to the window and look into her throat. She offers some resistance to this, like a woman who has a set of false teeth. I think, surely, she doesn't need them.—The mouth then opens wide, and I find a large white spot on the right, and elsewhere I see extensive grayish-white scabs adhering to curiously curled formations, which are evidently shaped like the turbinal bones of the nose.—I quickly call Dr. M., who repeats the examination and confirms it . . . Dr. M. looks quite unlike his usual self; he is very pale, he limps, and his chin is clean-shaven. . . . Now my friend Otto, too, is standing beside her, and my friend Leopold percusses her covered chest, and says: "She has a dullness below, on the left," and also calls attention to an infiltrated portion of skin on the left shoulder which I can feel in spite of the dress. . . . M. says: "There's no doubt that it's an infection, but it doesn't matter; dysentery will follow and the poison will be eliminated." . . . We know, too precisely, how the infection originated. My friend Otto, not long ago, gave her, when she was feeling unwell, an injection of a preparation of propyl . . . propyls . . . propionic acid . . . trimethylin (the formula of which I see before me, printed in heavy type). . . . One doesn't give such an injection so rashly. . . . Probably, too, the syringe was not clean (Freud, 1900).

By a careful analysis through free association of the "Irma Injection" dream, Freud noticed that the dream had actually fulfilled some of his own wishes. In the dream Freud had not been responsible for Irma's pain, because the pain was organic. Furthermore, Freud had taken revenge on Otto, and had accused Otto of careless medical treatment (the unclean injection), also comparing Otto with his colleague Leopold. In the dream Freud had even taken revenge on Irma by making her look "pale and puffy." Dr. M., who also disagreed with Freud's interpretation offered to Irma, was made to appear ignorant in the same dream. Freud had also been on bad terms with his older brother who had recently rejected the former's advice. In the dream Dr. M. had resembled Freud's brother.

"Irma's Injection" demonstrates some aspects of the concepts of manifest dream content and latent dream thoughts. In some cases the manifest dream element may be only a fragment or an illusion substituted for the total latent thought. In others the manifest dream may be not so much a distortion of the latent thoughts as a representation, using concrete imagery, of words remotely related to the latent thoughts. Some dreams reflect abstract thoughts that are substituted in the manifest dream by images that conceal or even contradict the latent thoughts. In some other dreams, the latent thoughts may appear unaltered, or even intensified, in the manifest dream.

The dreams of children demonstrate less distortion than those of adults, for their superegos are weaker. Freud reported a dream of his daughter after she had crossed the Aussee by boat. The trip was too quick an experience for her, and at night she dreamt that she went sailing on a lake. This dream, like children's dreams, shows that the dream thoughts are usually related to recent experiences, are meaningful, and fulfill a wish.

The dreams of all people, adults and children alike, convey unfulfilled wishes. The dream is a means of removing, "by hallucinatory experience, the mental stimuli which disturb sleep" (Freud, 1900, p. 409).

Dreams stimulated by physical needs are usually less disguised and the wish-fulfillment is more transparent. Freud could invariably expect a certain type of dream by consuming large quantities of salted food just before going to bed. He would become thirsty while asleep, and just before awakening he would have a dream in which he was drinking water. Such dreams are labeled by him "Dreams of Convenience." They fulfill a wish by attempting to provide the dreamer's need without waking him up.

One of Freud's patients dreamt that her husband suggested the tuning of their piano. The patient replied, "It is not worthwhile, for the hammers would have to be rebuffed as well." In free association, the patient called the piano "a disgusting old box" with a "bad tone." The

patient recalled that the previous day she had called on her girl friend.
When the hostess invited her to take off her coat, the patient replied,
"Thanks, but it isn't worthwhile." During her psychoanalytic session,
the patient took hold of her undone coat, as if saying, "Please don't
look, it isn't worthwhile." Free associations disclosed that box stood for
chest, and the patient recalled her adolescence when she was dissatisfied
with her own figure. Then the associations led further back to the anal
stage when "disgusting" and "bad tone" were connected with the frequent allusion to the two small parts of the chest and the two parts of
the buttocks.

Dream-Work and Symbolism

Analysis of dreams enabled Freud to discover the laws that govern
the "primary" unconscious processes and to find the differences between them and the "secondary" conscious processes. In primary processes the thought elements that are kept apart in the waking state are
condensated into larger units. A single element of the manifest dream
may stand for a whole conglomeration of unconscious, latent dream
thoughts. A short manifest dream content is usually an *allusion* to a
variety of unconscious thoughts.

In the waking state, instinctual energies are bound and cathected in
definite objects. In dreams those cathexes or mental energy loads drift
and shift easily from one object to another. In some dreams significant
issues are barely mentioned, or represented by trivia, or perhaps only
alluded to in the manifest dream content, while unimportant unconscious elements may be represented in the manifest dream in a very
clear manner. This process of the dream-work is called *displacement*.

The unconscious uses its own prelogical language. It is the irrational
language in which contradictory elements do not exclude one another.
Yes and no statements, true and false propositions, reality and imagination are brought together in a complete disregard for truth, logic, and
consistency.

The process of *secondary elaboration* in dreams puts nonrelated elements together and represents them as a whole. An idea may be represented by its opposite, and a causal relation may be substituted by a
coincidental sequence in time. Quite often the manifest dream goes

contrary to the wish, as if saying, "If only things could be the other way around." This distortion Freud called *inversion*.

Not only inversion of content, but inversion of time sequence as well can take place in a dream to fulfill the dreamer's wishes. Inversion can also be seen in the many words that have multiple, contradictory meanings, e.g., the Latin word *altus,* which means both high and deep.

The dream-work has certain definite limitations. It cannot create conversation, for any conversation included in the dream is usually that which has been recently heard; it cannot also confer judgment, or register surprise. The critical powers and the power of deductive reasoning are suspended in the dream-work. They are the province of the conscious, and after 1923, when Freud wrote *The Ego and the Id* (1923b), the prerogative of the ego.

The dream-work takes the dreamer back to the primitive era of intellectual development in which the individual's early childhood and the childhood of mankind are represented. Freud explained the regressive aspects of dreams by stating that our perceptions leave *memory traces* in the unconscious mind. In the waking hours, the censorship systems are too active to allow the preconscious to bring these repressed memories into the conscious. Yet in sleep, the memories gain access to the conscious through a regression from a complex ideation into the primary, raw material of the underlying memory traces. Since the mental energy has no outlet in any physical motion during sleep, it takes an active part in pushing the unconscious thoughts toward the conscious, providing the impetus upon which the dream-work makes the unconscious material palatable for the conscious. Here, again, Freud followed Herbart's psychological mechanics.

According to Freud the hallucinations of the paranoiac or hysteric corresponded to the regression present in the dream world of normal individuals. These hallucinations carry emotionally charged unconscious infantile memories. Almost no one remembers anything from his first five years of life, except for a few seemingly insignificant memories. (For instance, a man whom Freud's mother identified as the physician who took care of the psychoanalyst in infancy appeared in Freud's dreams.) Such "screen memories" seem trivial through the action of condensation and displacement.

The dream-work is particularly fond of representing two contrary

ideas by the same composite structure. Each element in the content of
a dream is *overdetermined* by material in the dream thoughts; it is not
derived from a single element in the dream thoughts, but may be
traced back to a complex aggregate of ideas not necessarily related to
one another. Just as connections lead from each element of the dream
to several other elements, so a single dream thought is usually represented by a variety of dream elements. Condensation, together with
the transformation of thoughts into imaginary actions (*dramatization*),
is one of the most peculiar characteristics of the dream-work.

In some complicated and confused dreams, condensation and dramatization alone are not enough to account for the whole story of the
manifest dream. In the course of the dream-work, the abovementioned phenomenon of displacement takes place, transforming the psychical intensity, the latent thoughts and wishes into sensory experiences. The more obscure and confused a dream appears to be, the
more displacement there was in the dream-work.

The Language of Dreams

The dream-work employs pictorial symbols to give disguised representation to the latent dream wishes. Undisguised wishes could not
pass; the "censor" would repress them. The symbols used in dreams are
a residue of forgotten identity; and symbolism in general is a reflection of an archaic mode of thinking. Conscious ideas are used as symbols to represent in a cryptic fashion an unconscious and objectionable
wish. This primary process of distortion is part of the prelogical thinking, and it uses regressive methods. The ego applies the same repressive
method when it distorts through the use of symbols.

The knowledge of symbolism is based on cultural-historical sources
such as mythology, fairy tales, folklore, folk songs, and so on. In ancient
Hebrew a woman is often described as a house; when she is no longer
a virgin her "door" has been opened. Since the fetus lives in a bag of
water, and mammals are descended from water-inhabiting organisms,
dreaming of water usually symbolizes birth. Dreams of travel often
represent death, the last journey. Little animals and vermin symbolize
siblings and young children in general.

Some symbols are more universal than others. A house symbolizes
the human body. When the house is smooth, it represents a male;

when there are balconies and ledges, it symbolizes a female. Parents usually appear in dreams as kings and queens or other authority figures.

A number of dream components relate to sexual organs and functions. Cupboards, boxes, carriages, ovens, flower pots and vases, receptacles, bags, purses, drawers, jars, doors, and gates are female sexual symbols. Entrances to rooms and stores symbolize female genitals. Watches and clocks symbolize periodical processes and intervals; snails and mussels symbolize women; a diamond symbolizes the open female genitals; chapels and churches usually represent women; apples, peaches, and oranges represent breasts. The number two stands often for the two breasts. Landscapes with rocks, woods, and water represent female organs.

Cloaks, sticks, and hats symbolize men. Weapons such as guns, swords, and knives; poles, pencils, guns, snakes, tree trunks, and hammers symbolize the male sexual organ. A bridge represents the male organ that connects parents during sexual intercourse. A bridge may also indicate birth or death—transition from life to death or womb to birth. Airplanes and balloons symbolize erection. Flying symbolizes sexual arousal. Machinery represents masculine organs. The number three stands for the penis and testicles. Medusa or a spider usually symbolizes the aggressive, phallic mother, and the fear of spiders represents the fear of incest and the abhorrence of female sexual organs.

Sliding, gliding, pulling, and so on may represent masturbation. Ascending stairs, climbing, riding, shooting, dancing, mounting a ladder, rhythmical movements, and some violent motions represent sexual intercourse. Falling out and extraction of teeth symbolizes castration as a punishment for masturbation.

In psychoanalytic treatment, the discovery of the latent dream thoughts reveals unconscious conflicts. The patient is asked to free himself from the impression of the manifest dream and to tell whatever crosses his mind in connection with various parts of the dream. This technique of *free associations* is based on the assumption that if the control apparatus is shut off, the unconscious thoughts and wishes will appear in the free-floating associations, memories, and ideas. Free associations are not a replica of the latent dream thoughts, but some of the latent thoughts will usually come out in the associations.

As previously indicated, dreaming is regressive, and includes early memories retained in the unconscious. Death wishes toward people who did not gratify the primary demands of the infant are also stored in the unconscious. Death wishes might have been directed toward competing siblings, and, in the Oedipal involvement, toward one or sometimes both parents. Early sexual desires, including incest, homosexuality, and any other perversion are part of infantile sexuality (see Chapter Two). As the child grows and matures, normal, adult sexuality develops; however, residues of infantile perversions are often included in the dreams of adults.

All dreams contain rejected or repressed wishes, but some of them also carry vehement inner conflicts. What represents a gratification for the unconscious id may be perceived as a threat to the preconscious or conscious ego. In anxiety dreams, the latent dream thoughts undergo little change, and the instinctual demands are too powerful to be warded off. In a nightmare, the threat to the ego is so great as to disrupt the sleep.

Dream-work results in *dream distortions*. It is a result of a compromise between the unconscious forces that press for a discharge of energy and the opposing forces of the ego, the *dream censor,* that inhibits, restrains, and counteracts these pressures. This dream censor is the same force that represses the unconscious wishes, keeps them repressed, and resists their expression in free associations necessary for dream interpretation in psychoanalytic therapy.

The interpretation of dreams is based on a deterministic assumption that everything has a cause and an effect. This strict determinism is conducive to a thorough investigation of the manifest contest of a dream. As irrational as a dream may sound, it always represents some unconscious processes that the dreamer does not know he knows and, moreover, believes that he does not know.

ERRORS OF EVERYDAY LIFE

Everyone makes mistakes, but repetition of error can hardly be attributed to chance factors, especially when the erroneous behavior is contrary to the conscious wish of the individual. *Slips of the tongue* are a case in point. Often we wish to say one thing and say something different. Freud wrote about many such cases: a soldier who said to a friend: "I wish there were a thousand of our men *mortified* [instead of *fortified*] on that hill, Bill"; a woman who complained that she had an "incurable *infernal* [*internal*] disease; a professor who said in his introductory lecture, "I am not inclined (*geneigt* instead of *geeignet*, that is, fitted) to estimate the merits of my predecessor"; the Speaker of a Parliament who opened a session with the words, "Gentlemen, I declare a *quorum* present and herewith declare the session *closed*" (1938, pp. 31 ff.).

Some people are aware of the inner conflict and sense it before their tongue slips. Some others say that they knew that they had made the slip, but deny that they were aware of it beforehand. Some others not only deny their inner conflict before the slip, but are also unaware of having made the slip.

Slips of the pen may follow the same pattern as slips of the tongue. A writer may make a slip of the pen to let the reader know of something that is on the writer's mind. *Misreading* represents substitution. *Forgetting* of decisions indicates inner opposition or resentment. *Losing or mislaying* objects may be due to an object's having lost its value, being damaged, or representing an unpleasant memory of someone; it may also be an impulse to sacrifice something to fate in order to avert a dreaded loss of something more important. *Forgetting of names* is often related to association of the forgotten name with some unpleasant personality traits of the one who forgot the name.

The motive for forgetting of past experiences reflects an unwillingness to recall something that may evoke painful feelings. In forgetting of resolutions, the conflict that led to the repression of the painful memory becomes tangible. The analysis of these cases points to a strong inner opposition that failed to put an end to the resolution. A similar conflict can be discerned in erroneously carried out actions. The impulse that manifests itself in the disturbances of the actions is frequently a counterimpulse. Quite often one expresses through an erroneous action his unconscious and repressed wishes. The acts of taking the wrong train and getting out at the wrong station illustrate the point.

One finds in the errors of the daily life the same condensations and the same compromise formations (*contaminations*) as in dreams. The situation is much the same, since unconscious thoughts find expression in a disguised fashion. The incongruity, irrationality, and absurdity of the manifest dream correspond to the irrationality of unconscious wishes that express themselves in the errors of everyday life.

FORMATION OF SYMPTOMS

Symptom-formation in mental disorder will be discussed in detail in the second part of this book. It must, however, be briefly described here because it helps to explain the nature of the unconscious. Neurotic symptom-formation is a compromise between the unconscious impulses and the reality-oriented censorship. The symptom represents a fulfillment of an unconscious wish, distorted by the same censoring forces that oppose the fulfillment of the wish. There is a distinct difference between symptom-formation and dream-formation.

The preconscious purpose in dream-formation is merely to preserve sleep and to allow nothing that would disturb it to penetrate consciousness. It does not insist upon confronting the unconscious wish-impulse with a sharp prohibiting "No, on the contrary." It can be more tolerant because a sleeping person is in a less dangerous position; the condition of sleep is enough in itself to prevent the wish from being realized in actuality (Freud, 1915-1917, p. 315).

Like errors and dreams, neurotic symptoms have a hidden meaning; and they are closely connected with traumatic events in the patient's life.

A traumatic experience is one that, within a very short space of time, subjects the mind to such an intense degree of stimulation that assimilation or elaboration of it cannot be effected by normal means, and lasting disturbances in the distribution of the available mental energy result. A vehement effort is exercised to prevent the traumatic and disturbing process from entering into consciousness. The trauma becomes repressed, that is, pushed into the unconscious; and there, as an unconscious conflict, it has the power to develop symptoms.

The main area of repression is related to sexual experiences and wishes. Experienced or imagined sexual traumas are the chief causes of symptoms. The precise cause of a trauma cannot always be ascertained; but the earlier a trauma takes place, the more serious is the damage to the personality. Resolution of hidden, traumatic conflicts is one of the main objectives of the psychoanalytic treatment. Every treatment success adds support to Freud's theory of the unconscious.

Resistance

All patients in the process of psychoanalytic treatment act as if they objected to being cured. Although the patients come for treatment voluntarily, expending time and money, they seem to avoid doing what they are requested to do. Consciously they cooperate with the psychoanalyst; somehow, however, they manage not to follow his instructions, as if opposing the unraveling of the unconscious conflict and the very process of cure.

An entire chapter in the second part of this book is dedicated to resistance. Obviously, resistance is a continuation of repression; the same forces that repress the dangerous impulses keep on repressing, and oppose the discovery of their sources.

Telepathy

Freud's staunch determinism allowed no loopholes in the study of mental phenomena. Whatever exists, Freud maintained, has a cause and an effect, and must not be dismissed. Even wit and jokes did not escape Freud's keen eye; jokes give vent to wishes that could not otherwise be expressed (Freud, 1905a).

Another area usually bypassed by research workers was telepathy— occult phenomena "force themselves" on our attention. Freud took an empirical approach. He wrote: "First, we have to establish whether these processes really occur, and then, but only then, where there is not doubt that these processes really occur, we can set about their explanation" (Freud, 1932, p. 40). Freud objected to too hasty a condemnation of telepathy; the fact that charlatans busy themselves with occult phenomena does not prove that these phenomena do not exist.

Freud cited several instances of telepathic dreams, intuitive knowledge, and transference of thought. There is no doubt that certain individuals have better access to their unconscious than others do, and that such people seem to be somehow aware of their unconscious feelings about others and of the feelings of other people about them. They may, for instance, display unexplainable foresight that is somehow related to anticipation of risks and dangers.

These deep layers of the unconscious require a cautious approach and objective investigation.

2
Sex and Love

At the meeting of the German Association of Neurologists and Psychiatrists in 1910 in Hamburg, Herr Professor Doktor Wilhelm Weygandt, a prominent neurologist and *Geheimer Medizinalrat* lost his temper when Freud's theories were mentioned. The professor clenched the fist, banged at the table, and shouted: "This is not an issue to be discussed at a scientific meeting! This is a matter for police!" (Quoted after Jones, 1953, II, p. 109).

Why police?

Because at that time Dr. Sigmund Freud of Vienna was under a barrage of accusations for writing with unheard of frankness about normal and abnormal sexuality. At the same time, when Freud's disciple and associate, Dr. Sandor Ferenczi, presented Freud's findings to the Budapest Medical Society, he was publicly rebuffed, and told that psychoanalysis was sheer pornography and prison was the right place for Dr. Freud and his followers.

In Freud's times sexuality was a topic to be avoided among educated people. Sex was a dirty word, not to be mentioned in the presence of women and children. The educated classes pretended to believe that sexuality was sort of a necessary evil; if they had the choice, they would prefer to stay away from sex, but the necessity of procreation lent married sexuality the vestige of a sacred act. Sexuality was believed to be vulgar and sacred at the same time.

When people unwillingly participate in embarrassing acts, they try to hide them. Early in the twentieth century, no self-respecting person could have disclosed the secrets of the marital bedroom. Children were told that their new brothers or sisters were brought by storks. Children's questions pertaining to childbirth and human genitals were met with silence and embarrassment, hushed away, or scorned. Whenever parents or educators noticed a child masturbating, they punished him severely and often threatened to cut off his penis. Older boys and girls were told that masturbation leads to insanity.

Children were not supposed to know anything about sex. Adolescent boys and girls had to hide whatever secret and distorted knowledge they had obtained. Many a girl in a "good home" was actually prevented from receiving any sexual information whatsoever prior to marriage: a girl was supposed to wait for a man's love to be presented coated in poetic words, bearing no relation to anything physical. Of course, she was expected to marry and bear her husband's children to promote the family's name and fulfill the good God's mandate to increase and multiply. Small wonder that the hysterical bride who ran away from her husband on the wedding night, seeking mother's protection existed in fact as well as in jokes. Yet, it would be naïve to assume that premarital and extramarital relations did not exist in this Victorian era. Sexual problems, normal and abnormal, are as old as humanity itself; but prudes and bigots the world over frowned at whoever dared to speak about them in a frank and honest way.

Where did Freud get his ideas? From his teachers, his patients, and from his psychoanalysis of himself.

"One day when I was a young house physician," wrote Freud in the essay *On The History of The Psychoanalytic Movement,* "I was walking with Breuer through the town, when a man came up who evidently wished urgently to speak to him. I fell back; as soon as Breuer was free, he told me in his friendly instructive way that this man was the husband of a patient and had brought him some news of her. The wife, he added, was behaving in such an extraordinary way in society that she had been brought to him for treatment as nervous. Then he concluded: "These things are always *'secrets d'alcove.'*" Astonished I asked him . . . and he answered by telling the meaning of the word *Alcove* [marriage by] (1914a).

Several years later, when Freud was lecturing in nervous diseases in the University of Vienna, a colleague, Dr. Chyobak, asked Freud to take care of a patient who suffered anxiety attacks. Dr. Chyobak told Freud that the patient's anxiety was caused by the absolute impotence of her husband. After eighteen years of marriage she was still a virgin. Freud's ideas of normal and abnormal sexuality grew out of his clinical work with patients. Prior to the invention of the psychoanalytic method, Freud used suggestion and hypnosis. Patients recalled their past experiences, and the stories told by them were loaded with sexual reminiscences. Some of these stories were correct reports of events that had actually happened in childhood while others were mere recollections of sexual wishes. In either case, sexual desires dominated the picture of the past and were closely related to the patients' emotional difficulties.

As noted above, the very idea of sexuality was taboo in Freud's times and the discovery of infantile sexuality was shocking to Freud himself. Memories of early childhood are usually skimpy and, unless one lets his thoughts float in free associations, in dreams, or in hypnotic trance, one may have little if any recollection of his early years.

Freud at first gave credence to his patients' stories of alleged traumatic childhood seductions. But soon he discovered that many of these stories were fabricated by the patients, and reflected not the real past but the patients' past wishes. The Oedipal wish colored past memories; and its fulfillment was reported by the patients as if fulfillment had been a real experience (Freud, 1887-1902, pp. 215 ff.).

Freud's patients' reports were reinforced by his own self-analysis. The theory of sexuality evolved partly out of Freud's experience with patients, and mostly through the arduous and danger-fraught process of self-analysis. Freud analyzed his own dreams and discovered sexual attachments in his own childhood. "I have found love of the mother and jealousy of the father in my own case too," he admitted, "and now I believe it to be a general phenomenon of early childhood. . . . The gripping power of Oedipus Rex . . . becomes intelligible" (Freud, 1887-1902).

In 1905, after years of work with mentally disturbed patients, and following completion of his own self-analysis, Freud published in Vienna his famous *Drei Abhandlungen zur Sexualtheorie*. The English translation, called today *Three Essays on the Theory of Sexuality,* was published in 1910 under the title, *Three Contributions to the Psychology of Love.*

Freud's *Three Essays* are based on the biogenetic principle introduced by the biologist Haeckel. According to Haeckel, ontogenesis (the development of the individual) is a recapitulation of phylogenesis (the development of the species). In prenatal life the zygote, and later the embryo and the fetus, go through stages similar to the phylogenetic evolution of organic life from protozoa through infrahuman species to *homo sapiens*. Thus, in the *Three Essays* Freud related the sexual development of the individual to the evolutionary development of the entire species.

Freud's sexual theory hinges on his over-all explanation of the driving forces in man.

MOTIVATION

In trying to understand Freud, one must never forget the man's background in neurology. Freud was for years a research worker in that discipline and he never renounced his monistic belief in the unity of mind and matter. Even when he developed his far-reaching psychological theories, Freud advocated the idea of transition from physical into mental energy; indeed his entire psychological theory is couched in physical terms such as tension, discharge, and thwarting, corresponding to the actions of the nervous tissues.

Newton's physics and Darwin's evolution served as Freud's frame of reference. Inertia was the basic law; bodies were inert unless exposed to forces that caused movement.

The forces acting in the organic nature were called *Triebe,* that is drives, sometimes translated as instinctual drives or instincts. These drives are inherited and are geared toward two main goals: namely, preservation of the individual life and preservation of the species. Until 1914 Freud called the first *ego drives* and the latter *libido drives;* in 1914 Freud introduced the idea of narcissism and modified the theory of instinctual drives.

The self-preservation drives help one to adjust to life. The libido or sexual drives are more impulsive, and it is years before they become (somewhat) subordinated to the reality considerations.

The self-preservation drives are not too flexible. One cannot indefinitely postpone the gratification of hunger or thirst; nor is there much latitude for change in the ways one can satisfy his thirst or hunger—the basic needs such as food, and fluids *must* include oxygen, certain nutritional elements, and water, respectively. Sexual instincts, however, can be altered with regard to the bodily zone, aim, and person with whom one seeks gratification. Sexual drives are full of conflicts, substitutions and deviations, and perversions. Self-preservation drives are clear-cut; sexual drives are much more modifiable.

The modifications in sexual drives are related to aims and objects. Transformation, fusions, and substitutions of instinctual gratifications are frequent and quite apparent. The evidence of analytic experience proves conclusively that instinctual impulses from one source can join on to instinctual impulses from another and share their further vicissitudes, and that in general the satisfaction of one instinct can be substituted for the satisfaction of another. . . . The relations of an instinct to its aim and to its object are also susceptible to alterations; both can be exchanged for others, but the relation to the object is the more easily loosened of the two (Freud, 1932, p. 133). In other words, the energy at the disposal of an instinct can be *cathected* into a certain person, withdrawn, and re-invested in another.

Sometimes the instinctual drive comes to a stop at a certain point and renounces its full gratification. This takes place when the instinctual drive becomes too powerfully cathected in a certain object. For instance, affection represents such a case of permanent object-cathexis, one that expresses itself in a constant care for the beloved person without sexual gratification. This process of suspension of gratification was named by Freud *aim-inhibition*. A genuine parental love is aim-inhibited; loving parents don't expect sexual gratification from their children.

Another modification takes place when libido is redirected from the search for sexual gratification into a socially useful channel; this modification is *sublimation*. Freud believed that creative art represents this process of sublimation. The energies put originally at the disposal of sex are redirected in another channel of creative work in art, music, or literature.

SEXUALITY

People are "bent upon *procuring pleasure and avoiding pain.*" Freud wrote: "We may venture to say that pleasure is *in some way* connected with lessening, lowering, or extinguishing the amount of stimulation present in the mental apparatus; and that pain involves a heightening of the latter. Consideration of the most intense pleasure of which man is capable, the pleasure in the performance of the sexual act, leaves little doubt upon this point" (1915-1917, p. 311).

Sexual instincts always follow the pleasure principle. The highest degree of gratification and relief is brought about by sexual orgasm.

The sexual instincts are "the purest example" of the instincts of life. One may use here an analogy that Freud himself never used: alcoholic beverages are mixtures of pure alcohol with other elements; if one wants to assess the true nature of alcohol, obviously he will look for the strongest available proof and not for a diluted one. Libido is found in many forms, but the "purest" one, or the strongest proof of it, is sex.

BEYOND THE PLEASURE PRINCIPLE

The popular view distinguishes between hunger and love, seeing them as representatives of the instincts that aim at self-preservation and reproduction of the species respectively. In associating ourselves with this very evident distinction we postulate in psychoanalysis a similar one between the self-preservative or ego-instincts on the one hand and the sexual instincts on the other; the force by which the sexual instinct is represented in the mind we call "libido"—sexual longing—and regard it as analogous to the force of hunger, or the will to power, and other such trends among the ego-tendencies. . . .

We have defined the concept of libido as a quantitatively variable force which could serve as a measure of processes and transformations occurring in the field of sexual excitation. We distinguish this libido in respect of its special origin from the energy which must be supposed to underlie mental processes in general, and we thus also attribute a qualitative character to it (Freud, 1905, p. 217).

Freud did not believe that there is a single streamlined drive that leads to fertilization and preservation of the species. He found that "sexual life comprises the function of obtaining pleasure from zones of the body" (1938, p. 26). There have always been several instinctual needs related to various somatic sources, striving to obtain gratification in their respective somatic zone or to *organ-pleasure*. In the process of ontogenetic development, some of them have merged with the proper sexual instinct and, subsequently, brought into the service of the function of reproduction. But the two functions "often fail to coincide completely" (*Ibid.*).

One should distinguish between source, object, and aim in the sexual drive. The *source* is a stimulation arising in some part or zone of the organism. The various parts of the body that react to sexual stimuli, such as the genitals, the mouth, and the anus, are called *erotogenic zones*. The usual *object* of sexual desires is an adult person of the opposite sex; but a person of same sex is the object for homosexuals.

In psychoanalysis the term "sexuality" comprises far more than it does as generally used, going lower and also higher than in the popular sense of the word. This extension is justified genetically; we reckon as belonging to "sexual life" all expressions of tender feeling, which spring from the source of primitive sexual feelings, even when those feelings have become inhibited in regard to their original sexual aim or have exchanged this aim for another that is no longer sexual. For this reason we prefer to speak of *psychosexuality,* thus laying stress on the point that the mental factor should not be overlooked or underestimated. "We use the word sexuality in the same comprehensive sense as that in which the German language uses the word *lieben* (to love)," wrote Freud in 1910 (1910c, p. 270).

Infantile Amnesia

According to Freud, the newborn child already carries the germs of sexual feelings which continue to develop for some time and then succumb to a progressive suppression, which is in turn broken through by the proper advances of the sexual development and which can be checked by individual idiosyncrasies (Freud, 1905c). Furthermore, infantile amnesia causes most people to reject this contention. This amnesia causes the individual to view his childhood years as if they belonged to a prehistoric time.

Infantile amnesia is actually a process of repression; the infantile sexual drives are incompatible with one's adult life and, as such, they must stay deeply buried in the unconscious. In dreams, these hidden sexual desires appear in a disguised manner. The first and most pleasurable activity of an infant is the sucking from the mother's breast. The nipple of a milk bottle is the prototype of all future pleasures. "He who sees a satiated child sink back from his mother's breast and fall asleep with reddened cheeks and blissful smile, will have to admit that this picture remains as typical of the expression of sexual gratification in later life" (Freud, 1905c). Those individuals who retain the action of thumb-sucking for a prolonged period of time may show a tendency in adulthood to intense or even perverse kissing, and experience the desire for excessive drinking and smoking.

Infantile Sexuality

Infantile sexuality is basically autoerotic, for the infant's own body is the main source of pleasure. Pleasure is the primary goal of sexuality and only after years of growth toward maturity does the acquisition of pleasure become associated with the function of propagation and parenthood.

The story of psychosexual development will be told in Chapter Seven, but a brief review is perhaps indicated at this point. The earliest stages of psychosexual development, in which the genital zones have not yet assumed the dominating role, are called *pregenital phases*. The first such pregenital phase is the oral, with the mouth being the first erotogenic zone. At this stage sexuality is not yet separated from the intake of food. The second pregenital stage is called anal-sadistic, with the anus being the erotogenic zone. The differentiation between active and passive attitude that will be later designated as "masculine" and "feminine," respectively, begins at this stage. The third stage is called phallic, related to the genital organs.

In puberty the psychosexual life outgrows the autoerotic concentration of childhood and gradually develops into adult sexuality and making of a lasting sexual choice.

The sexual impulses in childhood manifest themselves in single and short-lived impulses related to a particular erotogenic zone, and seeking a certain pleasure as a single sexual aim. At puberty all the partial impulses become subordinate to the primacy of the genital zone and the aim of sexual intercourse. Kissing, touching, onlooking, and caressing become forepleasure activities that elicit pleasure and increase sexual excitement.

ABNORMAL SEXUALITY

Freud's concept of sexuality includes perversions and infantile sexuality that do not lead to the usual aim of unification of the genital organs in the act of intercourse. A perverse sexual relation may end with orgasm and ejaculation analogous to the normal sexual intercourse. As mentioned before, the forepleasure activities of normal individuals include several elements that, if performed exclusively, and in place of normal intercourse, should be considered perverse. Kissing is an indispensable part of the sexual foreplay in normal individuals, though kissing is merely a contact of oral zones. The mouth is an erotogenic zone and, as such, it is capable of producing sexual excitation. Some individuals obtain orgasm by kissing, "deep kissing," or by oral-genital contacts. Kissing is a part of the sexual excitement and foreplay that ultimately leads to the union of the genital organs, and it is one of the most natural parts of sexual life. According to Freud, if kissing prevents normal sexual intercourse, it may become perverse. The normal and the perverse sexuality have the same roots.

The newborn child is a "polymorphous pervert" who must grow up to become normal. Some of his early sexual preferences must be modified, some elements must be discontinued, and others incorporated in the sexual foreplay, and subordinated to the main sexual aim—the unity of sexual organs. Thus onlooking, for example, is a widely practiced element of sexual foreplay; only if its practice excludes the union of genitals, does the foreplay become a perverted voyeurism. Another form of perversion is fetishism, in which an object of clothing, for example, takes the place of the genital organs.

The study of perverted forms of sexuality proves that sexuality is not limited to reproduction, nor to the function of genital organs; nor is it necessarily heterosexual. The functions of the genital organs may be replaced by the other organs for the purpose of gratification (as in the normal kiss), or by perverse practices, or by conversion symptoms of hysteria. Sexual deviations are not a "degeneration" but a sort of thwarting or regression of the sexual development. Studies in biology and embryology led Freud to assume, after Haeckel, that the child's sexual development is a recapitulation of the main phases in the evolution of sex.

Infantile sexuality contains all the potentialities for future development in any possible direction—toward normal sexuality, or becoming fixated on one of the early stages or functions.

If we are led to suppose that neurotics conserve the infantile state of their sexuality or return to it, our interest must then turn to the sexual life of the child, and we will then follow the play of influences which control the processes of development of the infantile sexuality up to its termination in a perversion, a neurosis or a normal sexual life (Freud, 1905b).

NARCISSISM

Freud wrote in his essay "On Narcissism": "There are various points in favor of the hypothesis of a primordial differentiation between sexual instincts and other instincts, ego-instincts. . . . This differentiation of concepts corresponds to the distinction between hunger and love. . . ." (1914, p. 77). After several years of clinical experience Freud discovered that libido may be directed to oneself and not necessarily to external objects only. Love-for-oneself precedes object-love. "The sexual instincts are at the outset supported upon the ego-instincts [for] the first autoerotic sexual gratifications are experienced in connection with vital functions in the service of self-preservation" (*Ibid.,* p. 84). It takes a while for infants to learn to divert part of the love primarily cathected (invested) in themselves and to cathect it in their mothers. This self-love was called by Freud *narcissism* after the legendary Greek youth Narcissus, who fell in love with himself. "In persons whose libidinal development has suffered some disturbance, as in perverts and homosexuals, that in the choice of their love object they have taken as their model . . . their own selves" (*Ibid.*).

Narcissism probably starts in the prenatal life and never entirely disappears. At the earliest stage of life, narcissism is the libido's only channel of cathexis; all mental energies are invested in oneself. This initial stage was called by Freud *primary narcissism*. Later in life, in cases when the object-love is being thwarted, the libido may turn back to one's own person and *secondary,* morbid narcissism may develop.

The discovery of the phenomenon of narcissism destroyed the barriers separating the libido from the ego instincts. From then on, the so-called ego-instincts had to be considered as special cases of the libido-cathexis, namely as an investment of libido in one's own person. With the essay "On Narcissism" Freud arrived at a monistic interpretation of the instinctual life: there is but one instinctual force, the force of love, the libido, that can be cathected (invested) in oneself in narcissistic love or in others, in object-love.

The conflict between sex and self-preservation instinct drives was reinterpreted by Freud as narcissism versus object-love. In order to be well-adjusted, one has to have a balanced distribution of libido cathexes between oneself and others. A balanced amount of narcissism is necessary purely for self-protection. In order to take care of others, one has to be capable of object-cathexis of libido. Some individuals suffer from disbalance in cathexes; some develop secondary and morbid narcissism after they have been seriously thwarted in the development of object-cathexis. Some are unable to take care of themselves due to insufficient narcissism or abundant object-cathexis.

Freud united under the name of Eros all the forces that serve pleasure and enhance the vital functions of the individual. Eros encompassed all sexual and egoistic drives, and libido became the name for all the energies, whether self- or object-directed, that are at the disposal of erotic force.

The Instinct of Death and Destruction

In the year 455 the German tribe of Vandals invaded Rome. They were the have-nots, while imperial Rome was rich and opulent. The Vandals stole, and carried away whatever they could. They apparently could not carry away the marble columns and beautiful temples of Rome, so they demolished them.

Why? What was the advantage of this senseless destruction?

In 1914 the German army attacked neutral Belgium. The Germans robbed and plundered Belgium and, in their unlimited greediness, they took away from Belgium's civilian population whatever they could put their hands on. But plunder was not enough, and they set fire to the beautiful cathedral of Louvain and slaughtered innocent Belgian hostages.

Why this senseless cruelty?

It seemed for a while that the theory of Eros and libido could explain the entire gamut of human motives. When one loves others, it is object-cathexis of the libido; when one loves himself, it is narcissism and self-cathexis. Self-cathected narcissistic individuals have no consideration for other people and may attack for gain and profit. Oral aggression can fit into the libido-cathexes theory; but senseless brutality and murder for their own sakes do not.

SADISM AND MASOCHISM

The matter becomes further complicated when one takes into consideration sexual brutality. Libido can be sexual or neutralized (desexualized). Sex is a sort of galvanized libido; it is love rooted in physi-cal attraction. Sexual desires lead to affection, kindness, and considera-tion; when two people desire each other physically and emotionally, they usually form a union sanctioned by society called marriage.

Mammalian males fight against each other for the possession of fe-males, but they don't fight against females. Some men, however, do fight against females and are unable to enjoy the sex act unless they in-flict pain on their female partner. Such behavior, called sadism, cannot be interpreted by the theory of Eros for it is not an act of love and af-fection. Love does not make people inflict pain on their love objects. The empirical fact of sadism forced Freud to reconsider his theory of instincts.

Masochism was even more difficult to understand than sadism. To love and to be loved is normally the source of greatest pleasure. How could one combine love with the wish to be hurt? How could pain be a prerequisite of the greatest sensual pleasure?

The desire to be hurt could easily lead to self-destruction. Suicidal impulses, so frequently met in mental patients, could not be interpreted in terms of the libido theory. Libido, as viewed by Freud in 1914, could serve either self-preservation (when self-cathected), or preserva-tion of love objects. It could not be a tool for the destruction of oneself or of others.

As early as 1897 Freud wrote that the hostile impulses against parents (a wish that they should die) are also an integral part of neuroses. They come to light consciously in the form of obsessional ideas. "In paranoia the worst delusions of persecution . . . correspond to these impulses. They are repressed at periods in which pity for one's parents is active—at times of their illness or death. One of the mani-festations of grief is then to reproach oneself for their death . . . or to punish oneself in a hysterical way by putting oneself in their posi-tion with the idea of retribution." (1887-1902.)

Freud was not sure whether hostile impulses and death wishes form a part of sexuality or are independent entities. The term *thanatotic* was used in the meetings of the Viennese Psychoanalytic Society formed by Freud in 1902 (Nunberg and Federn). In the *Three Essays on Theory of Sexuality* Freud wrote: "It may be assumed that the im-pulses of cruelty arise from sources which are in fact independent of sexuality but may become united with it at an early stage" (p. 193).

Adler suggested in 1908 a separate aggressive drive (Nunberg and Federn, p. 408). Freud never denied the existence of aggressive behavior, but at that time he linked aggression to libido. Moreover, Freud could not accept Adler's notion of self-assertion as the underlying principle of aggression.

Freud's concept of aggression was anchored to the general principle of equilibrium. Nature tends to retain its *status quo;* if the original equilibrium is disturbed, the tendency is to go back, and to restore the initial state.

Let us make a sharper distinction than we have hitherto made between function and tendency. The pleasure principle, then, is a tendency operating in the service of a function whose business it is to free the mental apparatus entirely from excitation or to keep the amount of excitation in it constant or to keep it as low as possible. We cannot yet decide with certainty in favor of any of these ways of putting it; but it is clear that the function thus described would be concerned with the most universal endeavor of all living substance—namely to return to the quiescence of the inorganic world (Freud, 1920a, p. 62).

EROS VS. THANATOS

Thus, Freud introduced a new theory of instincts. He explained it as follows.

With the hypothesis of narcissistic libido, . . . the sexual instinct was transformed for us into Eros, which seeks to force together and hold together the portions of living substance. . . . Our speculations have suggested that Eros operates from the beginning of life and appears as "life instinct" in opposition to the "death instinct" which was brought into being by the coming to life of the inorganic substance. These speculations seek to solve the riddle of life by supposing that these two instincts were struggling with each other from the very first. (*Ibid.,* Note 55)

Organic matter developed from inorganic matter. With the start of life, an instinct was born that aimed at the return of the inorganic state and destruction of life. According to Freud, the aim of Thanatos, the death instinct, is the re-establishment of inanimate nature. Life ends in death, and death leads to a new life. Eros and Thanatos are interwoven; and construction and destruction are inseparable. The process of life cannot be entirely free from the death-instinct. The erotic instincts try ". . . to collect living substance together into even larger unities, [and the death instincts act against this] and try to bring living matter back into inorganic condition. The cooperation and opposition of those two forces produce the phenomena of life to which death puts an end" (Freud, 1932, pp. 146-147).

The development of these new concepts was a major step in psychoanalytic theory:

> After long doubts and vacillations we have decided to assume the existence of only two basic instincts, *Eros* and the destructive instinct. . . . The aim of the first of these basic instincts is to establish ever greater unities and to preserve them, thus—in short, to bind together; the aim of the second, on the contrary, is to undo connections and so to destroy things. We may suppose that the final aim of the destructive instinct is to reduce living things to an inorganic state. For this reason we also call it the death instinct (1938, p. 20).

Freud put the emphasis on death rather than on murder. Death is the inevitable end of all, the inescapable consequence of the process of life. Death is the tragic aim of life and the final destiny of all living matter. Eros is affirmation of life, Thanatos brings its destruction. The sexual drive brings tension to a pleasurable relief, death brings all life processes to a peaceful end.

FREUD'S MODIFICATIONS OF HIS INITIAL MOTIVATION THEORY

In *Beyond the Pleasure Principle* (1930a), Freud introduced a series of new concepts deviating substantially from his early theory of motivation. The constancy principle, or the restoration of the initial state, became more important than the search for pleasure. People re-experience past tensions in dreams not because the dreams bring relief and pleasure, but because the dreamers are compelled to repeat past experiences. Repetition compulsion is the inescapable product of the principle of constancy. Past tensions, pleasurable or painful, tend to undergo repetition until they are resolved and an equilibrium is established. Repetition compulsion explains the tendency to reproduce painful and traumatic experiences. The instinctual forces produce continuous repetitions of the disturbing experience until a balance is restored.

One's natural aggressiveness against the self may be directed against the outer world. Thanatos is, primarily, an instinct of death and all of us carry a certain amount of self-destructiveness within ourselves. It seems that people have to destroy things and other people in order not to destroy themselves. In order to protect oneself from the tendency toward self-destruction, one must find external channels for aggressiveness.

As stated above all instincts turn out to be directed toward the reinstatement of an earlier state of things. As soon as a given state of being is upset, an instinctual action starts, aiming at the restoration of that state. In such an action, Eros and Thanatos may combine their resources, but no less often they fight each other. Eating is a process of destruction with the purpose of incorporation; sexual intercourse is an act of aggression that aims at the "most intimate union." Sexual impulses are rarely purely erotic; quite often they combine erotic and destructive instinctual demands.

In some cases, when the destructive instincts become the stronger part in the fusion of the two kinds of instincts, sadism or masochism results. In sadism, as we have seen, aggressive impulses thrust the sexual aims away, the goal of hurting the love-object becoming dominant over the normal sexual aim. Sexual gratification is possible only if pain is inflicted upon the sexual-object. Masochistic aggression is self-directed; sexual gratification depends upon being hurt and experiencing pain.

When an individual's behavior, under the control of Thanatos, is directed toward the outer world, he becomes hateful and aggressive, spreading destruction and death. When these forces are directed to oneself, self-defeat and self-destruction (suicide) may put an end to life.

4

Id: The Boiling Cauldron

Freud's topographic and economic concepts are fundamental parts of Freudian theory, but they do not tell the entire story.

For a while Freud identified the unconscious with the sexual impulses, the libido. He saw in the conscious the control apparatus related to the self-preservative ego forces, dividing, under the influence of Darwin, all motivating factors into the categories of libido and ego drives.

As mentioned before, in 1914 Freud united all instinctual forces under the name Eros, the symbol of love and life. Love supports life, and Eros is the god of love and life. The energy of Eros, the libido, can be self-cathected in a narcissistic way for the protection of one's own life or object-cathected for the protection of someone else's life. Libido can be aim-inhibited, desexualized, or sublimated, as love for one's relatives or country or art; it can be sexual, and then it may lead to the creation of new lives and the preservation of the species. In 1920 Freud added the concept of Thanatos and its destructive energy. The two instinctual forces, together with the three topographic strata of Ucs, Pcs and Cs, seemed to form a satisfactory theoretical framework.

Why, then, did Freud revise his theory again in 1923? The reasons were hinted at in the first chapter: they are related to the issue of censorship, repression, and resistance.

How are the unconscious processes regulated? First, by the pleasure-unpleasure mechanisms. "It seems probable," wrote Freud in "The

Interpretation of Dreams," that in the first instance the unpleasure principle regulates the displacement of cathexes automatically" (p. 616). Then comes the control of the Pcpt (perceptual systems) and the sense organs of the conscious itself.

"Excitatory material flows into the Cs sense organs from two directions: from the Pcpt systems, whose excitation, determined by qualities, is probably submitted to a fresh revision before it becomes a conscious sensation and from the interior of the apparatus itself, whose quantitative processes are felt qualitatively in the pleasure-unpleasure series when, subject to certain modifications, they make their way to consciousness (*Ibid.,* pp. 615-616).

CENSORSHIP

Any unconscious material has to pass double censorship to become conscious. First it must pass the censorship from the unconscious (Ucs) to the preconscious (Pcs). This censorship, "the assumption of whose existence is positively forced upon us by dreams, deserves to be recognized and respected as the watchman of our mental health" (*Ibid.,* p. 567).

The second censorship involves the preconscious and conscious.

Soon the idea that censorship must be conscious proved untenable. The same forces that repressed unacceptable desires also resisted the unraveling of the unconscious and repressed material. These repressing and resisting forces could hardly be believed to be conscious. When a patient comes for treatment, spends his time and money and yet is unable to cooperate, his difficulty in free association and recall is all but conscious. Obviously the repressing, censoring, and resisting forces are unconscious: yet they are not the same as the repressed wishes and desires. In 1915 Freud explained that "the reason for all these difficulties is to be found in the circumstance that the attribute of being conscious, which is the only characteristic of psychical processes that is directly presented to us, is in no way suited to serve as a criterion for the differentiation of systems" (1915b, p. 192). In other words, to be conscious or unconscious does not determine the fact of being repressed or doing the repression. The terms unconscious, preconscious, and conscious merely indicate the *quality* of mental processes and their respective *topographic* positions.

DISPOSITION AND EXPERIENCE

In 1923 Freud introduced a complex model of personality structure based on economic, topographic, and structural factors. This new model dealt with the distribution, balance, and interaction of the two instinctual forces, Eros and Thanatos, and the energies at their disposal, libido and destructive energy—that is, the economy of the mind. The new model included the three "mental provinces," previously described: the unconscious, the preconscious, and the conscious. Thus it delimited the topography of the mind. The new model introduced three parts of the mental apparatus, the id, the ego, and the superego. Thus it dealt with the structure of the mind.

The new model took into consideration both inherited dispositions and life experiences. "The determining causes of all the varying forms of human mental life are to be found in the interplay between inherited dispositions and accidental experiences," wrote Freud (1938, p. 84). An instinct may be "innately too strong or too weak," and an innate capacity may be "stunted or insufficiently developed in life." The totality of all the innate factors forms the *constitution* of an individual.

Each individual is exposed in his life span to environmental influences. The totality of these influences forms the *constellation* of one's life. A given constellation can be more, or less, favorable to the development of an individual and his successful adjustment in life; but one must not forget that how one handles his constellation depends largely on his constitution.

The somatic structure is the basic constitutional factor. Anatomical and physiological differences between the sexes determine, to a great extent, the psychological makeup of people. Constitution includes not only what can be found in neonates, but also the disposition-developmental tendencies that appear at a later stage. Accepting Haeckel's biogenetic principle, Freud believed that hereditary dispositions enable the infant to grow and develop into a civilized adult, passing through the evolutionary phases of human development "in an almost uncannily abbreviated form."

This development process is not entirely a matter of biological dispositions; it is also a learning process. Whether the child will or will not pass the developmental stages safely depends primarily on the child's innate dispositions, and upon his interaction with the physical and social environment. Freud did not believe in rigidly set universal developmental phases. He suspected that the way children develop is varied, depending on cultural patterns. The growth of human personality is largely determined by an individual's life experiences; these may or may not foster inherited potentialities, may encourage or prevent growth, may stimulate development or thwart it. One's mental health is only partly dependent upon his constitution. In most cases the environment, the constellation, and not the constitution have the final say about personality development.

The Pleasure Principle

Freud called the innate part of personality the *id,* the Latin word for "it." Whatever is inherited or fixed in the constitution, whatever originates in the body, finds its mental expression in the id. The id is the link between somatic and mental processes; it is "somewhere in direct contact with somatic processes, and takes over from them instinctual needs and gives them mental expression, but we cannot say in what substratum this contact is made" (Freud, 1915-1917, p. 104).

The id expresses the chief purpose of the individual organism's life, namely, the gratification of its innate needs. The id acts impulsively, irrespective of whether or not its actions protect the organism from danger. The id knows no fear and takes no precautions to insure survival. An immediate and unconditioned gratification of instinctual demands is pursued by the id. An id-inspired behavior may lead to clashes with the external world and to the death of the organism.

The entire mental energy, both libidinal and aggressive, is stored in the id. This energy is mainly put at the disposal of the two primal forces, Eros and Thanatos. The energy stored in the id is free, unbound, operating on the homeostatic Nirvana principle and the pleasure principle.

The term *pleasure principle* was used by Freud in two different though often overlapping connotations. Freud's theory is basically hedonistic, that is, it assumes that human beings (with some exceptions) pursue pleasure and avoid pain. This pleasure-pain continuum was related by Freud to mental economy. Freud followed in Fechner's footsteps and linked unpleasure to disbalance and pleasure to restoration of balance. In Freud's theory the tension-relief continuum corresponds to the pain-pleasure continuum.

In this sense, even repetition compulsion and the constancy principle do not contradict the pleasure-unpleasure principle. The maximum relief is attained in the restoration of complete peace, Nirvana. In dreams people repeat traumatic experiences in order to have them resolved, with unpleasant dreams occurring again and again as long as the tension of an unresolved conflict exists.

The id, as the seat of all vehement desires and seething impulses, tends to an immediate discharge of energies. The discharge of energies that restores the inner balance was called by Freud the *Lustprinzip,* that is, the principle of lust (usually translated as "pleasure principle"). Undoubtedly, an immediate discharge of libidinal or destructive energy brings relief, thus it is experienced as pleasure. The *Lustprinzip* emphasizes the urgent need to obtain an immediate gratification, come what may. The unbound, uncontrolled energies of the id lead to impulsive discharges of energies according to the pleasure principle. Thus the pleasure principle sometimes indicates the general striving for pleasure and avoidance of pain, while in another context it points to the urgency of obtaining such a pleasure through an immediate discharge of energy.

PRIMARY PROCESSES

At the beginning of an individual's life, everything is unconscious. The id stays entirely unconscious forever; but, under the pressure of the outer world, some of the unconscious material of the id develops into preconscious material, and the ego emerges. "Under the influence of the external world which surrounds us, one portion of the id has undergone a special development. From what was originally a cortical layer, provided with organs for receiving stimuli and with apparatus for protection against excessive stimulation, a special organization has arisen which henceforward acts as an intermediary between the id and the external world. This region of our mental life has been given the name of ego" (Freud, 1938, p. 15).

The id's unconscious material is usually composed both of the original unaltered, and almost inaccessible, unconscious nucleus, and of a relatively younger and more readily accessible material that has been repressed by the ego and thrown back into the id.

The mental processes in the id, called *primary processes,* defy the laws of logic. The id is cut off from the external world, but performs perceptory functions in its own interior. The very fact that the id always acts in the direction of procuring pleasure and avoiding unpleasure indicates that the id is capable of perception. Then self-directed perceptions and coenesthetic feelings disclose the economy of inner tensions and the balance of the mental apparatus. Whenever the economy or the equilibrium of the mental apparatus is disturbed, the instinctual forces react in the striving for immediate discharge of energy. Indeed, the id blindly obeys the pleasure principle. Id knows no values, no right or wrong, no moral standards, no consideration for other people. It is a "cauldron of seething excitement," Freud said. "Instinctual cathexes seeking discharge"—that is all that the id contains. Being unbound, fluid, capable of quick discharge, the id's energy is easily condensated and displaced.

The Id

The id does not change. "Conative impulses which have never gotten beyond the id, and even impressions which have been pushed down into the id by repression, are virtually immortal and are preserved for whole decades as though they had only recently occurred" (Freud, 1932, p. 104). The repressed material is hardly affected by the passage of time. Long-forgotten infantile memories come back in dreams, and early childhood experiences play a decisive role in the symptomatology of the mental disorders. The two other "agencies of the mind," the ego and superego, develop out of the id and become independent.

It remains certain that self-perceptions—coenesthetic feelings and feelings of pleasure-unpleasure—govern events in the id with despotic force. The id obeys the inexorable pleasure principle. But not the id alone. It seems as though the activity of the other agencies of the mind is able only to modify the pleasure principle but not to nullify it; and it remains a question of the greatest theoretical importance, and one that has not yet been answered, when and how it is ever possible for the pleasure principle to be overcome (Freud, 1938, p. 109).

The unbound energies stored in the id are irrational, uncontrolled resources of an individual's vitality. The id leads the individual to the most irresponsible of actions, resembling those of a neonate.

The core of our being, then, is formed by the obscure *id,* which has no direct relations with the external world and is accessible even to our own knowledge only through the medium of another agency of the mind. Within this id the organic *instincts* operate, which are themselves composed of fusions of two primal forces (Eros and destructiveness) in varying proportions and are differentiated from one another by their relation to organs or systems of organs. The one and only endeavor of these instincts is toward satisfaction, which it is hoped to obtain from certain modifications in the organs by the help of objects in the external world. . . . The id knows no precautions to insure survival and no anxiety; or it would perhaps be more correct to say that, though it can produce the sensory elements of anxiety, it cannot make use of them. The processes which are possible in and between the assumed mental elements in the id (the *primary process*) differ largely from those which are familiar to us by conscious perception in our intellectual and emotional life; nor are they subject to the critical restrictions of logic, which repudiates some of these processes as invalid and seeks to undo them (*Ibid.,* pp. 108-109).

MENTAL APPARATUS

Prior to 1923, as we have seen, Freud's theory of personality was mainly topographic, based on the Ucs, Pcs, and Cs systems. Freud never abandoned this division; but as we know, in addition to it, he introduced the "structured" theory of the id, ego, and superego. The new theory had to take into account (1) the driving forces Eros and Thanatos, and the mental energies of libido and destruction attached respectively to Eros and Thanatos; (2) the three mental layers, unconscious, preconscious, and conscious; and (3) the three parts of the mental apparatus, the id, ego, and superego. One can present this complex personality model as follows:

FREUDIAN MODEL OF PERSONALITY

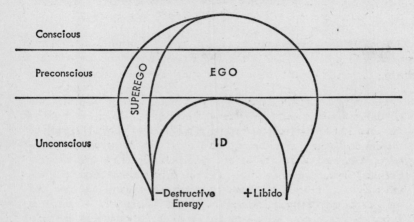

Conscious

Preconscious   EGO

SUPEREGO

Unconscious   ID

−Destructive   +Libido
Energy

The id is entirely submerged in the unconscious. But the two parts or agencies of the control apparatus, the ego and the superego, are topographically spread over all three layers of Ucs, Pcs, and Cs. The driving forces, the positive energy of libido and the negative destructive energy, are originally seated in the id. When the ego and the superego develop, they derive their energies from the id.

5

Ego: The Control Apparatus

Freud described the ego as

a poor creature owing service to three masters and consequently men-
aced by three several dangers: from the external world, from the libido
of the id, and from the severity of the superego. It only too often yields
to the temptation to become sycophantic, opportunist and lying, like a
politician who sees the truth but wants to keep his place in popular
favor (Freud, 1923b, p. 56).

But the ego is not a servant. It is a master that applies all its might
to control the irrationality of the id and the superego (Freud, 1926, pp.
95 ff.). While the id contains human passions, the ego represents reason
and sanity. Keeping a precarious balance between the instinctual demands of the id and the moralistic demands of the superego, the ego
clings to reality and guides behavior in a rational way.

The ego is, actually, "merely a specially differentiated part of [the
id]" (*Ibid.*, p. 97). At the beginning was the id, for the id is the only
innate part of personality. The ego and the superego gradually evolve
and develop; they are the acquired parts of human personality.

DERIVATION OF THE CONCEPT OF EGO

For a long time Freud believed that whatever is repressed is unconscious and whatever represses is conscious. As mentioned above,
this distinction proved invalid, and there was a need for considering

a factor that was repressive yet not necessarily conscious. This factor or agency was called the ego.

From this ego proceeds the repression, too, by which an attempt is made to cut off certain trends in the mind. . . . In analysis these trends which have been shut out stand in opposition to the ego and the analyst is faced with the task of removing the resistances which the ego displays against concerning itself with the repressed. . . . During analysis . . . the patient gets into difficulties; his associations fail when they ought to be getting near to the repressed. We then tell him that he is dominated by a resistance, but he is quite unaware of the fact. . . . However, there can be no question that this resistance emanates from his ego and belongs to it. . . . (1923b, p. 14).

Freud had no alternative but to conclude that unconscious does not coincide with what is repressed and that a part of the repressing force is itself unconscious. "It is still true," he wrote, "that all that is repressed is Ucs, but not the whole Ucs is repressed. A part of the ego, too—and heaven knows how important a part—may be Ucs, undoubtedly is Ucs" (*Ibid.,* p. 15).

But if a part of the controlling ego is unconscious, then the topographic division into Ucs, Pcs, and Cs loses some of its importance. Small wonder that several psychoanalytic thinkers (Arlow and Brenner, 1964; Gill, 1963) found the entire topographic theory superfluous. Freud, however, found room for both the old topographic division and the new "structural" theory of id, ego, and superego.

Freud explained his views as follows: "It gives rise once more to a doubt whether we are really justified in referring the whole of consciousness to the single superficial system Pcpt-Cs" (1923b). The ego starts with the preconscious, out of memory residues, but it is also partly unconscious. The ego is the control apparatus that regulates human behavior; it is, however, important to be aware of the fact that human behavior is partly Ucs, partly Pcs, and partly Cs. The innate id is entirely unconscious, but the acquired parts of personality structure spread to all three mental layers, the Ucs, Pcs, and Cs.

The simple equation "perception = reality (external world)" cannot hold any longer, since perception may also stem from within—from memories, and from inside the body. At the early stages the ego confuses inner stimulation with stimuli coming from the external world. These confusions are called illusions and hallucinations, and they take place whenever the ego is not fully alert (as is often the case in neonates, always true of people in dreams, and often of psychotics).

The ego derives its energy from the id. The instinctual demands of the id lead to investment of parts of its energy in objects. By identifying itself with the cathected objects, the ego "recommends itself to the id in the place of the object and seeks to attract the libido of the id on to itself. . . . In the course of a person's life the ego takes into itself a large number of such precipitates of former object-cathexes" (Freud, 1938, p. 108).

ORIGIN OF THE EGO

The neonate is exposed to excitations that he cannot master. He becomes somehow dimly aware of them and feels uncomfortable and unhappy. Hunger, thirst, cold, noise, and other tension-producing stimuli flood the infant's mental apparatus and produce a state of anxiety. The infant wishes to get rid of the disturbing stimuli, but he is unable to do so. Infants are helpless and cannot survive without being taken care of. The help must come from without; and the disturbing stimuli of hunger can disappear only with the satisfaction of hunger.

The neonate's mental apparatus, the id, resembles a body floating in water. Under the influence of environmental forces that act on the surface of the id, this surface changes and develops into a sort of protective shell, called the ego. The surface unconscious material of the id becomes preconscious, and part of the primary mental processes are gradually transformed into secondary processes of the ego. But, Freud stressed, "the ego is not sharply separated from the id; its lower portion merges into it" (1923b, p. 24).

The Infantile Ego

The infantile, "archaic" ego knows and loves only itself: it is primarily narcissistic. The infantile ego is only dimly aware of the external world. Gratification of needs must come from without, and hunger is satisfied by mother's milk. The infant is wrapped up in himself and in his own needs and, when his needs are gratified and tension removed, he falls asleep.

In this early stage the craving for objects and the craving for removal of unpleasant stimuli seem to be one and the same thing. Satisfaction of the hunger tension restores the narcissistic state of equilibrium and gives the infant a feeling of bliss and omnipotence. The desire for milk and the gratification of this need regulate the infant's self-esteem, which is so significant for the future growth of his ego.

This sequence of events leads to some sort of inner contradiction. When the infant is free from disturbing stimuli, he falls asleep. Then the stimuli come again: there are pangs of hunger, pressures in bowels and bladder, irritation of skin, and craving for objects. It seems that at the earliest stage of life, the infant craves for a contact with the outer world but he is unable to face too much contact with the outer world. This is the point at which a contradiction of basic importance in human life arises, the contradiction between longing for complete relaxation and longing for objects (stimulus hunger) (Fenichel, 1945, p. 35).

Only gradually does the infant give up his narcissistic feeling of omnipotence and ascribe omnipotence to those who satisfy his needs. The adults around him seem to have unlimited power, and the infant may hope to share their omnipotence via fantasies about incorporating them or being incorporated by them.

The love of oneself by incorporation, or secondary narcissism, expresses itself in the longing for unification with the omnipotent adults or other external forces believed to be omnipotent. The infantile ego is unable to distinguish clearly between self and other objects and narcissistic-love and object-love are not yet separated.

The Emerging Ego

As the child grows, his ego gradually becomes more capable of protecting the organism against threats coming from within and without.

The emerging ego gradually draws the line between self and the external world. The undeveloped, primitive ego *introjects* objects and makes them part of self or *projects,* i.e., ascribes parts of itself to the outer world.

A child is usually prone to accept pleasant stimuli as part of self and to ascribe unpleasant ones to the outer world. Thus, contrary to one common misinterpretation of psychoanalytic teaching, Freud stressed that a reasonable amount of frustration is necessary for a normal development. A child whose *every* wish comes true can never develop a proper distinction between himself and the outer world. The wall that does not move away when the child pushes it, and the rain that pours against the child's wishes, help him to distinguish between himself and the outer world, called by Freud *reality*.

The Main Role of the Ego

Self-preservation is the chief task of the ego. The ego must learn to cope with the external world—

. . . by avoiding excessive stimuli (through flight), by dealing with moderate stimuli (through adaptation) and, finally, by learning to bring about appropriate modifications in the external world to its own advantage (through activity). In regard to internal events and in relation to the id, the ego performs its task by gaining control over the demands of the instincts, by deciding whether they shall be allowed to obtain satisfaction, by postponing that satisfaction to times and circumstances favorable in the external world or by suppressing their excitations completely. Its activities are governed by consideration of the tensions produced by stimuli present within it or introduced into it. The raising of these tensions is in general felt as *unpleasure* and their lowering as *pleasure*. . . . The ego pursues pleasure and seeks to avoid unpleasure. An increase in unpleasure which is expected and foreseen is met by a *signal of anxiety* (Freud, 1938, p. 15).

The id seeks pleasure, come what may, but the ego is concerned with discovering the most favorable and least dangerous method for satisfaction. The id is blind, but the ego takes into consideration the external world. Both the id and the ego are ruled by the pleasure-unpleasure principle. But in contradistinction to the id, the ego calculates the consequences of its behavior. The id is bound by the necessity of seeking immediate gratification of instinctual demands, while the ego is capable of logical reasoning, of considering causal relations, and of learning by experience.

Due to these activities, the ego applies a modified pleasure-unpleasure criterion. Ego's main task is *self-preservation,* thus the ego must control; it suppresses and postpones those instinctual demands that threaten the existence of the organism. Ego does not object to instinctual gratification, but refuses to risk displeasure and defeat.

As indicated, the id operates on the principle of immediate gratification of instinctual demands, the pleasure-principle. The ego operates on the reality principle, that is, a cautious pursuit of pleasure. If the attainment of satisfaction jeopardizes survival, the ego, in order to protect, will renounce pleasure. In most cases, however, a delay of satisfaction or a modification of the ways in which it is obtained will suffice.

In order to protect the organism the ego has to perform several functions. The first is *testing of reality*—acting as a constant watchdog, perceiving the outer world and thus making possible avoidance of confusing inner and outer stimuli. The second task is the control of the unconscious impulses coming from the id and the superego. This control requires powerful *anticathexes*. The third task is the control of the *motor* apparatus.

These three main tasks affect cognitive processes, impulses and emotions, and motility.

REALITY-TESTING

The infant's perception of the world is vague, inexact and undifferentiated. Parts are taken for wholes, wholes for parts. Objects are perceived in a diffuse manner, overlapping each other.

> The id "has its own world of perception. It detects with extraordinary clarity certain changes in its interior, especially oscillations in the tension of its instinctual needs, oscillations which become conscious as feelings in the pleasure-unpleasure series. It is, to be sure, hard to say by what means and with the help of what sensory terminal organs these perceptions come about (Freud, 1938, p. 109).

But the id is "cut off from the external world" and it is the task of the ego to distinguish between the inner, id-originated stimuli, and the stimuli from without, perceived by sensory apparatus. The archaic ego and the failing ego of psychotics may not be able to distinguish between inner and outer stimuli and may fall prey to delusions and hallucinations.

The mature ego is capable of *reality-testing,* that is, checking its perception against the outer reality and eliminating from the picture of the outer world any elements that may stem from "inner sources of excitation." The mature ego separates wish from reality thus making possible adjustment to real situations. In sleep, when the ego's reality-testing function is suspended, inner and outer stimuli merge in the world of fantasy and wish-fulfillment of dreams.

The ego resembles a driver who must keep his eyes on the road, always aware of the condition of his car—its power, size, weight, roadability, and so on. He must also keep moving along the road, considering the necessary adjustment of his own speed in view of the external conditions, such as the road being wet, other cars, men working, and so on; exercise adequate control over his own car; and go toward his destination, trying to make the best possible time and enjoying a safe and economical ride.

The task of the ego seems to be even more complex, because the id is not an engine but a "seething cauldron," and the demanding and critical superego is the backseat driver.

The most important task of the ego is contact with the outer world through a correct perception of what is going on. The perception of one's own body is the first step in this direction. The infant dimly perceives some tensions stemming from within, as from "inside something"; this perception enables the formation of his own *body-image.* The perception of one's body as a definite object is an important step toward the perception of the outer world.

Infantile perceptual and motor functions are diffuse and intertwined. Gradually, the infant's passive experiencing of excitations is transformed into observation, retention of perception (memory), and motor responses. The growing ego becomes an organized entity with differentiated functions, one of them being protection of the organism from too many or too strong stimuli.

Perception of the external world starts with the ego's primary, archaic *identification* with perceived objects. Several functions are included in this archaic identification. The infant puts the perceived things into his mouth, in fact and in effect introjecting his first love objects. This *oral introjection* shows that several distinct functions such as perception, motility, and emotionality have not separated from one another. Identification is an effort to master stimuli that are too intense by adjusting one's body to them and imitating them.

As noted above, the dim picture of the outer world is accompanied by the infant's feeling of his own omnipotence: when his perception of the outer world becomes more precise, the infant begins to realize that satisfaction of his needs depends on external factors.

The "surface" part of the ego is the perceptual-conscious or Pcpt-Cs system. This system "is directed on to the external world, it mediates perceptions of it, and in it is generated while it is functioning, the phenomenon of consciousness. It is the sense organ of the whole apparatus, receptive not only of excitations from without but also of such as proceed from the interior of the mind" (Freud, 1932, p. 106).

The mature ego controls the cognitive functions and can perform reality-testing. It is possible, for instance, to test reality by closing one's eyes, or by putting cotton in the ears; if such detachment from the outer world removes the perception, then it is obvious that the perception came from the outer world. If a visual or auditory perception is not affected by the elimination of a given outer stimulus, then the stimulus must have come from the organism itself.

Thought and Speech

Verbalization is of crucial importance in the development of several functions of the ego. The use of words facilitates a more precise communication with other people, more adequate reality-testing, and better control of impulses. In very early childhood and in cases of severe mental deterioration an *autistic* language develops, understandable to the speaker only.

Speaking helps thinking. There are, undoubtedly, preverbal ways of perceiving and thinking. Logical thinking, however, requires verbal symbols applicable to logical manipulations such as comparison, generalization, and abstraction.

Primitive and archaic thinking tolerates contradictions and it is ruled by emotions; it is guided by wishing and magic beliefs. Preverbal thinking puts together things that do not belong to one another, takes parts for wholes, similarities for identities, and confuses itself with the outer world. Archaic thinking operates with primitive symbols, pictures, distortions, and substitutive figures. The symbols are pictorial, representative of definite objects rather than of classes of objects (see Panel, 1959).

When the ego takes over the control of thought processes, the symbolic, prelogical, pictorial way of thinking is retained only in dreams and other unconscious processes. In severe mental disorders there is some regression to these primitive, prelogical forms of thinking, and disturbance in verbalization (Arieti, 1955; Bellak and Benedict, 1958; Wolman, 1966a).

"Thinking is an experimental dealing with small quantities of energy, just as a general moves miniature figures about over a map before setting his troops in motion," Freud wrote (1932, p. 124). The ego brings together, unifies, and organizes thought processes, and eliminates inner contradictions. Instead of the hallucinatory images of the infant, a correct picture of reality evolves, preparing the individual to cope in a realistic fashion with problems of living.

ANTICATHEXES AND THE CONTROL OF IMPULSES

The task of the ego is to meet the inner demands of the id and the superego, and the external demands of reality. At the same time, the ego has to preserve its own organization and maintain its autonomy. The economic task of the ego is to reduce the forces that act upon it and to bring to them a degree of harmony and balance. The pressure coming from the id may either disrupt the ego and turn it back into id, or, by forcing the ego to disregard reality, expose the entire organism to external dangers.

The ego expends considerable amounts of energy in anticathexes to keep down the instinctual pressures coming from the id. On the other hand, the superego may become too powerful and press the ego. Sometimes the id and the superego join forces against the ego, and the hard-pressed ego barely manages to keep its relation with reality. When the ego is weakened by the internal conflict, it loses its contact with reality and slips down into psychosis.

Something similar happens in dreams. When the ego becomes detached from reality, dreams represent a state of mind analogous to psychosis. The inner world is perceived as the outer world, and wish takes the place of fact.

Even when the ego "goes to sleep, it continues to exercise a censorship" (Freud, 1923b, p. 14). In sleep the ego withdraws its cathexes from the sensory organs and reduces the contact with the external world. The withdrawal of inhibiting anticathexes directed against the id is harmless, for the ego controls the motor apparatus. In sleep the reduction or withdrawal of inhibitions allows the id considerable but harmless freedom; the forbidden wishes that are warded off in the waking state "occupy the stage" in dreams. In some pathological cases, such as somnambulism, the motor apparatus performs unconscious actions of which the individual is unaware.

The neonate does not have the ability to control the impulse for immediate discharge of energy, nor can the archaic ego master excitation. The mature ego has the ability to absorb greater amounts of excitation, and to check panic reactions by anticathexes. The stronger the ego, the greater is its tolerance of frustrating experiences, and its ability to control emotional reactions. The strength of the ego is a good indicator of mental health.

CONTROL OF MOTILITY

"We have here formulated the idea," Freud wrote in *The Ego and the Id*, "that in every individual there is a coherent organization of mental processes which we call his *ego*. The ego includes consciousness and it controls the approaches to motility, i.e., to the discharge of excitations into the external world" (Freud, 1923b, p. 13).

One of the main tasks of the ego involves adjustment to the organism's environment. Adjustment means action, and the mature ego, which controls the motor apparatus and the cognitive functions, inhibits and regulates the motor functions of the organism. In infancy, external stimuli elicit an immediate and unorganized mass reaction of the entire organism. One of the most important functions of the ego is to "bind" the instinctual impulses and to convert their mobile cathectic energy into a predominantly quiescent, tonic cathexis. An infant's actions are impulsive; adult behavior is controlled.

The ego postpones motor reaction and abides by the *reality principle* (Freud, 1911a). The reality principle, as mentioned before, is not contradictory to the pleasure principle; it is, rather, a development of the latter. The ego pursues pleasure as much as the id does; but the ego is concerned with the avoidance of displeasure and the prevention of disastrous consequences of blind pursuit of pleasure. Ego seeks the best ways for procuring of maximum of pleasure with a minimum of unpleasure; an immediate discharge of energy in an act of love or hate may bring temporary relief, but its consequences may be disastrous. Therefore, the ego weighs the possible outcomes before responding to a given stimulus. A mature ego can withstand a certain amount of tension; it discharges energy in a way that guarantees the least risky gratification of instinctual needs.

The functions of walking and talking increase the infant's contact with the outer world. The walking infant can reach objects he could not reach before; he can meet new people and experience new situations. His narcissistic and self-centered world gradually gives way to a world of objects and people; no longer bound to a passive and hallucinatory imagination and expectation, the child moves around, becomes acquainted with the world, and tries to master it. The development of the speech function enables the child to exchange information with the outer world, and to enlarge his field of knowledge. The child begins to anticipate the reactions of adults, and his growing ego learns to avoid unpleasurable experience.

> [The ego] controls the path of access to motility, but it interpolates between desire and action the procrastinating factor of thought, during which it makes use of the residue of experience stored up in memory. In this way it dethrones the pleasure principle, which exerts undisputed sway over the processes in the id, and substitutes for it the reality principle, which promises greater security and greater success (Freud, 1932, p. 106).

The ego carries out the intentions of the id but only under conditions that safeguard survival and prevent disastrous consequences. In well-adjusted individuals, the ego is not the servant but the master that satisfies the legitimate needs of the id and superego and thwarts their irrational demands.

6

Superego and the Guilty Conscience

How does one explain self-criticism, self-reproach, one's feeling of inadequacy and guilt?

As early as in 1896 Freud noticed that people use socially accepted norms for self-criticism. This self-criticism (called "censor" in *The Three Essays*) is the inner force that prevents dangerous and morally inacceptable ideas from appearing in one's conscious. The "censor" was held responsible for repression and dream-work.

The concept of *censor* has always had two not too clearly delineated connotations: one suggesting restriction of wishes that jeopardize an individual's wellbeing and survival, the other being related to moral norms and conscience.

In 1914 Freud introduced the term *ego-ideal*, defined as a "critical faculty" within the ego. This ego-ideal was described in 1921 as the heir to the original narcissism, a sort of self-serving legislative organ. The ego-ideal is formed under the influences of the environment and represents the demands which that environment makes on the ego and which the ego cannot always rise to. It is the individual's conscience, the critical self-attitude of a part of the ego. It exercises the power of censorship in dreams and it serves as the main force in repressing instinctual wishes (Freud, 1921).

The superego evolves out of two highly important factors. One is biological and the other is cultural-historical. The differentiation of the superego from the ego is a product both of the development of the individual and of the species. The ego-ideal (later called the superego) sets behavioral norms: "thou shalt" do this, and "thou shalt not" do

61

that. As will be explained in the following chapter, the superego is, in a way, the heir of the Oedipus complex and, therefore, it carries the most powerful impulses and libidinal vicissitudes of the id. The ego is essentially the representative of the external world—reality— whereas the superego is the representative of internalized cultural values. The conflicts between the ego and the ego-ideal reflect the contrasts between the individual, realistic, here-and-now situation and the cultural-historical heritage.

In earlier works the term ego-ideal was synonymous with what Freud called later superego; in the later works, however, the ego-ideal represented a part of the superego and its craving for perfection. Thus Freud wrote in 1938:

> [The picture of the ego] which mediates between the id and the external world, which takes over the instinctual demands of the former in order to bring them to satisfaction, which perceives things in the latter and uses them as memories, which, intent upon its self-preservation, is on guard against excessive claims from both directions, and which is governed in all its decisions by the injunctions of a modified pleasure principle—this picture actually applies to the ego only up to the end of the first period of childhood, till about the age of five (p. 121).

Origins of the Superego

Around the age of five, at the phallic stage (to be more fully discussed in the following chapter), the clash between the id and the superego that represent instinctual demands versus the fear of punishment respectively, leads to the formation of the superego.

The ego grows and develops from a state of merely perceiving instincts toward actually controlling them; from yielding to instincts toward inhibiting them. In this development a large share is taken by the ego-ideal, which is partly a reaction formation against the instinctual processes of the id.

Furthermore, through its work of identification and sublimation, the superego gives the death instincts in the id some assistance, while the ego represents the Eros and the desire to live, to love, and to be loved. The superego develops as a result of the weakness of the infantile ego. At the anal stage (see Chapter Seven) the child undergoes toilet training. The fear of punishment and the need for affection and protection force the child to accept the parental demands and to "internalize" them, that is, to consider them as his own. As a result, the child may develop a dislike for playing with feces because his parents dislike him to do this.

These internalized prohibitions and self-restraints are "forerunners of the superego"; they contain the elements of the future superego, namely the fear of punishment, and tendency to conform to parental demands. Needless to say, as long as parental restrictions are not enforced, the child tends to disregard them.

DEVELOPMENT OF THE SUPEREGO

The actual development of the superego takes place toward the end of the phallic period. The fear of punishing parents comes to its peak at that point in the Oedipus complex when the little boy, shocked by castration fear, is forced to give up his mother as a love object, and the little girl, under the threat of losing her mother's love, is forced to abandon the father as her love object. The frustrated child of either sex regresses from object relationship to identification by introjection. The introjected parental figures are idealized and seem to be more powerful and more glorious than they may be in reality. In most cases the father's image (which usually encompasses the images of both parents) plays the greater role in child's superego. Originally a new element added to and introjected into the ego, forming a part of it, the superego gradually becomes a separate mental agency, often opposed to the ego. For, in contradistinction to the ego, the superego carries a great amount of destructive energy.

The superego is the "voice" of the parents and their moral standards as perceived by the child; it also represents parental wrath and punitive attitudes. The superego is partly irrational, imposing rigid restrictions not related to present situations.

The ego-ideal is one of the elements of the superego that carries the child's admiration for his parents. The superego reflects striving toward perfection, and an effort to live up to the expectations of the parents. Freud described the ego-ideal as the "sum of all limitations in which the ego has to acquiesce, and for that reason the abrogation of the ideal world must necessarily be a magnificent festival for the ego, which might then once again feel satisfied with itself."

The id is the sole source of instinctual energies; all the energy that the ego uses for its inhibiting and anti-instinctual functions is drawn from the id; the anti-instinctual forces of the superego are, furthermore, derivatives of the instinctual forces of the id. Since the child's rebellion and resentment against parental prohibition can hardly find satisfactory discharge, the superego becomes cathected with some of the destructive energy, originally directed against the parents, but later internalized and directed against the individual's own ego.

The ego's attitude to the superego is, to a great extent, a replica of the child's attitude toward his parents. The ego needs love and affection, and its self-esteem depends on the approval of the superego. When the ego lives up to the expectation of the superego, the superego reacts with approval experienced as elation. When the superego disapproves of the ego, the aggressive forces stored in the superego turn against the ego, creating guilt feelings. Depression is self-directed aggression; it is the result of the ego's being torn down by the superego. Manic bliss is caused by a fusion of the ego and superego. (See Chapter Eleven.)

The Mature Superego

In well-adjusted individuals, the superego plays the role of self-critic; it represents the conscience and socially approved norms and standards: the superego represents the moral code of the individual.

The adult superego must outgrow the initial parental prohibitions. The superego of a little child represents

> . . . not merely the personalities of the parents themselves but also racial, national, and family traditions handed on through them as well as the demands of the immediate social milieu which they represent. In the same way, an individual's superego in the course of his development takes over contributions from later successors and substitutes of his parents, such as teachers, admired figures in public life, or high social ideals (Freud, 1938, p. 17).

No longer a replica of infantile images of the parents the superego of a mature individual becomes more impersonal, related to objective social and ethical standards by which the adult person abides. In well-balanced adults there is little if any conflict between the moral standards of the society carried by the superego on the one hand, and the realistic considerations of self-protection and survival as represented by the ego on the other.

7

Oedipus Complex and
Personality Development

Mythology is the memory of nations. It conveys the irrationality of human nature, the everlasting impulses, and their eternal vicissitudes. A study of ancient myths and folklore, therefore, may shed light on unconscious motivation.

Sophocles immortalized the ancient Greek story of a man who murdered his father and married his mother. Oedipus acted unaware of the true nature of his deeds and was, therefore, innocent: he did not know that Laios, whom he had killed, was his father, nor that Iocasta, whom he married, was his mother.

Greeks were not alone in portraying the mythological family drama. The Judean King David had an experience similar to that of the Greek King Laios. King David was obliged to escape from Jerusalem, and from his rebellious son Absalom, who had slept with his father's wives.

Freud's principle of constancy applies to personality development. Life starts with conception, and intra-uterine life goes through pre-human evolutionary stages in a sheltered environment. (This principle is related to Haeckel's biogenetic principle, discussed earlier.) To be born is a traumatic experience that disrupts this sheltered life. Birth is a trauma and, as such, is the prototype of all anxiety feelings in later life.

The newborn infant's mental apparatus is exposed to stimuli far beyond his handling capacity; the natural tendency, therefore, is to restore mental economy through withdrawal from contact with the outer world. Immediate gratification of the infant's narcissistic needs gives rise to his feeling omnipotent whenever his wishes are gratified. Failure to satisfy his wishes creates a feeling of hopelessness and despair. The newborn infant experiences an objectless longing and craving for the outer world. This unspecified yearning was called by Freud the *oceanic feeling*. Probably the infant somehow craves to restore the previous state, to returns to the uterus, or even to nonexistence. Eros and Thanatos are united in this primary striving toward the soothing, well-balanced Nirvana passivity that ultimately means death.

The Oral Stage

The first pleasure-producing objects are the nipples of the mother's breasts or the bottle, and the first part of the body that experiences the pleasure of sucking is the mouth: the *oral* stage is the first erotogenic, or pleasure-producing, stage of development.

Pleasure and sexuality are closely interlocked areas in Freud's theory. Certainly not all pleasure is sexual, and pathological sex can be unpleasant; but the greatest pleasure is related to sexuality, and non-genital infantile sexuality, when various wishes and desires exist independently, is the forerunner of adult sexuality. In childhood several bodily zones may strive for their own pleasure; in adulthood the genital zone dominates. Adults whose sexuality has remained infantile are polymorphously perverted.

Every human being goes through developmental stages reflecting the level of libidinal organization and the respective erotogenic zone. The infant's first libidinal excitations are connected with the feeding process. As the infant falls asleep at the breast completely satisfied, "it bears a look of perfect content which will come back again later in life after the experience of the sexual orgasm." Many an infant continues to suck after an intake of food; sometimes in hunger, and sometimes for the pure pleasure of sucking.

Sucking is the "prototype of every later sexual satisfaction." The desire to suck includes within it the desire for the mother's breast, which is therefore the first libidinal *object*. At this stage love is intertwined with hunger, and sucking brings gratification both of hunger and of love. Initially the infant is unable to distinguish the mother's breast from his own body. Gradually, the breast is given up as a love object and is replaced by the infant's own body. The infant may suck his own thumb or tongue. Whether breast-fed or bottle-fed, weaned early or late in life, every child longs after the mother's breast and the mother as a whole. The mother's image stays in his memory as his first love object and the prototype for all future love.

At the oral phase the attitude toward the outer world is ambivalent and contains elements of both Eros and Thanatos. The infant swallows what he loves and loves what he swallows. His love is destructive and cannibalistic; cannibals, said Freud, have "a devouring affection" for their enemies, and devour people of whom they are fond.

Oral love is destructive and self-terminating; the infant does not care any longer for the milk he drank. As soon as the tension stimulated by hunger is removed, the infant falls asleep. Oral love is a primitive love; it is a love for a while, a love that terminates itself immediately after gratification.

Some adults who have not outgrown the oral stage may retain these destructive elements in their adult love life. They love their love objects inasmuch as they can exploit them, and love them as long as they can exploit them.

The *primary identification* is one of the earliest emotional attitudes toward others; it is a wish to be like another person. Identification is the wish to possess the other person. Identification is not necessarily love: "It can turn into an expression of tenderness as easily as into a wish for someone's removal" (Freud, 1921, p. 121).

The oral introjection leads to the primary identification. At the oral stage the infant takes things into his mouth, thus incorporating whatever he loves. When he incorporates an object, he may believe that he himself is like the incorporated object. Savages believe that they become as brave as the lions they eat.

Primary identification in the oral stage is a normal phenomenon that must be distinguished from *secondary identification* that may develop at a later stage in pathological cases. Loss of love object may cause desexualization of love, and introjection of the beloved person or object. In such a case a normal object relationship gives way to identification.

Freud and Abraham suggested a division of the oral phase into *oral-passive* and *oral-aggressive* (Abraham, 1911). The oral-passive phase extends over several months of the first year of life; toward the end of the first year, and in the second year of life the oral-aggressive phase of libido develops. The oral-passive or oral-dependent stage is characterized by pleasure derived from sucking—the oral-passive infant may not be able to distinguish between himself and the external world, so experiencing sucking as a self-gratifying phenomenon.

The oral-aggressive phase usually coincides with teething. The infant becomes aware of the fact that the mother's breast is not a part of himself and that it is not always available. The infant does not take the breast for granted, and, whenever frustrated, he grabs, bites, and seeks oral gratification by acts of aggression.

The fusion of Eros and Thanatos in the oral stage is accomplished in the cannibalistic act of swallowing. (At the oral-passive stage the infant is less aggressive and takes the supply of milk for granted.) At the oral-aggressive phase teeth are used as a weapon in procuring gratification.

THE ANAL STAGE

In the second and often the third year of life, infants derive considerable pleasure from excretion, and learn to increase this pleasure by a delay in emptying the bowels, with concomitant stimulation of the mucous membranes of the rectum.

Infants experience pleasure in the evacuation of urine and the content of bowels, and they very soon endeavor to contrive these actions so that the accompanying excitation of the membranes in these erotogenic zones may secure them the maximum possible gratification. . . . The outer world steps in as a hindrance at this point, as a hostile force opposed to the child's desire for pleasure. . . . He is not to pass his excretions whenever he likes but at times appointed by other people. . . . In this way he is first required to exchange pleasure for value in the eyes of others (Freud, 1915-1917, p. 276).

The infant sees in feces "part of his own body and is unwilling to part with them." He may offer resistance to the maternal demands, and try to exercise sole control over them. Many an infant acts aggressively in elimination; libido and hate are combined in anal eroticism in the sadistic holding and expelling of feces. Resistance against bowel training is an expression of rebellion against adults.

The anal stage is ridden with another ambivalence besides expulsion-retention. Masculinity and femininity are distinguished at this stage by activity and passivity respectively. Masculine impulses are scoptophilia (gazing), onlooking, curiosity, desire to manipulate and to master; these impulses may develop into cruelty and sadism. Feminine impulses represent a passive desire connected with the anal and the feminine erotogenic zones. The rectum can be easily stimulated by accepting a foreign body that enters it. The anal ambivalence of masculine-active expulsion and feminine-passive reception of a foreign body may lead to a confusion of sexual roles in adulthood.

Abraham (1911; 1924) suggested a subdivision of the anal stage into the anal-expulsive and the anal-retentive stage. In the early and expulsive phase, the infant enjoys the sadistic pleasure of expulsion. Folklore and slang bear witness to these anal-aggressive tendencies as preserved in the scatological language used by adolescents and some adults.

At the anal-retentive stage, the infant may develop affection for feces. Feces are the first possession that the infant may give away to his beloved mother. Feces is the prototype of a gift, and subsequently of gold and money. In dreams feces may symbolize babies, since most children believe that childbirth is a process similar to elimination. Often the penis is considered by children as being analogous to the column of feces that fills the mucous tube of the bowel.

The anal-retentive phase is considered to be the source of *tenderness,* that is, the wish to preserve and to take care. Freud accepted Abraham's suggestions on this point, and elaborated on the concept of tenderness as distinguished from the oral type of love.

Although tenderness originates from the wish to keep and to preserve feces, gradually the care spreads to all pleasurable objects and grows into a consideration for the mother whom the infant wishes to keep and preserve as a source for a future and continuous flow of gratification. According to Abraham, the "retention pleasure" outweighs the "elimination pleasure." With the spread of tenderness, the child begins to care for his property and pets, handling them carefully and with tenderness.

THE URETHRAL PHASE

The urethral phase is transitional to the phallic phase (when genital organs become the main avenue of libido gratification). The urinary tracts are closely related to the genital tracts in both sexes, and children's sexual fantasies and dreams confuse urine with semen and sexuality with urination.

Urethral eroticism is basically autoerotic; one's own body is the love object. Urethral eroticism may turn toward other objects with fantasies about urinating on them or being urinated on by them.

Urethral eroticism in girls often leads to holding on and retention, but usually aims at the expulsion of urine; emptying of the bladder gives pleasurable sensations. Urination itself may be as active and aggressive as urinating on someone. Urethral eroticism in boys develops gradually into normal and active genital eroticism. Urethrality in girls leads to a conflict concerning their sexual role, and often becomes later on associated with penis envy. The passive nature of urination, experienced as "let it go," or loss of control over the bladder in boys, is related to confusion about their sexual role. Often one may find passive and feminine traits in men who were bedwetters in their childhood.

Bladder-control training often leads to conflicts with parents. The child's lack of self-control, and his delays in developing full control are often punished by parents. Urethral conflicts often hurt the child's self-esteem and elicit feelings of shame. Bedwetting children become often overambitious as if struggling against the feeling of shame and trying to re-establish their self-esteem.

The Phallic Phase and the Oedipal Conflict

The term "phallic" is derived from *phallos* which means erected penis. The boy discovers, as it were, the genital organs and learns to derive pleasurable sensations by manual stimulation. The genital organs become powerfully cathected, although it is some time before all sexual excitement becomes concentrated in the genitals, and is discharged by their interaction in sexual intercourse.

The most important conflict at the phallic stage is the Oedipus complex. The tragedy of Oedipus was not a result of malevolence on his part, but a product of inevitable fate. When Oedipus realized what he had done, he punished himself by pulling out his eyes. Freud saw in the myth a symbolic description of the prehistoric development of human society and, in accordance with the biogenetic principle, a necessary stage in the lives of individuals.

Every four- to five-year-old boy desires to possess his mother physically in the ways which he has derived from his observations and intuitive surmises of sexual life, and tries to seduce her by showing her the male organ of which he is the proud owner. The boy tries to take over his father's place, for, though he loves and admires his father, at the same time he views his father as a competitor and wishes to get rid of him.

At the phallic phase the penis becomes the main source of pleasurable sensations. In contradistinction to the urethral (passive) desire to be fondled, a definite need emerges for active pursuit and thrust with the penis.

The little boy is aware of his inferiority in comparison to his father, whose penis is larger. The little boy is afraid that his father may punish him for masturbation, and for desiring mother. If the boy has had a chance to notice the difference between male and female organs, the castration threat becomes something very realistic and shocking. The boy believes that all people originally have a penis but that it is sometimes cut off by an omnipotent father. Castration fear is much stronger than the (oral) fear of being eaten or the (anal) fear of losing the body content.

The fear of castration forces the boy to abandon his incestuous desire for his mother. Some boys give up masturbation altogether and develop a passive attitude similar to that of the mother. The passive attitude conceals an increased fear of and hatred for the father. This resentment toward the father often develops into a defiant attitude against all men in authority. The affection for the mother often turns into a dependence relationship, into a passive need to be loved. Overattachment to the mother—its feminine components, and partial identification with the mother—may lead, in turn, to a submissive attitude toward women in the future.

In some cases, when the mother is strong and aggressive and the father is weak, the little boy represses his phallic strivings toward his mother. Instead of trying to possess her, he identifies with her and forms a passive affection for his father. This *negative Oedipus* complex may lead to homosexuality.

The Electra Complex

The Oedipus complex in boys creates castration fears that lead to its resolution; in girls there are no castration fears. As soon as the little girl realizes the organ differences between the sexes, she develops *penis envy,* which accentuates her love for the father. This is the feminine version of the Oedipus complex, called the *Electra complex.*

Originally the little girl believes that everyone's body is like hers. As soon as she discovers that men have penises, she wishes to have one. In most cases girls fantasize that they had a penis but lost it. The little girl "begins by making vain attempts to do the same as boys, and later, with greater success, makes efforts to compensate herself for the defect —efforts which may lead in the end to a normal feminine attitude" Freud wrote (1938, p. 97). Girls often masturbate using the clitoris as a penis-substitute. If the little girl clings to her wish to have a penis, she may develop masculine tendencies and become domineering and aggressive. If she goes so far as to develop a negative Electra complex, she will become homosexual.

Many a girl becomes hostile to her mother, blaming the mother for not giving her a penis or for taking it away from her. Of course, jealousy of the mother for the possession of the father is always present. The girl wishes to annihilate her mother and to possess her father's penis. The feminine Oedipus complex differs significantly from the masculine one; it is jealousy and penis envy. The girl's love for the mother turns into hate; the mother is no longer a love object, and the girl reacts to the loss of the love object by identifying with it. She wishes to take mother's role and, instead of wanting to have a penis, desires to be given a baby, which is a penis substitute. Her role now becomes passive and receptive, paving the road for normal feminine sexuality.

The sexual pleasure at this stage is focused in the clitoris. Clitoral masturbation is typical for this age, and it sometimes is accompanied by masculine fantasies in which the clitoris plays the role of a penis. Penis envy leads to an inner conflict related to clitoral masturbation. A girl with a negative Electra complex may dream about taking the role of the father, inserting her clitoris into the mother's vagina and having a baby with her.

Normally, resentment toward the mother and love for the father (the positive Electra complex) lead to giving up the wish for the penis, identification with the mother, acceptance of the feminine-receptive role, and the wish to have (to "incorporate") a baby.

EMERGENCE OF MASCULINITY AND FEMININITY

The differences between masculine and feminine traits are described by Freud as follows:

When you say "masculine," you mean as a rule "active" and when you say "feminine" you mean passive. . . . The male sexual cell is active and mobile; it seeks out the female one, while the latter, the ovum, is stationary, and waits passively. This behavior of the elementary organisms of sex is more or less a model of the behavior of the individuals of each sex in sexual intercourse. The male pursues the female for the purpose of sexual union, seizes her and pushes his way into her (1932, p. 156).

Femininity does not imply all-out passivity. In several areas, women can be as active as men. In some mammalian species, the female is stronger and more aggressive than the male. Even the function of caring for the infant is not always feminine. Moreover, the function of feeding, caring for, and protecting the infant usually performed by mothers is anything but a passive waiting. It is only in the psychosexual relationship where men must be active and women receptive.

One of the best methods for the study of the differences between the sexes is to observe how the characteristics of adult men and women gradually emerge out of the bisexual behavior of infants. In earliest stages, little girls are usually more dependent and docile, learning earlier to control bowels and bladder. Girls in the anal-sadistic stage are no less sadistic than boys. In the phallic phase, girls act as if they were little men and all their masturbatory activities concentrate around the clitoris which, at this stage, is a penis equivalent.

According to Freud, the boy does not have to change his love object, which is always the mother, nor the erotogenic zone, which is the penis. The girl, to the contrary, has to change both. To become a woman, the girl has to substitute father for mother as a love object, and vagina for clitoris as the erotogenic zone. In boys the fear of castration leads to the overcoming of the Oedipus complex. Girls have no fear of castration but the feeling that they were castrated, thus there is less motivation for the resolution of the Oedipus conflict. In the pre-Oedipal stages girls are attached to their mothers just as boys are. Girls go through the ambivalent feelings of love and hate toward the mother in the oral, anal, and phallic stages. The Oedipus complex in girls comes, therefore, *after* a period of negative Oedipus complex. The turning away from the mother in the post-Oedipal phases may develop into a bitter resentment against her, a resentment that is very common in girls. The main reason for this is that the girl holds her mother responsible for her lack of penis (Freud, 1931).

The difficulties and hazards of the phallic phase in girls are summarized by Freud:

> The discovery of her castration is a turning point in the life of the girl. Three lines of development diverge from it; one leads to sexual inhibition or neurosis, the second to a modification of character in the sense of masculinity complex, and the third to normal feminity. The little girl . . . finds her enjoyment of phallic sexuality spoilt by the influence of penis envy. . . . She gives up the masturbatory satisfaction which she obtained from her clitoris, repudiates her love toward her mother, and at the same time often represses a good deal of her sexual impulses in general (*Ibid.*, p. 172).

In contradistinction to boys, the Oedipus complex in girls is not terminated but created by castration.

Many a woman takes her father as the model for her choice of a husband or assigns her father's place to him, yet in her married life repeats with her husband her bad relations with her mother. The mother-relation was actually the one upon which the father-relation was built up; in married life the original basis emerges from repression. For her, development to womanhood has consisted mainly in transferring affective ties from the mother to the father-object.

> With many women we have the impression that the period of their maturity is entirely taken up with conflicts with their husbands, just as they spent their youth in conflicts with their mothers. . . . Childish love knows no bounds, it demands exclusive possession, is satisfied with nothing less than all. . . . It has no real aim; it is incapable of complete satisfaction and this is the principal reason why it is doomed to end in disappointment and to give place to a hostile attitude (Freud, 1931, p. 231).

LATENCY

The resolution of the family drama depends on interaction between the child and his parents. Although Freud assumed that the developmental stages are biologically determined, he believed that in each particular culture the Oedipus drama is played in a different way. Moreover, how far and how well the Oedipal conflict will be resolved depends in each case on the child's constitution, his pre-Oedipal experience, the personality types of his parents, and specific patterns of intrafamilial interaction.

The fear of loss of parental love, combined with castration fear, and reinforced by primeval sources, forces the child to give up his incestuous Oedipal wishes. The child "introjects" the parental prohibitions and usually identifies himself with the parent of the same sex. This identification with parental wishes, and acceptance of their standards, leads to the establishment of conscience and superego (see Chapter Six).

When the child perceives his father as loving yet punishing, fear of and love for the father merge into a feeling of awe which facilitates the resolution of the Oedipal involvement.

At the age of about five or six to eleven or twelve, the *latency period,* the incestuous and aggressive Oedipal feelings are repressed and neutralized. Part of the instinctual forces is incorporated in the superego and used as anti-instinctual guards. The "internalized" parental prohibitions that form the core of the superego keep under severe control the repressed Oedipal cravings. The child identifies himself with the threatening parental figure which is, in most normal cases, the parent of the same sex. The sexual desires of the school-age child subside to some extent. Inhibitions, repressions, and sublimations play the decisive role in tempering the impulses. The child still loves his parents, but the love is desexualized and aim-inhibited, that is, the sexual aim of intercourse is removed. Some sexual elements are preserved in the unconscious, though once the sexual aim becomes inhibited, the child's feelings toward the parents are more tender than passionate.

Most children in latency give up their interest in persons of the opposite sex. During the early school years boys play with boys, girls play with girls. Children tend to associate and identify with parents, adults, and peers of the same sex, and develop interests that increase their identification with, and feeling of belonging to their own sex.

ADOLESCENCE

The onset of puberty signals a new outburst of libidinal cravings and increased interest in the opposite sex. This development, determined by biochemical and physiological changes, brings an upsurge of sexual desires and the beginning of courtship. Rapid physical growth and glandular changes make the adolescent excitable and sexually active. The identification with the proper sex is, to a certain extent, attained in the latency period; now the adolescent strives toward heterosexual relations patterned after the actions of the parent of the same sex.

Normal adolescents learn to combine the uninhibited and bursting sexual urge with deeply inhibited feelings of care, tenderness, and consideration for the love object. They grow gradually into adulthood and become more and more interested in a permanent union with a person of the opposite sex. Such a union leads to marriage.

In some cases, however, adolescents and sometimes adults keep their affectionate feelings and admiration for women separate from the sexual urge and become aroused and potent only with women for whom they have neither respect nor tender feelings. Apparently in such cases the affectionate and aim-inhibited attachment for the mother, normal for the latency period, is not overcome during the teen-age years, and continues into adulthood.

Needless to say, unresolved Oedipal attachments prevent normal sexual adjustment and affect adversely personality development. Chapter Eleven contains a fuller discussion of this matter.

Adult Personality

Permanent and consistent patterns of overt and covert behavior, and the totality of ways in which the individual faces frustrations, overcomes hardships, and relates to other individuals, is called character. Although Fenichel (1945) believes that the term character is almost identical with the term ego, Freud's writings imply that ego and character are two different, though closely related terms. Ego is a "structural" term; the ego is a part of the mental apparatus that includes the id and the superego. As Freud used the term, *character* is more descriptive, dealing with the entire behavior of an individual. Character encompasses the history of an individual's libidinal development, his fixations and regressions, defense mechanisms and adjustments, and the totality of interactions between the individual and his environment. The term character is not a function of the ego, although it is certainly overlapping with the ego. Fenichel believes that:

Character, as the habitual mode of bringing into harmony the tasks presented by inner demands and by the external world, is necessarily a function of the constant, organized, and integrating part of the personality which is the ego. The question of character would be thus the question of when and how the ego acquires the qualities by which it habitually adjusts itself to the demands of instinctual drives and of the external world, and later also of the superego (Fenichel, 1945, p. 467).

The term character, as used by Freud, has a broader meaning than the one described by Fenichel. Freud, to a certain extent, was influenced by the "cultural school" in psychology, specifically by Dilthey and Spranger (cf. Wolman, 1960, Chapter Eleven). In Freud's writings, character represents the quality, the "how" of personality. Each individual personality contains diverse elements; but how these work together—how the individual functions as a whole, and in what ways he differs from other individuals—all this is his character.

In the complex psychoanalytic theory of personality, the interdependence of the various mental forces and agencies is of primary importance. The strength of the character is determined by the relative strength and position of the id, ego and superego. Needless to say, development of the ego and superego depends upon environmental influences.

The ego can deal with the instinctual impulses either in a *cathectic* or in an *anticathectic* manner. In well-adjusted adults the instinctual demands find proper outlets, that is, the ego cathects them. Instinctual energies are cathected in the natural functions of the organism and in the objects of these functions. This type of behavior, the *cathectic* character, perpetuates the instinctual demands and finds avenues of gratification in which the demands of the id, the ego, the superego, and of the external world are brought to a rational harmony.

An individual has a cathectic character if he handles the instinctual demands in a rational way. Those impulses that jeopardize the inner harmony become either "successfully repressed" or sublimated, that is, channeled into new and more acceptable channels. The Oedipal situation lends itself to a cathected solution; under normal circumstances, the child gives up the love object and the sexual and destructive aims of his Oedipal wishes; the energies related to the incestuous and destructive desires are not blocked but cathected in substitute aims and objects. The libidinal energy continues to flow, but it becomes desexualized. Part of this energy becomes sublimated, the success in sublimation depending on the strength of the ego and the chances of identification with the parents. Adequate sublimation of impulses reduces the tension, and what is left of the unacceptable instinctual aims and objects can be successfully repressed.

When the ego is unable to act in a cathected way, an anticathectic—a reactive or defensive—type of behavior develops. In the *reactive* type of character, the ego cannot handle the unconscious impulses and wards them off by anticathexis. This involves a substantial expenditure of energy that must affect one's mental economy and reduce one's efficiency. In reactive behavior, repeated anticathexes are required to block the unacceptable impulses. Anxiety accompanies the conflict between the ego and the repressed impulses, limiting the ability of the individual to obtain full satisfaction in life.

The main mechanisms used in the reactive character type are reaction formations and phobias. Both defense mechanisms, to be explained in Chapter Eleven, develop into habitual behavioral patterns or character traits. Some reactive character types seem to be frigid, as if they had a "feeling phobia" or fear of letting themselves experience the usual human emotions. Some other reactive character types seem to be hyperemotional, as a reaction formation against emotions. Some develop reaction formations against reaction formations. The reactive, anticathectic character traits seem to be a kind of "armor" used by the ego in its struggle against both instincts and environment (Reich, 1945).

The development of an individual's character depends on his life history. When an individual retains the libidinal organization of one of the early developmental phases, he is said to have become *fixated* in that stage. Abraham (1924) suggested the following character types related to the developmental stages and points of fixation. Oral fixation, for instance, results in an *oral character*. This fixation is a result of either abundant or insufficient oral satisfaction. In the first case, the oral character develops an overdependent but rather optimistic attitude; such a person believes that the world owes him a living and will supply it. Oral deprivation usually leads to depressive, self-aggressive, and hostile attitudes. In either case oral individuals expect that their narcissistic needs will be met by the environment; the oral type of individual is demanding, self-centered, and requests others to take care of him. The oral-erotic fixation makes one a compulsive eater, drinker, smoker, and talker. The oral characters are selfish takers, hungry and acquisitive, who desire to swallow more food or more love objects, depending on the specific nature of their oral cravings.

Abraham suggested the division of the oral phase into early-passive and the late-aggressive substages. The oral-passive fixation relates to sucking in the first months of life. An adult with an oral-passive fixation is passive and overdependent, easily disappointed and unable to take frustrations. He seems to believe that the world owes him tender maternal love and care, and in his optimistic daydreaming he hopes to receive whatever he wishes. The traits of the oral-aggressive type are related to frustrations in nursing and to biting; the oral-aggressive type is critical, hostile, negativistic and overdemanding, and tends to destroy his love objects. He too seems to believe that the world owes him support and affection, but, for certain reasons, refuses to fulfill this debt. The oral-aggressive type is disagreeable and offensive, as if trying to force the world to give him the love and the affection that, he feels, is owed to him.

Abraham suggested a division of the anal stage into the anal-expulsive and the anal-retentive substages (Freud, 1908). Orderliness, parsimony, and obstinacy are the three main *anal character* traits. Exaggerated and overly harsh toilet training may lead to compulsive behavior in washing, and hyperconcern for personal cleanliness, neatness, and orderliness in work and household duties. The excessive parsimony that develops in the anal-retentive stage is expressive of the tendency to retain what one possesses, and feces is the prototype of all transferable possession. At the anal-retentive phase, the child learns to postpone elimination and to enjoy retention, as if keeping his cherished possession for a future and more enjoyable use. Anal-fixated adults are stingy and unwilling to part with even useless objects, as if hoping that someday they will enjoy their possessions even more. The first rebellion against the mother occurs at the anal stage, when the infant refuses to give her the feces or eliminates indiscriminately in disregard of toilet training demands. Hence negativism, obstinacy, and cruelty belong to the character traits of the anal-fixated types.

The *urethral character* type is ambitious, impatient, and envious, yet urethrality also includes the tendency toward passivity. Urethral personality types have been usually punished for enuresis by being put to shame. The bedwetter would like to hide what has happened and avoid shame; hence the "burning ambition" not to be ashamed any more, and the feeling of envy for all those who have been successful and have avoided humiliation. The urethral type lacks, however, the necessary persistence and aggressiveness. He often expects, in an oral fashion, that a magic wand will help him to attain success and glory.

The development of the *phallic character* type is a reaction formation to the castration fear. Self-assuredness, boastfulness, and aggressiveness are the main phallic personality traits, combined with a narcissistic self-love, vanity, and sensitivity. Exhibitionistic and overtly aggressive behavior is a reaction formation to castration fear. The phallic character is torn by ambivalent feelings of needing love and fearing it, of courage and timidity. The phallic character tries to overcompensate his inner fear of castration and doubts concerning his own masculinity by being overtly aggressive and boisterous. But this bold and ostensibly daring behavior serves as a façade behind which insecurity, inner doubts, and anxiety are hidden.

If penis envy in girls is not resolved or sublimated, a reactive anti-cathectic character develops. Unresolved penis envy may be channeled into the assumption of a masculine role or into vindicative feminine behavior displaying the tendency to be humiliated by, and in revenge, to humiliate men.

Normal adulthood is attained by the *genital character*. The supremacy of the genital zone over other erotogenic areas, the subordination of all genital aims to the normal heterosexual urge, and a rational choice of a heterosexual love object are the main elements of the genital character. The mature genital character accepts his or her psychosexual role as a husband-father or wife-mother, within the framework of a particular culture.

Sublimation of libidinal and aggressive impulses is facilitated when great quantities of excitation have already been discharged along normal channels. When too much instinctual energy is blocked, sublimation is rather difficult, and reaction formation usually takes place. In the genital character, sexual and aggressive energy find adequate and socially acceptable outlets; emotions are not warded off, but controlled and utilized by the ego. The pregenital impulses are partly subordinated to the normal heterosexual function, and partly sublimated; they can, however, serve as a forepleasure. The ego becomes the master of the total personality. The diversified instinctual impulses become coordinated, the Oedipus complex resolved, and reasonable harmony established between id, ego, and superego. The more harmonious the personality structure, the better the individual's mental health.

8
Theoretical Considerations

Psychoanalysis can be presented as a stimulus-response theory. Stimuli act upon the organism and the organism reacts to them. What goes on inside the organism between the moments of stimulus and response is the subject matter of psychoanalytic study. Freud's set of hypothetical constructs enables us, given the stimulus, to understand and to predict the response or, given the response, to discover the stimulus. Psychoanalysts apply this method in their therapeutic practice. When patients report their past history (the stimulus being the independent variable), psychoanalysts apply psychoanalytic hypotheses and interpret the patients' symptoms. Quite often the analysts can anticipate the symptoms from the life histories. When a patient describes his symptoms, the psychoanalyst views the symptoms as a reaction (dependent variable) and reconstructs the patient's past as the stimulus that elicited the response (that is, the symptoms).

Freud's theory evolved gradually out of his work with patients, and out of his own psychoanalysis. Out of his observations emerged a body of hypotheses aimed at filling the gaps between existing clinical data, and binding them into a coherent system.

The chief difficulty in psychological theory was presented by the concept of conscious or consciousness in its relation to physical data.

[Psychological processes] are in themselves just as unknowable as those dealt with by the other sciences, by chemistry or physics, for example; but it is possible to establish the laws which those processes obey and to follow over long and unbroken stretches their mutual relations and interdependences—in short, to gain what is known as an "understanding" of the sphere of natural phenomena in question. This cannot be effected without forming fresh hypotheses and creating fresh concepts (Freud, 1938, pp. 36-37).

METAPSYCHOLOGY

Every theoretical system goes beyond observable data. Freud's system operates with five categories of statements or propositions:

1. Propositions describing *observable* facts, for example, such overt symptoms as impotence, bedwetting, homosexuality, catatonic stupor, and so on.

2. Propositions describing *introspective* data, such as depression, elation, feeling of inadequacy, and so on.

3. Propositions describing *unconscious* phenomena, such as repression, condensation, displacement, and so on. These three categories deal with facts: the first one with facts observable from without; the second, from within; and the third, unobservable under usual circumstances.

4. This category of propositions does not report facts, but includes assumptions, postulates, hypotheses, logical constructs, and models used in theory formations. *Theoretical* propositions are used by all sciences including psychology.

5. The last category of propositions, called *praxiological,* deals with application and clinical practice, such as what an analyst should do, how and what to interpret, and so on (Wolman, 1964; 1965a).

The fourth category of propositions, the theoretical principles, has been called by Freud *metapsychology.* Freud himself had doubts about this term. In a letter to Fliess in 1897 Freud wrote: "Incidentally, I am going to ask you seriously whether I should use the term 'metapsychology' for my psychology which leads behind consciousness" (1887-1902, p. 246).

Freud did not use the term metapsychology with great consistency. In 1915b he wrote that metapsychological presentation should include the "dynamic, topographical, and economic aspects of mental processes."

Most psychoanalysts accepted the term metapsychology as indicative of general concepts of Freud's theory that reach beyond clinical observations, and set the stage for a deeper understanding of Freud's contribution to psychological theory.

Rapaport (Rapaport & Gill, 1959) has extracted from Freud's work the following metapsychological principles:

1. The *dynamic* principle—that all behavior is driven by forces
2. The *economic* principle—that all behavior is a result of transformation of mental energies
3. The *structural* principle—describing the three parts of the mental apparatus
4. The *genetic* principle—stressing the origin of mental phenomena and their developmental stages
5. The *adaptive* principle—describing human behavior in terms of people's interaction with the environment, and adjustment for life

Perhaps the term metapsychology should be abandoned in favor of psychological theory of theoretical postulates. It seems that the following principles form the theoretical backbone of Freud's work (Wolman, 1960; 1964a; 1965a; 1967a) :

Empiricism
Epistemological Realism
Monism
Energetism
Principle of Constancy
Principle of Economy
Pleasure-Unpleasure Principle
Determinism

EMPIRICISM

Freud (1856-1939) was educated in and surrounded by an atmosphere of natural sciences. The natural sciences scored great achievements during the second part of the nineteenth century and dominated Freud's *Weltanschauung*. The splendid progress of the physical, chemical, and especially the biological sciences—witness the appearance of the theory of evolution, and the advances in anatomy and neurophysiology—gave rise to the hope that the riddles of life and of human nature would soon be solved. The searching minds of scientists armed with precise research tools began to storm the fortresses of philosophy and religion, struggling with the perennial problems of human destiny, will, and emotions.

The optimistic outlook of Darwin, and Spencer's *Zeitgeist* enhanced Freud's preference for a biological approach to psychology and instilled in him a dislike for armchair philosophical speculations. Freud observed human behavior in a clinical setting and, as did all other therapists of mental disorders in his time, he sought the roots of the trouble in the nervous system.

Freud was originally trained as a neurologist, but when, in 1885, he went to study in France with the great Charcot, he became acquainted with phenomena we now think of in connection with psychiatry—suggestion, hypnosis, and hysteria. Back in Vienna, Freud was guided in the study of these matters by Josef Breuer.

Freud's research method was a continuation of British and French empiricism. His teachers and masters were Francis Bacon and John Stuart Mill, the fathers of the empirical method. Freud's research proceeded from observable phenomena to generalization and interpretation. But Freud was never a naïve empiricist, shying away from the study of unobservables. Unconscious phenomena had to be inferred, and the new hypotheses had to be verified by whatever observation was available. Whenever his clinical observations did not corroborate his hypotheses, or whenever his hypotheses failed to interpret the empirical data, Freud changed his hypotheses and constructed new ones.

The nature of Freud's approach can be seen in the way he studied dreams. He said:

> If the dream is a somatic phenomenon it does not concern us; it can only be of interest to us on the hypothesis that it is a mental phenomenon. So we will assume that this hypothesis is true in order to see what happens if we do so. The results of our work will determine whether we may adhere to the assumption, and uphold it, in its turn, as an inference fairly drawn (1915-1917, p. 106).

Freud followed the objective methods of scientific inquiry, assessing empirical data to establish the connections between them, and interpreting them by a set of hypotheses.

> Reality will always remain "unknowable." What scientific work elicits from our primary sense perceptions will consist of an insight

into connections and interdependences which are present in the external world, which can somehow or other be reliably reproduced or reflected in the external world of our thoughts, and the knowledge of which enables us to "understand" something in the external world, to foresee it and possibly to alter it. Our procedure in psychoanalysis is exactly similar (Freud, 1938, p. 106).

EPISTEMOLOGICAL REALISM

Epistemology seeks criteria of truth. Epistemological realism assumes the existence of the universe independently, whether people perceive it or not. A realist insists on checking data against the world of facts; the results of empiricism are used as the sole evidence of truth.

Freud believed in the transcendent truth, that is, dependence of truth upon experience:

> Scientific thought, [endeavors] to eliminate personal factors and emotional influences, carefully examines the trustworthiness of the sense perceptions, manages to have new perceptions unobtainable by usual means, and isolates the determinants of these new experiences by purposely varied experimentation. Its aim is to arrive at correspondence with reality, that is to say, with what exists outside of us and independently of us. . . . This correspondence with the real external world we call truth. It is the aim of scientific work. . . . (1937, p. 233).

Adherence to the principle of correspondence of science with the external world puts Freud in the camp of positivistic thinking developed by Auguste Comte, as against the German critical idealism initiated by Immanuel Kant. Freud's empiricism is faithful to the assumption that any scientific inquiry starts with sensory perception of facts. Sensory perceptions themselves could and should be enlarged by means of the microscope, telescope, and other tools. Observation is the fundamental approach to any scientific inquiry. Yet there is not much in common between Freud's belief in the *transcendent truth* and the neopositivists or logical positivists or physicalists, who emphasize the principles of immanent truth. Freud was highly critical of these philosophers. He wrote:

> According to this anarchistic doctrine there is not such a thing as truth, no assured knowledge of the external world. . . . Ultimately we find only what we need to find, and see only what we desire to

see. We can do nothing else. And since the criterion of truth, correspondence with an external world, disappears, it is absolutely immaterial what view we accept. All of them are equally true and false. And no one has a right to accuse anyone else of error (*Ibid.,* p. 240).

MONISM

All his life Freud believed in the unity of mind and body. Even when, under the influence of Charcot, Freud shifted to an emphasis on the psychological factor, he continued to seek organic elements in mental disorders. Freud's theory of personality was influenced by physics; his theory of libido was modeled after hydraulics; and human behavior was described in terms of tension and relief, equilibrium and disequilibrium.

In 1894 Freud wrote that it is scarcely possible to avoid picturing mental processes as being in the last resort of a chemical nature. Later on when Freud introduced some nonreductionistic concepts, he hoped that future research would close the gap between the physico-chemical and mental data.

According to Freud, all mental activities are discharges of mental energy. Mental energy was conceived as a sort of derivative of the physico-chemical energy.

Freud never overlooked the gap between the physical and mental processes and opposed a naïve reductionism that says that mental processes *are* physical. Freud believed in the monistic structure of the universe, but Freud's monism allowed for a gradual *transition* from body to mind. (See Wolman, 1965b.)

Freud wrote:

> We know two things concerning what we call our psyche or mental life: firstly, its bodily organ and scene of action, the brain (or nervous system), and secondly, our acts of consciousness, which are immediate data and cannot be more fully explained by any kind of description. Everything that lies between these two terminal points is unknown to us and, so far as we are aware, there is no direct relation between them. If it existed, it would at the most afford an exact localization of the processes of consciousness and could give us no help toward understanding them (1938, pp. 13-14).

Freud was always aware of the organic foundations of mental life. At best, Freud believed, one can assume—and never do more than assume—that mental processes utilize a form of energy that is at the disposal of the living organism. This energy is analogous to any other energy, and that is all we know. "We assume, as the other natural sciences have taught us to expect, that in mental life some kind of energy is at work; but we have no data which enable us to come nearer to a knowledge of it by analogy with other forms of energy" (*Ibid.,* p. 44).

Being a monist, Freud never gave up hope for a monistic interpretation that would combine both physical and mental processes in one continuum. But, at the present state of scientific inquiry, a radical reductionism must be rejected. Psychology must continue to do what Freud actually did: develop new hypothetical constructs independent of the physical sciences. Freud knew that his later theoretical constructs were nonreductionistic, and irreducible to any of the constructs of physics or chemistry. Although he believed that the future might prove that chemical substances influence the amount of energy and its distribution in the human mind, work on such an assumption would not be too productive at the present time.

Quite late in his life Freud arrived at the conclusion that psychology must develop its own conceptual system, since the processes with which psychology is concerned

> . . . are in themselves just as unknowable as those dealt with by the other sciences, by chemistry or physics, for example; but it is possible to establish the laws which those processes obey and follow over long and unbroken stretches, their mutual relations and interdependences. . . . This cannot be effected without framing fresh hypotheses and creating fresh concepts . . . (1938, p. 36).

Fenichel, one of the leading thinkers in psychoanalysis, summarized as follows the scientific task of psychoanalysis:

> Scientific psychology explains mental phenomena as a result of interplay of primitive physical needs . . . and the influences of the environment on these needs. . . . Mental phenomena occur only in living organisms; mental phenomena are a special instance of life phenomena. The general laws that are valid for life phenomena are also valid for mental phenomena; special laws that are valid only for the level of mental phenomena must be added. . . . Scientific psychology

investigates, as does any science, general *laws*. It is not satisfied with a
mere description of individual psychic processes. . . . Its subject is not
the individual but the comprehension of general laws governing mental
functions (p. 5).

ENERGETISM

Freud believed that there is one kind of energy in nature and that all
observable actions are either produced by this energy or exist as its
variations or transformations. If this holds true in physics, it holds true
also in other sciences, such as chemistry, biology, and psychology.
This must not be construed in a radical reductionistic vein, for human
thoughts are not electrical processes and cannot be reduced to terms of
amperes, or watts, or volts. Mental processes cannot be reduced to anything that is not mental, but they develop from the same physical
source as everything else in the world. Mental energy is energy in the
physical meaning of the word, that is, something that can be transformed into another kind of energy in a manner analogous to the
transformation of mechanical into electric energy in generators. Energy can be accumulated, preserved, discharged, dissipated, blocked; but
it cannot cease to exist. The law of *preservation of mental energy*, its
transformability, and its analogousness to physical energy, is one of
the guiding principles of psychoanalysis.

Among the psychic functions there is something which should be
differentiated (an amount of affect, a sum of excitation), something
having all the attributes of a quantity—although we possess no means
of measuring it—a something which is capable of increase, decrease,
displacement and discharge, and which extends itself over the mem-
ory-traces of an idea like an electric charge over the surface of the body.
We can apply this hypothesis . . . in the same sense as the physicist
employs the conception of a fluid electric current (Freud, 1894, p. 61).

Freud postulated that psychic energy is not an entirely new or a completely different type of energy. Mental energy is a derivative of physical energy, though no one can really tell how the "mysterious leap"
takes place, either from body to mind or vice versa.

THE PRINCIPLE OF CONSTANCY

The idea of equilibrium was not invented by Freud. It is an old idea,
as far back as Ecclesiastes:

> The wind goeth toward the south and turned about
>   unto the north;
> It whirleth about continually,
> And the wind returneth again according to its
>   circuits. (I, 6)

The thing that hath been it is that which shall be;
And that which is done is that which shall be done
And there is no new thing under the sun. (I, 9)

In physics the idea of equilibrium was expressed by Newton in his principle of inertia. Cannon introduced the idea to biology under the name homeostasis. Pavlov called it equilibrium; Kurt Goldstein, equilibration.

This idea was expressed first in *Studies on Hysteria* (Breuer and Freud, 1895). Breuer defined it as the "tendency to maintain the intra-cerebral excitation at a constant level." Freud credited Fechner with the introduction of the "tendency toward stability."

Both instinctual forces, Eros and Thanatos, were explained by Freud as particular aspects of the everlasting tendency of the living matter to restore the former state. All instincts are conservative.

The principle of constancy serves as the general framework of his theory of motivation. It represents a tension-relief continuum and explains the compulsion to repeat first experience. This "repetition compulsion" is responsible, and manifests itself in several aspects of human life.

The attributes of life were at some time evoked in inanimate matter by the action of a force [of] whose nature we can form no conception. . . . The tension which then arose in what had hitherto been an inanimate substance endeavored to equalize its potential. In this way the first instinct came into being: the instinct to return to the inanimate nature. It was still an easy matter at that time for a living substance to die. For a long time, perhaps, living substance was thus being constantly created afresh and easily dying . . . (Freud, 1920a, p. 40).

Freud invoked the constancy principle also in regard to the sexual instincts. Since "science has little to tell us about the origin of sexuality," Freud reported a myth that "traces the origin of an instinct to a need to restore an earlier state of things" (*Ibid.*, pp. 57-58). In Plato's *Symposium,* Aristophanes tells that "Everything about these primeval men was double; they had four hands and four feet, two faces, two privy parts, and so on. Eventually Zeus decided to cut these men in two. . . ." After the division had been made, "the two parts of man, each desiring his other half, came together, and then their arms about one another eager to grow into one" (*Ibid.,* p. 60).

A similar myth concerning the origins of love was quoted by the Indian *Upanishads.* Atman was the only man. "But he felt no delight. Therefore a man who is lonely feels no delight. He wished for a second. He was so large as man and wife together. He then made this his Self to fall in two, and thence arose husband and wife. Therefore Yagnavalka said: 'We two are thus (each of us) like half a shell: Therefore the void which was there is filled by the wife'" (*Ibid.,* p. 2).

Freud hypothesized that living matter was broken down into small particles "which have ever since endeavored to reunite through sexual instincts." Several biological processes may be interpreted in the light of this tendency to restore an earlier state of things.

THE ECONOMY PRINCIPLE

Freud's theory is faithful to the principle of preservation of energy, and this principle is applied to the mental energy. Mental energy can be transformed, released, or accumulated; but it can never disappear entirely. When a degree of energy is invested into something, this object becomes loaded or charged with a certain amount of mental energy in a manner analogous to that in which bodies become charged with electricity. This process of charging *ideas of objects* with mental energy was called by Freud *cathexis,* and objects in which mental energy was invested were *cathected.* Cathexis can be applied to external objects as well as to one's own organism.

Energy is transformable and displaceable. Mental processes are processes of *mental energy economics,* that is, *quantitative* processes of transformation, accumulation, investment, and discharge of mental energy. Some processes consume more energy, some less. When powerful instinctual drives mass for an immediate discharge of energy, a great amount of energy is needed for anticathexis. Individuals torn by inner conflicts cannot be very efficient because considerable amounts of their energy are being tied in inner struggle.

Mental economy depends on the comparative strength of the external stimuli, instinctual drives, and the inhibitory forces. Human behavior can be presented as a series of reflex-arcs. A stimulus acts on the organisms causing a disequilibrium (perceived as tension), and the tension leads to an action, that is, to a discharge of some amount of energy. The discharge of energy restores the equilibrium and is experienced subjectively as relief and pleasure.

Between the tension and discharge of energy two contradictory types of forces step in, one facilitating the discharge of energy that brings relief, the other preventing or postponing this discharge. The forces that urge and facilitate discharge are called by Freud *drives* or *instincts*. The instincts, or instinctual drives, press for discharge of energy, for lowering the level of excitation, and reduction of the tension in the organism. Thus these forces help to restore the equilibrium. Since homeostasis, or the tendency to keep equilibrium, seems to be a general property of living matter, the instinctual drives must be basic, innate, and primary biological forces.

When Freud postulated Eros, the instinct of life, and Thanatos, the instinct of death, in 1923, he concluded that the counterforces oppose the immediate discharge of energy, ward it off, or repress it. *Inhibitory forces* originally come from outside the organism; but in the process of an individual's growth and development they become internalized. The neonate is endowed with instinctual forces that are the guardians of its mental equilibrium. The adult's mental mechanism is far more complicated. Between the stimulus and response, a complicated process of interaction between instinctual and inhibitory forces takes place.

THE PLEASURE-UNPLEASURE PRINCIPLE

Freud credited Fechner with the idea of pleasure and unpleasure as related to the mental economy of excitation. Freud quoted Fechner as follows:

Insofar as conscious impulses always have some relation to pleasure or unpleasure, pleasure and unpleasure too can be regarded as having a psycho-physical relation to conditions of stability and instability. This provides a basis for a hypothesis [that] every psycho-physical movement crossing the threshold of consciousness is attended by pleasure in proportion as, beyond a certain limit, it approximates to complete stability, and is attended by unpleasure in proportion as, beyond a certain limit, it deviates from complete stability; while between the two limits, which may be described as qualitative thresholds of pleasure and unpleasure, there is a certain margin of aesthetic indifference (1920a, p. 8).

The ideas of constancy and economy were derived from clinical observations of pleasure and unpleasure, though from a logical point of view, the pleasure-unpleasure continuum should follow the principle of constancy. The mental apparatus endeavors to keep the quantity of excitation low, and any stimulus that increases the stimulation is felt as unpleasant.

> We have decided to relate pleasure and unpleasure to the quantity of excitation that is present in the mind but is not in any way "bound"; and to relate them in such a manner that unpleasure corresponds to an *increase* in the quantity of excitation and pleasure to a *diminution*" (*Ibid.*).

This, it will be recognized from previous chapters, is how pleasure and unpleasure are experienced by an infant.

An organism is in a state of equilibrium unless it is stimulated by inner or external factors that cause disbalance of energy, which is perceived as tension. Tension is experienced by human beings as unpleasure. The instinctual forces press for a discharge of energy, bound to re-establish the equilibrium that existed prior to the disturbance. This discharge of energy brings relief and is experienced by the individual as pleasure, or gratification of the instinctual demands.

DETERMINISM

Freud thought it possible that, in early animistic times, men had more self-confidence than has modern man.

Although the demons of animism were hostile to men, men have derived considerable self-confidence from magic practices. In their fight against the forces of nature, men used magic, which is "the first forerunner of our modern technology." Men believed in the omnipotence of their thoughts and ascribed magic power to the spoken word. It took quite a long time for men to learn to observe natural phenomena and to interpret these with scientific caution. Scientific inquiry has gradually substituted magic; empirical observation has taken the place of anthropomorphic images; and criticism and logic were introduced, following the wishful thinking of earlier ages. Science is never as certain as magic. Unfortunately, the philosophy of our times has still preserved

. . . essential traits of animistic modes of thought such as the overestimation of the magic of words and the belief that real processes in the external world follow the lines laid down by our thoughts. It is, to be sure, an animism without magical practices (Freud, 1932, p. 211).

As mentioned before, Freud was opposed to the idealistic German philosophy of Kant and to Hegel and rejected the idea that the universe is ruled by the laws of logic.

According to Freud, objective and verified observation is the sole source of knowledge. The results of these observations can be "intellectually manipulated" and put together into a system of generalizations and laws that form a system of propositions that explain empirical data.

One of these general principles is the principle of *causation*. Natural sciences, especially microcosmic physics, struggle with the difficulties arising from a strict application of the causal principle. No such difficulties have been encountered in any of the areas of scientific psychology. All students of psychology apply a more or less strict deterministic point of view. Freud preferred a rigorous determinism that accepts no causes without effects, no effects without causes.

Determinism cannot be proven; it must be postulated and corroborated by empirical research. Once determinism is postulated, it forces the research worker to continuous efforts in seeking for causes and predicting outcomes. Every successful case serves as evidence that one is on the right track, encouraging further efforts that promise to bring additional evidence. Lack of success indicates that one has to check and double-check his methods, and look for additional data. Strict determinism helped Freud in the study of the most irrational areas of dreaming and symptom-formation in neuroses. The principle of "whatever is, has its causes" forced Freud to give up the early theory of instincts that juxtaposed sex to self-preservation in order to assume the existence of destructive instincts. Causal considerations also put him constantly on guard in searching for minute details that might have been partial causes in mental development and mental disorder.

FORMATION OF MODELS

Freud himself was not pleased with the way his theory has developed. A theory does not add facts but binds them into a coherent system. The topographic model based on the distinction between Ucs, Pcs, and Cs proved to be inadequate in view of the fact that repression, being itself an unconscious process, could not be administered by the conscious. The concept of censorship, originally believed to be the function of Cs, needed further refinement.

The control apparatus obviously was partly unconscious, and partly preconscious and conscious. This apparatus was called the ego. But with the introduction of the ego, Freud had to reshape his personality theory and suggest an entirely new structural model. The id-ego-super-ego concepts do not represent empirical data. They are a theoretical *model* of personality structure that helps to organize the body of empirical findings into a coherent conceptual system.

9

Humanity on the Couch

Human beings are a gregarious species; they live in families, groups, and societies, and have close face-to-face relationships. One can hardly comprehend human life outside the complex fabric of human interactions. Every human being carries the blessings and curses of his times and is deeply involved with other human beings, their manners, and morals. The inherited constitution is but a part of one's personality; the sociocultural context is the other.

In 1913 Freud wrote *Totem and Taboo*. The main purpose of the book was to analyze the sociocultural elements of human nature. In this book Freud related his studies of the individual unconscious to the manifestations of man's collective irrationality. The direct impetus to write the book was, as stated by Freud in the preface, provided by Wundt's and Jung's works in collective psychology.

Freud chose the aborigines of Australia as a case study. These people do not build houses, do not cultivate soil, nor do they keep any domesticated animals other than dogs. They subsist on roots and the flesh of wild animals. The most influential people in their tribes are the elder members of the tribe. The Australian aborigines do not have chiefs or kings, nor do they worship any higher being. One would certainly not expect such a people to have a sexual morality in accordance with modern ideas, or to exercise restrictions of any kind upon their sexual impulses. Yet, one is surprised to learn that they seem to be obsessed with preventing any kind of incest. In fact, their whole social organization seems geared to this cause.

TOTEM

Each tribe is divided into small clans, each taking the name of its totem which is either an animal, plant, or a force of nature. The totem represents the tribal ancestor and protector of the clan. The totem is always hereditary either on the maternal or paternal side, but in most cases the maternal.

The totem system is associated with laws that forbid sexual relations between members of the same totem. Sexual relations between brother-sister, mother-son, or other family combinations are thus proscribed; and, furthermore, almost all other members of the tribe are forbidden to have sexual relations with each other. These laws are enforced with a strictly administered death penalty. Taboo rules that prohibit incestuous behavior go as far as to forbid young men to speak informally with their mothers; they also compel brothers and sisters to avoid each other's company, and married men to avoid their mothers-in-law.

Freud believed that the incest dread exhibited by these people is a subtle infantile trait and is in striking agreement with the psychic life of the neurotic. Marriage and sexual relations among the members of a totem clan were punished by death. The severity of the punishment indicates how strong the savage's wish for incest must be. These incestuous desires correspond to infantile, incestuous fixations of neurotics in our civilization (Freud, 1913a).

The members of a totem clan are not necessarily blood relations, and thus incest is a special case of breaking the exogamic rule. Since one's totem does not change with marriage, the line of transmission of the totem is the deciding factor as to whether father-daughter or mother-son incest is most strictly prohibited and, therefore, most feared. Freud inclined toward the supposition that matrilineal descent is the more primitive, thus, mother-son incest would be feared more than father-daughter incest. This fear of incest explains the above-mentioned restrictions on mother-son relations, and mother-in-law—son-in-law-relations.

TABOO

The concept of taboo is related to things and people that are holy and "uncanny, dangerous, forbidden, and unclean" at the same time;

it may be attached to the ruler, or any unusual state of health, birth, death and so on. Taboo manifests itself through prohibitions that are irrational and without any apparent mechanism for enforcement. Cases of transgressors who died shortly after committing a transgression are cited as evidence of an inescapable punishment. The transgressor becomes taboo, too.

Freud compared compulsion neurosis to the primitive taboo rules: in both cases, behavior is unconsciously motivated and seemingly absurd. The compulsive rituals attached to the neurotic and taboo situations are comparable, as are the mechanisms of contagion or displacement. Compulsion neurosis is the result of an impulse whose gratification was prohibited in early childhood, for example, an impulse relating to touching. The impulse to touch remains with the child, as does the prohibition imposed by the beloved and feared parental figure. By replacing the individual with the group, one can extrapolate a tentative explanation of taboo.

The first taboos considered are those involving the treatment of enemies. Killing of enemies is marked not by cruelty, but rather by a certain deferential attitude. Sacrifices and other rituals attempt to reverse the relation with the slain person from enmity to friendship. Murder must be expiated by purifications and by submission to restrictions, usually with regard to sex and food.

Rulers of primitive tribes are placed in a most ambivalent position. They are the chief persons in the tribe, yet they are quite commonly subject to the most restrictive measures. Priests and rulers are believed to possess great powers and to be responsible for the survival of the tribe; therefore they should be guarded from exposure to danger. Not uncommonly, however, this process is so restrictive as to give the impression that the tribe is protecting itself from the power of the ruler. In certain cases the "protective" measures are so restrictive that being chosen ruler is considerably closer to being a punishment than a pleasure.

Ghosts and spirits are believed to be associated with the dead. Murdered enemies are often sought as friends, but deceased friends and relatives may become enemies. Contact with the dead is restricted, sometimes even to the point of prohibiting the mention of the dead person's name.

According to the phylogenetic principle, narcissism in children is parallel to animism in religion; animism corresponds to the dependence of the child on his parents, as the scientific stage of humanity corresponds to maturity in individuals.

Totemism is similar to the actions of certain children toward animals. Unlike adults, children generally are unable to make a sharp distinction between themselves and animals; some children develop a considerably more specialized relation, that of a phobia with regard to a particular species of animal. The etiology of these phobias lies in a displacement of the child's fear of the father. Apparently totem restrictions and the Oedipus complex have the same underlying motivation, and totemism developed from the Oedipal conflict.

SOCIAL ORDER AND LEADERSHIP

Under the influence of Darwin's ideas, Freud believed that primitive societies were ruled by a despotic male, the arch-father who owned all females of the tribe. The primal father prevented his sons from gratification of their sexual needs. When the father died, he was succeeded by the youngest son, the mother's favorite.

The males who had no females formed a brotherhood clan and rebelled against the tyrant. The paternal horde was transformed into a brotherhood of sons who killed the father, cut his body in pieces, and distributed his women amongst themselves. In order to preserve the new social order, and to prevent another tyranny, it was decided that no one would ever take the father's place. Apparently, however, members of the brotherhood could not prevent each other from forming new families with the male as the head of the family. Now, instead of one large family with a tyrannical father, there were several families whose fathers had, to some extent, come to terms with each other; and all of them worshiped in the totem the memory of the arch-father.

Admiration for the father combined with hatred for him led to an ambivalent reaction to the father's murder. This murder was commemorated and imitated by the totem feast and indeed was the starting point of all the collective psychic phenomena considered previously.

At this point Freud made a generalization:

> The totem religion had issued from the sense of guilt of the sons as an attempt to palliate this feeling and to conciliate the injured father through subsequent obedience. All later religions prove to be attempts

to solve the same problem, varying only with the stage of culture in which they are attempted and according to the paths which they take . . . (1913a).

Freud believed that "a group is a collection of individuals who have introduced the same person in the superego, and on the basis of this common factor have identified themselves with one another in their ego. This naturally holds only for groups who have a leader" (1932, p. 96). Family is the arch-pattern for any group, a group leader is a father-substitute, and the group members are united in their admiration for and obedience to the primal father. They are acting under the assumption of being equally loved by the powerful father. "The indestructible strength of the family as a natural group formation rests upon the fact that this necessary presupposition of the father's equal love can have a real application in the famliy" (Freud, 1921, p. 140). The phenomena of transference and hypnosis are explained on similar lines: the therapist is perceived by the patient as the benevolent and omnipotent father figure.

Group Behavior

Freud pointed to two main features of group behavior. First, a distinct inhibition of criticism, judgment, and logical reasoning. Second, a definite increase in emotionality. These two symptoms are also typical for the transference situation in psychoanalytic therapy. As soon as the patient sees in the therapist the parent-substitute, his intellectual functions become inhibited, and his emotions intensify. This temporary regression creates a necessary climate for psychoanalytic treatment. Freud interpreted group behavior in a similar fashion: the members of a group admire the leader and obey him, while their critical capacity is reduced and their emotionality enhanced.

Freud used the Church and the army as examples of group formations and leadership. Both are artificial groups, which means that some "external force is employed to prevent them from disintegration." The leaders are respectively Christ for the Church and the commander-in-chief for the army. Christ loves all Christians equally, and the commander-in-chief loves all his soldiers. The army hierarchy corresponds to the hierarchy of the Church. Members of both organizations have libidinal ties to the leader and to the fellow members. When a tie with the leader is broken, the libidinal ties with members of the group break automatically.

CIVILIZATION

In 1930 Freud gave full expression to his views on civilization. The superior forces of nature, the inevitable decay of human bodies, and difficulties in interpersonal relations are the three causes of human suffering. Any means we use to defend ourselves against misery is part of our culture.

Society starts when the group unites against the individual, imposing its might upon the individual's exercise of his freedom. Society must dominate the individual in order to survive. Every individual faces the conflict between his own instinctual demands and the group demands. Civilization is built upon man's renunciation of his individual demands; and the isolated person is torn down by the same mechanism. The antithetical roles played by community protection, on the one hand, and by community restriction of satisfaction on the other hand, are hard to reconcile.

There is only a certain amount of mental energy available. Since genital love affords man the greatest gratification, man has a tendency to try to find all his pleasure along the same path. However, because of the great psychic danger involved in such a unilateral course, it remains a doubtful one. The death or defection of an individual's sole love object would be a deadly blow.

Sexual Restrictions

Civilization thwarts the uninhibited outflow of libido. It restrains part of the libido; it allows the use of some parts toward a love object that is really a substitute love object; and it sublimates part of the energy toward art. Aim-inhibited love also leads to the development of friendships and feelings of community belonging.

The love of humanity is an inadequate type of aim-inhibited love. Upon consideration, we realize that if we love blindly, we are not placing much value on our love. It is quite unsatisfactory to love a band of men without good reason. The further one is inhibited away from the prime choice of love objects, the less one gets out of the love relationship. If our limited mental energy were to be put entirely to love, we wouldn't have enough for our own protection. If civilization is to progress, we need to sublimate our sexual energy; and we pay a price for this. "On the one hand, love opposes the interests of culture; on the other hand, culture menaces love with grievous restriction" (Freud, 1930).

Sexual restrictions are a necessary source of the energy of nonsexual expression. However, such restriction is not the sole source of impingement on human nature. The bit of truth behind all this—one so largely denied—is that men are not gentle, friendly creatures wishing for love, who simply defend themselves if they are attacked, but that a powerful measure of desire for aggression has to be reckoned as part of their instinctual endowment.

Civilized man has forfeited some of his happiness for a greater chance of security. As times goes on, our civilization will contain less avoidable discomfort, with many deleterious social institutions being eliminated or reduced in unpleasant effect. But there is a certain irreconcilable line of irreducible problems and inherent contradictions: civilization has its price.

Social Restrictions

Society cannot permit full freedom of action for each individual because absolute freedom for one may mean slavery for other individuals. Curtailment of individual freedom, and inhibition of the instinctual wishes is necessary for the survival of the society. Social norms grew out of this necessity.

It is quite easy for a barbarian to be healthy: for a civilized man the task is a hard one. The desire for a powerful and uninhibited ego may seem to us intelligible, but, as it is shown by the times we live in, it is in the profoundest sense antagonistic to civilization. And since the demands of civilization are represented by family education, we must remember to find a place too in the etiology of the neuroses for this biological character of the human species—the prolonged period of its childhood dependence (Freud, 1938, p. 85).

The long childhood of humans and the inability of the human child to face the exigencies of life calls for protective and restrictive actions of the parent. The parental restraint of the child's freedom, and the thwarting of his instinctual wishes must lead to an inner conflict in the child's mind.

At this point, Freud concluded: "We cannot escape the conclusion that neuroses could be avoided . . . if the child's sexual life were allowed free play, as happens among many primitive races." But, on the other hand, this early repression must effect one's readiness for cultural growth, because "the instinctual demands, being forced aside from direct satisfaction, are compelled to take new directions which lead to substitutive satisfaction . . . and may become desexualized." One may conclude "that much of our most highly valued cultural heritage has been acquired at the cost of sexuality and by the restriction of sexual motive forces" (*Ibid.,* p. 114).

The restriction of the destructive instincts is even more important than the restrictions of sexual behavior. No society could ever survive without instituting definite prohibitions on the use of force. Since inner conflicts and fights could destroy the social organization, taboos have been imposed on the use of force within the boundaries of family and tribe. The thwarted aggressiveness becomes internalized and stored in the superego; from there it may turn against one's own person in acts of self-destructiveness. Freud explained this danger as follows:

> When the superego begins to be formed considerable amounts of the aggressive instinct become fixated within the ego and operate there in a self-destructive fashion. This is one of the dangers to health to which mankind becomes subject on the path to cultural development. The holding back of aggressiveness is in general unhealthy and leads to illness. A person in a fit of rage often demonstrates how the transition from restrained aggressiveness to self-destructiveness is effected, by turning his aggressiveness against himself . . . (*Ibid.,* p. 23).

Culture means restraint. Social order developed out of restrictions imposed upon two driving forces: sex and destruction. Incest and murder were forbidden. The killed father became totem, and all females inside the tribe became taboo.

Prior to the killing of the father, the sons lived under a permanent castration threat. After killing him, the castration threat became internalized in the form of guilt feelings. Some rituals have to be related to the castration complex. Freud discusses this problem as follows:

> Castration has a place, too, in the Oedipus legend, for the blinding with which Oedipus punished himself after the discovery of his crime

is, by the evidence of dreams, a symbolic substitute for castration. The possibility cannot be excluded that a phylogenetic memory trace may contribute to the extraordinarily terrifying effect of the threat—a memory trace from prehistory of the human family, when the jealous father would actually rob his son of his genitals if the latter interfered with him in rivalry for a woman. The primeval custom of circumcision, another symbolic substitute for castration, is only intelligible if it is an expression of subjection to the father's will (compare the puberty rites of primitive people). No investigation has yet been made of the form taken by the events described above among races and in civilizations which do not suppress masturbation among children (*Ibid.*, pp. 92-93).

RELIGION

According to Freud, men cannot imagine Providence in any other form "but that of a greatly exalted father, for only such a one could understand the needs of the sons of man, or be softened by their prayers and placated by the signs of their remorse" (1927). Freud saw in religious feelings a craving for protection. Though the primary narcissism of an infant is accompanied by the feeling of omnipotence, through inevitable frustrations infants learn to give up this feeling and ascribe omnipotence to parents. Unsatisfactory object relations and undue frustrations lead to a secondary narcissism, associated with a wish to become omnipotent and, at least, to win the favors of omnipotent beings. Frustrated and weak individuals strive to attain power by introjecting powerful figures, or by being incorporated by them. This, according to Freud, is the psychological source of religious feelings.

> [Religion is] an attempt to get control over the sensory world in which we are placed by means of the wish-world which we have developed inside us as a result of biological and psychological necessities. But it cannot achieve its end. Its doctrines carry with them the stamp of the times in which they originated, the ignorant childhood days of the human race. Its consolations desire no trust. Experience teaches us that the world is not a nursery (Freud, 1932, p. 229).

Religions, as indicated above, are based on an "illusion" that there is a head or spiritual being who loves all the members of his group with equal love. This head is the "Father-in-Heaven" and the believers are his "children." Several religious rituals speak of "brotherhood" and "sisterhood." Religious beliefs contain the elements of regression and reflect the childlike wish to be taken care of by a loving parent. The promised hereafter resembles a childhood paradise where family members live in love under the protection of the omnipotent father (Freud, 1927).

Those who do not belong to the community of believers, those who do not pray to God and are not loved by him, are necessarily outsiders. According to Freud, any religion, even if it is believed to be a religion of love, must be unloving and even hostile to those who do not belong. Every religion is a religion of love for those who belong and a religion of intolerance toward anyone else.

If today that intolerance no longer shows itself so violent and cruel as in former centuries, we can scarcely conclude that there has been a softening in human manners. The cause is rather to be formed in the undeniable weakening of religious feelings and the libidinal ties which depend upon them. If another group tie takes the place of the religious one—and the socialistic tie seems to be succeeding in doing so—then there will be the same intolerance toward outsiders as in the age of the Wars of Religion; and if differences between scientific opinions could ever attain a similar significance for groups, the same result would again be repeated with this new motivation (Freud, 1921, p. 101).

Religion assures men of protection from dangers and promises a happy end to their misfortunes. Religion fosters illusion, while science tries to help people to overcome hardship. Religion guides human behavior and sets a system of do's and don't's. Science does not offer such guidance. The business of science is the discovery of truth; some practical devices can be deduced from scientific facts and theories, but science does not offer guidance. Religion combines mythological stories of the origin and nature of the universe with ethical norms, and assurances of happiness as a reward for obedience to these norms.

Freud maintained that the religious man's picture of the creation of the universe is the same as his picture of his own creation. The ideas of cosmogony of the God-Creator-Father are combined in religion with ethical commandments and promises of comfort and protection. The Father, the symbol of parenthood, is the creator of life, the source of ethical norms, and the punishing and protecting force.

An Analysis of Judaism

Freud assumed that Moses was an Egyptian prince, one of the followers of the reformer King Tutankhaton, the heir of Ikhnaton who introduced the monotheistic religion. The Egyptian word "Mose," in Hebrew *Mosche* (which could be read as Mose), means a child. Also, the custom of circumcision has its origin in Egypt where it had been practiced long before Moses's time.

Freud maintained that the biblical story of Moses needing Aaron as a spokesman because he, Moses, had a speech defect may indicate, instead, that Moses spoke another language and needed an interpreter in order to speak with the new rulers of Egypt (Freud, 1939, p. 37).

The biblical account of Moses being a person of humble birth discovered and raised by a noble family resembles mythological accounts of other nations. According to Freud, however, Moses was a member of the Egyptian nobility and a close associate of the Egyptian King Ikhnaton (1375-1358 B.C.), who instituted the first recorded monotheistic religion, Aton. After the death of Ikhnaton, the ancient polytheistic Egyptian religion was reinstated by the priests. Moses, an ardent follower of the monotheistic Aton religion, sought people to whom he could give this religion. His choice was one of the Semitic tribes that had immigrated to Egypt several generations before.

Moses guided the Hebrew tribe in the principles of the Aton religion, taught them the Egyptian custom of circumcision, and led them forth from their bondage. While leading the tribes of Israel out of Egypt, Moses encountered several instances of resistance to the new religion. The Golden Calf incident (in which, it will be remembered, the people reverted to practices of the old religion) led to increased hostility to Moses, ending with the murder of Moses in the desert. The Israelite tribe abandoned the religion they had received from Moses and went back to polytheism.

Several generations later, after settling down in the land of Canaan, the Israelites adopted from a neighboring Midianite tribe the God Jahve. Jahve was a god of warriors (Adonai Tzvaoth), a god who led his people to territorial conquest.

The memory of Moses's murder was later denied in the Pentateuch, wherein Moses is represented as a shepherd, a son-in-law of a Midianite priest, to whom Jahve revealed himself on the Sinai Mountain. According to the Bible, it was Abraham, and not Moses, who introduced the custom of circumcision.

Centuries later the Prophets adopted the principles of the Aton religion. The Jews did not admit their sin, though the Jewish concept of God, the Great Father, is a result of this dramatic event. The Christians, however, were more fortunate in this respect due to the insight of Paul. According to Paul, Jesus the son of God, though himself innocent, sacrificed himself and assumed the guilt of the world. Thus Paul unconsciously but correctly traced the origin of the world's guilt back to guilt over the death of the primeval father. Christianity has admitted the murder of the father-substitute, Christ. Christians, by confessing their guilt, have solved the mass neurosis that originated with the murder of the primeval father. But "the poor Jewish people . . . with their usual stiff-necked obduracy continue to deny the murder of their father . . ." (Freud, 1939, p. 114). This denial is one of the main reasons for the popular hatred of the Jews, for the anti-Semitic person says, "You won't admit that you murdered God." Persecution of Jews stems from this denial; the envy that the Jews elicit in other people by maintaining that they are the first-born, the chosen children of God; and the fact that they have always been a minority.

THE MEANING OF HISTORY

Freud saw in human emotions and impulses the driving force in human history. But human impulses do not grow in a vacuum. Belonging to a group brings an individual into a complex involvement with other people whose impulses, wishes, and plans cooperate and compete with, fuse with, and contradict one another.

Group living creates a whole set of mental phenomena. Ascendance and submission, love and hate, aggression and surrender go through developmental stages resembling, to a certain extent, the life story of an individual.

In the history of the human species something happened similar to the events in the life of the individual. That is to say, mankind as a whole also passed through conflicts of a sexual-aggressive nature, which leave permanent traces, but for the most part are warded off and forgotten; and after a long period of latency come to life again and create phenomena similar in structure and tendency to neurotic symptoms (*Ibid.*, p. 101).

Freud believed that the patterns of the development of neurosis are somewhat analogous to the development of religious convictions; and the history of humanity is a history of human desires and passions, sane and insane. Men make history; men and their instincts, emotions, inhibitions, reaction formations, and sublimations determine the course of history. Men have been always lovers and haters; and Thanatos, the god of death and hatred, has never ceased to incite men to wars.

There are two sources of hostility. One is the primary force of threats, of the instinct of death and destruction which may be directed either against self or against the other man. The other is self-love, or narcissism. Narcissism works for the self-assertion of the individual and, in group processes, for the aggressive attitudes of the group toward people who do not belong.

This is why "closely related races keep one another at arm's length. . . . We are no longer astonished that greater differences should lead to an almost insuperable repugnance. . . ." One cannot be too optimistic about the future of mankind, nor expect a miraculous solution of human conflicts.

Freud was highly critical of abstract interpretations of history, and notably of the "obscure Hegelian philosophy." Man and not *"der absolute Geist,"* men and not dialectics, men and not logical systems make history. Can men harness their instinctual forces and make them work for peace? The future of mankind depends on whether and to what extent the cultural process developed in it will succeed in mastering the arrangements of communal life caused by the human instinct of aggression and self-destruction. In this connection perhaps the phase through which we are passing at this moment deserves special interest. Men have brought their powers of subduing the forces of nature to such a pitch that by using them they could now very easily exterminate one another to the last man. They know this—hence arises a great part of their current unrest, their dejection, their mood of apprehension. And now it may be expected that the other of the two "heavenly forces," the eternal Eros, will put forth his strength so as to maintain himself alongside of his equally immortal adversary (Freud, 1930, p. 101).

Freud never dismissed the role of physical environment, nor has he overlooked man's struggle for survival and his breadwinning efforts. However, he thought that a purely economical interpretation of history was too narrow.

It is probable that the so-called materialistic conceptions of history err in that they underestimate this factor. They brush it aside with the remark that the "ideologies" of mankind are nothing more than results of their economic situation at any given moment or superstructures built upon it. That is the truth, but very probably it is not the whole truth. Mankind never lives completely in the present; the ideologies of the superego perpetuate the past, the traditions of the race and the people, which yield but slowly to the influence of the present and to new developments, and, so long as they work through the superego, play an important part in man's life, quite independently of economic conditions (Freud, 1932, pp. 95-96).

Freud was understandably critical of Karl Marx for his economic interpretation of history that overlooked the cultural and psychological factors. Freud maintained that Marxism in Russia has acquired an "almost uncanny resemblance" to the Czarist absolutism. Freud admitted that economic factors play a considerable role in human affairs, but human emotions, unconscious and conscious, have always been the driving power in history.

SOCIALIZATION AND EDUCATION

According to Freud, the neonate is neither social nor antisocial. He is asocial, or presocial. His first feelings and motions are toward himself, in a narcissistic love. Need-gratifying objects and people lure his libido, which becomes gradually invested (cathected) in them. The infant "loves" whatever gives him pleasure.

Object-love is the prototype of social relations. The socialization of the child depends on his environment. An unfavorable environment thwarts the development of object-love, and facilitates narcissistic fixations. Under normal circumstances the child passes through the oral, anal, urethral, phallic, latency, and puberty stages, gradually becoming a mature individual capable of sustaining normal social relations.

Incorporation and identification represent the early, oral pattern of interpersonal relations. Some degree of consideration for the loved object begins at the anal stage, when the infant begins to preserve the love object. The feeling of "tenderness" starts when the pleasure of retention becomes stronger than the pleasure of elimination.

Tenderness and aim-inhibition are fundamental factors in social relations in adulthood. Aim-inhibited desires enable individuals to relate to one another in a nonsexual manner. Aim-inhibition starts at the anal stage, but develops more fully in the latency period. To become a well-adjusted adult one must renounce parents as love objects and identify with their norms and standards. Thus the child-parent relationship, after the resolution of the Oedipus complex, becomes aim-inhibited and tender. The same applies to normal parent-child relations. Aim-inhibited impulses are the main factor in friendship between individuals. Since these aim-inhibited impulses

> . . . are not capable of really complete satisfaction, they are especially adapted to create permanent ties; while those instincts (drives) which are directly sexual incur a loss of energy each time they are satisfied and must wait to be renewed by a fresh accumulation of sexual libido, so that meanwhile the objects have been changed. The inhibited instincts (drives) are capable of any degree of admixture with the uninhibited [instincts]. . . . It is well known how easily erotic wishes develop out of emotional relations of a friendly character, based upon appreciation and admiration (Freud, 1921, p. 141).

The superego is the carrier of social norms and values within one's mental system. The superego develops toward the end of the phallic stage as a result of the Oedipus conflict. The image of the beloved parent becomes internalized in the child's mind and forms the superego. The beloved and feared parents stand as symbols of perfection and as models to be imitated.

> [In some cases] the object serves as a substitute for some unattained ego ideal of our own. We love it on account of the perfections which we have striven to reach for our own ego, and which we should now like to procure in this roundabout way as a means of satisfying our narcissism. . . . The ego becomes more and more unassuming and modest, and the object more and more sublime and precious, until at last it gets possession of the entire self-love of the ego, whose self-sacrifice thus follows as a natural consequence. The object has, so to speak, consumed the ego. Traits of humility, of the limitation of narcissism, and of self-injury occur in every case of being in love; in the extreme case they are only intensified, and as a result of the with-

drawal of the sensual claims they remain in solitary supremacy (*Ibid.*, p. 139).

Not every individual attains this level of love, but society must bring all individuals to some degree of acceptance of social norms. This task is performed by education.

> One of the most important social tasks of education is to restrain, confine, and subject to an individual control (itself identical with the demands of society) the sexual instinct when it breaks forth in the form of reproductive function. . . . Without this the instinct would break all bounds and the laboriously erected structure of civilization would be swept away (Freud, 1915-1917, p. 273).

Later on, as he developed the theory of the death instinct, emphasis was put on the need to restrain the death instinct and the aggressive instinct, especially the latter.

Civilization is built up at the cost of aggressive and sexual impulses that must be partly repressed and partly sublimated. Each society demands that individuals limit aggression and mitigate their sexual activity. No society can survive without inhibition of instincts. The child must learn this inhibition: he must be educated in a way that will enable him to live in a society.

> The child has to learn to control its instincts. To grant it complete freedom, so that it obeys all its impulses without any restriction, is impossible. . . . The function of education, therefore, is to inhibit, forbid and suppress, and it has at all times carried out this function to admiration. But we have learned from analysis that it is the very suppression of instincts that involves the danger of neurotic illness. Education has therefore to stem its way between the Scylla of giving the instincts full play and the Charybdis of frustrating them. . . . If we can find an optimum of education which will carry out its task ideally, then we may hope to abolish one of the factors in the etiology of neurotic illness, *viz.* the influence of accidental infantile traumas (Freud, 1932, p. 204).

OUTLOOK ON LIFE

Freud's outlook on life in general and on Western civilization in particular was far from optimistic. Most people admire power and success, subscribing to material values. There are, however, some individuals who are not concerned with these goals and feel akin to the whole world in an "oceanic" sensation of eternity.

Love is the single nonpathological state in which "oceanic" feelings exist. Normal individuals, when in love, experience the feeling of identity with the external object, and they treat the love object as if it were one with themselves. It is true that in infancy there was an ego-feeling that embraced the universe, a feeling of inseparable union with the external world. But as the child matures, a sharp division appears between the internal and external worlds. In the state of love there is no clear barrier between oneself and the beloved one.

All men seek happiness, that is, the attainment of pleasure and the avoidance of pain. This goal is often at odds with reality. In the first place, the most intense form of pleasure can be experienced occasionally at best, and then only in periods of short duration; and prolonged pleasures are much less enjoyable, and very difficult to maintain. Furthermore, we are virtually always in danger of pain, which may come from three sources: one's own organism, the physical environment, and the social environment.

It would be expected that men striving for happiness would spend a great deal of their energy avoiding dangers to their well-being. Freud described several methods men use in dealing with the world —isolation, to avoid danger in human contact; intoxication, to avoid the sensation of unpleasure; control of internal drives (repression and regression); and sublimation of drives, to make satisfaction easier to attain. Happiness is an "economic" problem; it involves some sort of balance between pleasure and security, between immediate satisfaction and less intense, long-term well-being. There is no one uniform solution; each individual must find his own ways, according to his particular constitutional and environmental circumstances.

Civilization encourages intellectual, scientific, and artistic endeavors; but it requires some sacrifice of the individual's liberty to the demands of the society. The denial of free satisfaction of instinctual drives is a prerequisite of civilization, and that is why complete happiness is impossible in a civilized society. Civilization started when the sons, after killing the arch-father, were wise enough to establish taboos to prevent similar occurrences directed against themselves. This primary taboo was directed against the Oedipal wish of son for the mother. Thus, the institution of "Thou shalt not kill" and "Thou shalt not

covet" commandments became the first act of civilization, and a beginning of further control of instinctual drives in the interests of the
society as a whole.

Civilization must rely on mutual love among its members. Civilization needs aim-inhibited love rather than sexual love, as exemplified
in the commandment to "Love thy neighbor as thyself." Such aim-
inhibited love denies the sexual element inherent in all love (or at
least restrains it), for the main tasks of civilization are to serve Eros
and to promote cooperation among people. Needless to say, civilization's arch-enemy is Thanatos, the drive to destruction and death.
In the historic Oedipal act of killing, the destructive impulses over-
came those of love; remorse or feelings of guilt followed the act of
murder, and introjection, that is, internalization of the father's image
was the point that marked the beginning of civilization. The superego
was established, and became the agency of conscience representing
human guilt feelings.

The feeling of guilt harbored by the superego is used as an internal
punishment. It differs from remorse, for it is directed against the mere
hostile impulse before any act of aggression has been performed. The
superego prevents the repetition of the act of patricide and protects
civilization; however, at the same time it causes a great deal of suffering for the individual because of the guilt feeling it engenders. This
sense of guilt, while it is the bulwark of civilization, detracts from
the happiness of the individual.

In its efforts to serve Eros, civilization is in constant conflict with
Thanatos. Every individual experiences the inner struggle; he must
renounce some of his instinctual drives and comply with the norms
of civilization. In *Civilization and Its Discontents* (1930), Freud described the price paid for civilization.

Moral Values

Freud seemingly avoided ethical and philosophical problems, but
he could not altogether escape them. Freud thought that it would
be improper for a psychoanalyst to impose his moral standards on
his patients, or to offer them his own set of values. Psychoanalytic
treatment aims at helping the individual to overcome infantile fixa-

tions and regressions and to become a mature adult. It does not seek converts to the analyst's philosophy of life.

Freud was critical of the idea of a superhuman origin of moral standards:

> The philosopher Kant once declared that nothing proved to him the greatness of God more convincingly than the starry heavens and the moral conscience within us. The stars are unquestionably superb, but where conscience is concerned, God has been guilty of an uneven and careless piece of work, for a great many men have only a limited share of it or scarcely enough to be worth mentioning (1932, p. 88).

Little children are notoriously amoral; the first source of morality is the parents, who restrain the infant's pleasure-seeking impulses. The fear of punishment and loss of love, and the reward for obedience are the two main sources of children's moral development. To be bad means to do things that annoy parents; and to be good means to do things the parents approve of.

This reasoning is often applied by adults with regard to deity. Many people believe that there is a superior, father-like power that rewards people for good behavior and punishes wickedness. Each child is "brought up to know its social duties by means of a system of love-rewards and punishment, and in this way it is taught that its security in life depends on its parents (and subsequently other people) loving it and being able to believe in its love for them" (*Ibid.*, p. 224).

Moral standards are imposed by the society on the individual and become inner restraints. An individual is "virtually an enemy of culture," and morality must be imposed on him. Moral and cultural restraints stem from without, and the majority of men obey cultural prohibitions "only under the pressure of external force . . . as long as it is an object of fear. This also holds good for those so-called moral cultural demands" (Freud, 1927, p. 18).

But there is a second source of moral behavior, in addition to restraint. This second source is love for another person. "Love for oneself knows only one barrier—love for others, love for objects. . . . Love alone acts as the civilizing factor in the sense that it brings a change from egoism to altruism" (Freud, 1921, p. 119). Cathexis of libido in others necessarily limits narcissistic love for oneself.

10

In Freud's Footsteps

Freud's theories have stimulated a great many minds and inspired a host of ideas that are partly related, partly independent and dissident. The present chapter will describe the works of some of Freud's disciples who have added certain new ideas while remaining faithful to the main body of Freud's theories.

Two volumes, published shortly before Freud's death, set the pace for post-Freudian developments. Both were, in a way, a continuation of the ideas expressed by Freud in *The Ego and the Id* (1923b) and in *Inhibitions, Symptoms and Anxiety* (1926). The concept of the ego became the focal issue in psychoanalytic research and theory formation.

Anna Freud's *The Ego and the Mechanisms of Defense* (1936) elaborated upon the idea of defense mechanisms. Her work announced, as it were, the direction of the future psychoanalytic thought. The structural theory was gaining prominence in psychoanalysis, and the way the ego faced onslaughts from within and without became the main issue. Anna Freud's work clarified the role of the ego as the censor and control apparatus.

HARTMANN'S EGO PSYCHOLOGY

Heinz Hartmann's *Ego Psychology and the Problem of Adaptation,* published in 1939, went beyond Freud's original concept of the ego. Freud saw the ego as a "servant of three masters," namely the id, the superego, and the outer world, which he called "reality." Hartmann's ego was no longer a servant; it became the synthesizing power, the over-all coordinator of personality.

In 1937 Freud had suggested that not only the instinctual drives but perhaps also the ego may have a hereditary core. Hartmann went beyond this hypothesis and assumed that there are inborn forces in the ego which he called *primary autonomy*. These primary autonomous apparatuses of the ego in maturation constitute the foundation for the ego's relation to external reality. The hereditary core of the ego includes inhibitory forces that delay discharges of energy.

According to Hartmann, the early ego development appears in a new light if one accepts the idea that the ego may be more than a mere byproduct of environmental influences on the instinctual drives, and that the ego may have at least a partly independent origin. Hartmann's idea of the autonomous factor in ego development parallels the concept of the id's autonomous drives.

One should note that, prior to 1937 psychoanalysts believed that the ego developed out of the growing infant's id drives as a result of contact between the id and external reality. Hartmann stressed that the neonate is endowed at birth with a number of inborn capacities for development. These capacities are above and beyond those that spring from contact between id drives and the environment. These inborn capacities—perception, motility, and memory—have an inherent maturational timetable and do not arise out of conflict. Hartmann called them "ego apparatuses of primary autonomy." Hartmann offered the concept that the infant has only a simple, primary id, viewing the developmental potential at birth as an undifferentiated id-ego matrix.

According to Freud, the id is the source of all energy and the ego works with a desexualized libido, borrowed from the id. Freud felt that he could "make no headway" in accounting for the varied activities of the ego without assuming "a displaceable energy" which, of itself, is neutral but can join forces with an erotic or with a destructive impulse. Freud speculated that the neutral energy came from Eros and could be conceived as desexualized libido. According to Hartmann, Kris, and Loewenstein the energies of the aggressive instincts of Thanatos could be neutralized and placed at the disposal of the ego. Aggressive as well as sexual energy may, therefore, be neutralized; and in both cases this process of neutralization takes place through mediation of the ego. Thus, this energy contributes to the development of the ego and makes possible continuing interest in environmental objects regardless of their immediate relation to sexual or aggressive needs (Hartmann, Kris, and Loewenstein, 1949).

The ego's functions develop by learning and maturation. That the ego regulates relations with the environment, that it can organize to find solutions that fit the environmental situation, and the very nature of its psychic system became, therefore, of primary importance for man's self-preservation (Hartmann, 1948).

Hartmann did not assume that the ego is just as inherited as the id; he merely stressed the point that the development of the ego can be traced not only to the impact of reality and of the instinctual drives, but also to a set of factors that are probably genetic and cannot, in any case, be identified with the forces of reality and instinctual drives (Hartmann, 1950a).

The development of the ego, being partly based on the process of maturation, is not entirely traceable to the interaction of drives and environment; indeed, it can become partly independent from the drives in a secondary way. Hartmann terms these factors in ego development primary and secondary autonomy, respectively. The secondary autonomy of functions of the ego has a bearing on the stability of its developmental acquisitions.

The autonomous factors may also come to be involved in the ego's defense against instinctual tendencies, against the outer reality, and against the superego. What developed as a result of defense against an instinctual drive may grow into a more or less independent and more or less structured pattern of behavior. These relatively stable patterns are referred to by Hartmann as *secondary autonomous*.

The relative independence of the ego from the id pressures can be expressed in terms of distance from ego-id conflicts, or distance from the regressive trends exerted by the id determinants. The newly acquired ego functions, the secondarily autonomous, show a high degree of reversibility in the child who uses special devices in his effort to counteract regression.

Regression

Hartmann states that occasional regressions in the service of the ego can be tolerated by the adult ego if its functions are unimpaired.

Also, the healthy ego, for certain purposes, has to be able to abandon itself to the id, as in sleep, or in sexual orgasm.

Neutralization is a continuous process. In Hartmann's conception, it includes Freud's sublimation of both the libidinal and the aggressive drives.

Neutralization of energy is to be postulated from the time when the ego evolves into a more or less demarcated structure within the personality. The development of constant object relations presupposes some degree of neutralization. But it is quite possible that the use of this form of energy starts even earlier than at the moment of neutralization just described, and that primordial forms of postponement and inhibition of discharge have previously been fed by a neutralized energy. Some countercathectic energy distributions probably arise in infancy; and there are, probably, transitional states between instinctual and fully neutralized energy. The optimal functioning of the ego depends on the degree of neutralization.

The ego combines the archaic mechanisms of its own and those of the id into an integrated psychic process. The ego does not function only by means of rational and logical processes, but also through primitive feelings and mechanisms. Playful activities, artistic creativity, and fantasies are what Hartmann called a sort of *controlled regression.*

This "regression in the service of the ego," can be exemplified by the history of science. Friedrich August Kekulé, was unable to establish a formula for the arrangement of carbon atoms in the benzene compound. One night he dreamed of a snake that was swallowing its own tail. Upon awakening, Kekulé realized he had a schematic formula for benzene, having visualized in his dream the structure of the benzene ring.

Adaptation and the Intrasystemic Approach

An assumption that all reactions to the external world are processes of adaptation would be too broad. Hartmann felt, nevertheless, that attempts should be made to restudy the evolution of the ego in terms of adaptation. As stated above, the newborn infant is not entirely a creature of drives, but has inborn apparatuses (perceptual and protective mechanisms) that perform a part of the functions that, after the differentiation of ego and id, are attributed to the ego. "The consideration of the conflict-free ego sphere leads us to the functions which are more or less clearly related to the tasks of reality mastery, that is, adaptation" (Hartmann, 1939, p. 22).

According to Hartmann, ego is a complex system and its various inner conflicts are not as significant clinically as those between the ego and the id, or the ego and reality. Psychoanalysts did not think of them as conflicts, at any rate. Hartmann called the intra-ego conflicts "intra-systemic" in distinction to the intersystemic, ego-id or ego-superego conflicts.

The intrasystemic correlations and conflicts in the ego have hardly ever been studied. There are several inner conflicts in the ego: the ego has from its start the tendency to oppose the drives, yet one of its main functions is to help to achieve their gratification; then too, insight may border on rationalization, for while it provides objective knowledge, it may convey conventional prejudices of the environment.

The intrasystemic approach becomes essential if such concepts as the dominance of the ego, ego control, or ego-strength are to be clarified. These terms must remain ambiguous until a differential consideration of the ego functions is carefully scrutinized. Consider, for example, the concept of ego-strength. The strength of the ego is commonly judged on the basis of its behavior in typical situations, irrespective of the fact that these situations may be more related to the id, the superego, or outer reality than to the ego proper. According to Hartmann, the autonomous aspect of the ego must be considered. A variety of factors must be taken into account—the strength of the drives, narcissism, tolerance or intolerance against unpleasure, anxiety, guilt feelings, and so on. Hartmann studied the interrelations between the different areas of ego function such as defenses, organization, and autonomy. Whether the defense mechanisms lead to exhaustion of the ego's strength is determined not only by the force of the drive in question, and by the defenses at the ego's frontiers, but also by other factors. A definition of strength must include the autonomous functions of the ego, their interdependence and structural hierarchy and, especially, whether (or how far) they are able to withstand impairment through the processes of defense. This is one of the main elements of how Hartmann conceives of ego-strength. It is probably not only a question of the amount and distribution of ego energy available; doubtless it also has to be correlated with the degree to which the cathexes of these functions are neutralized (Hartmann, 1950a).

Hartmann introduced the idea of flexibility in the structural system; he called his idea *change of function*. According to Hartmann, a certain "behavior form which originated in a certain realm of life may, in the course of development, appear in an entirely different realm and role" (1939, p. 26).

In 1950, Hartmann went further. He wrote:

> It seems reasonable to assume that these mechanisms do not originate as defenses in the sense we use the term once the ego as a definable system has evolved. They may originate in other areas, and in some cases these primitive processes may have served different functions, before they are secondarily used for what we specifically call defense in analysis. The problem is to trace the genetic connections between those primordial functions and the defense mechanisms of the ego. Some of these may be modeled after some form of instinctual behavior: introjection, to give you but one example, probably exists as a form of instinct gratification before it is used in the service of defense. We will also think of how the ego can use, for defense, characteristics of the primary process, as in displacement (1950a).

We have seen that, according to Hartmann, the development of the ego is due partly to learning and partly to maturation. He considers the ego a partly primary, independent variable, not entirely traceable to the interaction of drives and the environment, as well as a quantity that becomes partly independent from the drives in a secondary way. This is what Hartmann means when he uses the terms primary and secondary autonomy in ego development. The secondary autonomy of the ego's functions has a bearing on the stability of its developmental acquisitions.

Social Considerations

Furthermore, according to Hartmann, man does not come to terms with his environment anew in every generation. Man's relation to the environment is guaranteed by hereditary factors, as well as by the influence of tradition and the survival of works of man, which Hartmann considers an "evolution peculiar to man." People take over from the past a great many methods for solving problems, so that man lives "in past generations as well as in his own" (Hartmann, 1939, p. 30). From this arises a network of identifications and ideal-formations having great significance for the forms and ways of adaptation. Thus, the "task of man to adapt to man is present from the very beginnings of life" (Hartmann, 1939, p. 31).

The fabric of social interrelations, the process of division of labor, and the individual's social position determine together the possibilities of adaptation; these qualities also regulate the elaboration of instinctual drives and the ego's development. Social structure determines which behavioral forms will have the greatest adaptive chance. The relation of the individual to his environment is "disrupted" from moment to moment, and must constantly be returned to an equilibrium. Every organism is capable of maintaining or re-establishing its equilibrium and, according to Hartmann, "we can picture the process as an oscillation around the equilibrium" (1939, p. 38).

Hartmann believes that the superego emerges in the Oedipal conflict, but, though genetically related to earlier anal phenomena, it must not be confused with them. The superego is not a part of the system ego, but it does include the ego-ideal. The contents of the superego are differentiated from superego functions; certainly the same applies to their respective cathexes. There may be, moreover, tensions and conflicts between the major systems (id, ego, and superego), as well as conflicts within the superego itself (Hartmann and Loewenstein, 1962).

Work with Kris and Loewenstein

Freud's structural theory was further elaborated by Hartmann, Kris, and Loewenstein. They wrote:

> *Functions of the id* center around the basic needs of men and their striving for gratification. These needs are rooted in instinctual drives and their vicissitudes (we do not here deal with these drives themselves and the theory of instincts as developed by Freud). Functions of the id are characterized by the great mobility of cathexes of the instinctual tendencies and their mental representatives, i.e., by the operation of the primary process. Its manifestations are condensation, displacement, and the use of special symbols.

Functions of the ego center around the relation to reality. In this sense, we speak of the ego as of a specific organ of adjustment. It controls the apparatus of motility and perception; it tests the properties of the present situation at hand, i.e., of "present reality," and anticipates properties of future situations. The ego mediates between these properties and requirements, and the demands of the other psychic organizations.

Functions of the superego center around moral demands. Self-criticism, sometimes heightened to incentives to self-punishment, and the formation of ideals, are essential manifestations of the superego (1946, p. 15).

Hartmann has developed most of his ideas in collaboration with Kris and Loewenstein. They have developed together a new version of the psychoanalytic theory of aggression and related it, analogously to the libido, to a source, aim, and object. The erotogenic zones serve as sources for sexual stimulation, discharge of energy, and gratification. The destructive instinct uses the body as a tool and as an instrument for the discharge of energy.

The plasticity of aggression manifests itself in the control of the body, in the control of reality and in the formation of psychic structure. . . .

Libidinal impulses may be aim-inhibited under two conditions: the inhibition may be temporary; may induce an accessory and preparatory stage of impulse completion; or it may substitute for the uninhibited action. In the first case discharge is delayed but under certain conditions mounting pleasure is experienced; in the second case, in which behavior is permanently aim-inhibited, there occurs, in addition to the damming up of libido, substitute-formation or sublimation (Hartmann, Kris, and Loewenstein, 1949, p. 18).

Hartmann, Kris, and Loewenstein conclude their discussion of the aggressive instinct as follows:

In rounding off our discussion it seems appropriate to enumerate four types of conflict through which the aims of aggression are modified. (1) Aggression and libido may be involved in conflict when the cathexis of both drives is vested in the same object (instinctual conflict). (2) The reaction of the object to attempts at completion of aggressive acts may endanger the individual (conflict with reality). (3) This danger may be anticipated by the ego, which is in part already identified with the object, and the ego might be opposed to the completion of aggressive acts (structural conflict, involving the ego). (4) The conflict may involve moral values (structural conflict, involving the superego) (*Ibid.*, p. 19).

ERIKSON'S EIGHT AGES

In his book *Childhood and Society,* Erik Erikson scrutinized Freud's timetable of libido development, relating it to what is known about the ego and what is beginning to be learned about society. Freud felt that there were "psychologically uncharted regions of the body's orifices as zones of vital importance for emotional health and illness." Freud found that neurotics and perverts were not only infantile in their attitudes toward their fellow men, but also regularly impaired in their genital sexuality, and given to overt or covert gratifications and comforts from nongenital body zones. All this seemed to be related to their early childhood, and to clashes between the impulses of their infantile bodies and the training methods of their parents. He felt that during stages of childhood, zones providing special gratification were endowed with libido, a pleasure-seeking energy that became genital only at the end of childhood.

Freud stressed the fact that sexuality does not just spring into being at a certain time in the life of the individual; rather, it is the result of step-by-step staged growth and development. He felt that if a stage is hindered from developing properly, it will then hinder the outcome of other stages.

Erikson endeavored to relate child development to sociocultural factors. He sought to identify the criteria "by which the individual demonstrates that his ego, at a given stage, is strong enough to integrate the timetable of the organism with the structure of social institutions" (Erikson, p. 246).

Erikson distinguished the eight ages of man as follows: (1) basic trust vs. basic mistrust, (2) autonomy vs. shame and doubt, (3) initiative vs. guilt, (4) industry vs. inferiority, (5) identity vs. role confusion, (6) intimacy vs. isolation, (7) generativity vs. stagnation, and (8) ego integrity vs. despair.

Erikson believes that "to understand either childhood or society, we must expand our scope to include the study of the way in which societies lighten the inescapable conflicts of childhood with a promise of some security, identity, and integrity" (*Ibid.,* p. 277).

At the first stage of life an infant needs continuous care and protection that will enable him to attain a peaceful satisfaction of his basic needs as related to, for instance, the intake of food, bowel movements, and sleep. Motherly care can provide the necessary comfort. "Consistency, continuity and sameness of experience provide a rudimentary sense of ego identity" (*ibid.,* p. 247).

The presence or absence of the feeling of security or, as Erikson calls it, trust, is an important factor in mental health. Parents must convey to the children the basic feeling of trust. The amount of trust does not depend on the quantity of food given to the child, nor on demonstrations of love, but on the quality of maternal care that "combines sensitive care of the baby's individual needs and a firm sense of personal trustworthiness within the trusted framework of their culture's life style" (*Ibid.,* p. 249).

The second stage ("autonomy vs. shame and doubt) is related to muscular maturation of the capacities of holding and letting go (Freud's retention and expulsion). Holding can mean care and protection, but it may also mean restraint and cruelty. Toilet training may lead to a tender care of the infant, or to shaming and doubting him.

This stage, therefore, becomes decisive for the ratio of love and hate, cooperation and willfulness, freedom of self-expression and its suppression. From a sense of self-control without loss of self-esteem comes a lasting sense of good will and pride; from a sense of loss of self-control and of foreign over-control comes a lasting propensity for doubt and shame (*Ibid.,* p. 254).

At the "initiative vs. guilt" stage the emphasis is on attack and conquest in boys; it is the "phallic-intrusive" mode. In girls it is making oneself attractive and endearing and, in more aggressive modes, it is "catching."

Infantile sexuality and incest taboo, castration complex and superego all unite here to bring about that specifically human crisis during which the child must turn from an exclusive, pregenital attachment to his parents to the slow process of becoming a parent, a carrier of tradition. Here the most fateful split and transformation in the emotional powerhouse occurs, a split between potential human glory and potential total destruction. For here the child becomes forever divided in himself. The instinct fragments which before had enhanced the growth of his infantile body and mind now become divided into an infantile set which perpetuates the exuberance of growth potentials, and a parental set which supports and increases self-observation, self-guidance, and self-punishment (*Ibid.*, p. 256).

The fourth stage, "industry vs. inferiority," corresponds to the child's school age, and the Freudian latency period.

This is socially a most decisive stage: since industry involves doing things beside and with others, a first sense of division of labor and of differential opportunity, that is, a sense of the technological ethos of a culture, develops at this time. [There is a] danger threatening individual and society where the schoolchild begins to feel that the color of his skin, the background of his parents, or the fashion of his clothes rather than his wish and will to learn will decide his worth as an apprentice, and thus his sense of *identity*—to which we must now turn. But there is another, more fundamental danger, namely man's restriction of himself and constriction of his horizons to include only his work to which, so the Book says, he has been sentenced after his expulsion from paradise. If he accepts work as his only obligation and "what works" as his only criterion of worthwhileness, he may become the conformist and thoughtless slave of his technology and of those who are in a position to exploit it (*Ibid.*, pp. 260-261).

The fifth stage, adolescence, is called by Erikson "identity vs. confusion." Physiological revolution is but one aspect of the dangers typical of this stage. The ego has to integrate childhood identifications with the vicissitudes of the libido, with endowed aptitudes, and with social roles and opportunities related to the prevailing culture. The adolescent has to develop his sense of identity in his sociosexual role and group identification.

The sixth stage, "intimacy vs. isolation," reflects the problems of young adults. Freud was once asked what a normal person should do well. His answer was short: *lieben* and *arbeiten;* that is, a normal adult is capable of loving and of working. "Satisfactory sex relations," Erikson wrote, "make sex less obsessive, over-compensation less necessary, sadistic controls superfluous."

The seventh stage presents the conflict between "generativity and stagnation," or productivity and aridity. An individual's mature age may lead to stagnation, or it may open the best chances for productive work and creativity.

The full realization of oneself is presented dramatically by Erikson as "ego integrity vs. despair." Lack of ego integration is signified as fear of death. Integrity of the ego is "a postnarcissistic love . . . he partakes" (*Ibid.*, p. 268).

ALEXANDER AND FRENCH: THE INTEGRATIVE FUNCTIONS

Franz Alexander followed three principles in interpreting the integrative functions of the ego: the constancy principle of Freud, and the ideas of inertia and surplus energy. Life consists of a continuous supply and output of energy. Energy is consumed and must be regularly replaced; and this requires a continuous flow, or a fresh supply from the environment. The primary function of the central and autonomic nervous systems in higher animals is the maintenance of this dynamic equilibrium, which is frequently challenged both by external stimuli and by the very processes of growth and living.

Disturbances of equilibrium are experienced by the individual as needs and wishes that motivate voluntary behavior. All organisms tend to keep these psychological tensions at a constant level. Freud borrowed this principle from Fechner and called it the "constancy principle."

The Alexander and French version of psychoanalytic theory maintains that the chief task of the ego is to fulfill the principle of constancy. The ego is the governing head of the organism. By its intrasensory perceptions, it registers internal disturbances of the equilibrium, grasping them as needs and sensations. The sensory perceptions of the outer world register the environmental conditions upon which the fulfillment of its needs depends. The ego also performs integrative and executive functions. It is the center of motor control, and by confronting its internal perceptions with its external perceptions, it integrates them, and becomes capable of gratification of subjective needs within the realistic limits set by external conditions. The ego serves, too, as protection from excessive and harmful external stimuli.

The constancy principle does not distinguish the quality of different instincts, drives, or emotions; it is applicable to all of them, however, whether they represent needs as fundamental hunger and sex, or more complex impulses like curiosity and creativity, conflict and revenge, or emotional experiences that find expression in such processes as weeping, laughing, or sighing. Thus, according to Alexander, the principle of stability is identical with the instinct of self-preservation; but it is more precise since the organism tries to keep internal conditions at an optimal balance.

Alexander stressed the importance of learning in personality development. Behavioral patterns that proved adequate in maintaining biological and psychological homeostasis are repeated until they become automatic, and can be performed with minimum effort. This process of learning consists of two phases: groping experimentation through trial and error, and repetition of the adequate behavior patterns that have been found useful by trial and error. The learning process is therefore based on two dynamic principles: (1) the constancy principle, in accordance with which the organism is compelled to try out behavioral patterns that reduce internal tensions experienced as needs and wishes by gratifying them; (2) the economy principle, in accordance with which adequate behavioral patterns are repeated and repeated so that gradually they become automatic, requiring no conscious mental effort.

The constancy principle expresses merely the tendency of the organism to attain optimal conditions for survival; but this principle alone cannot constitute a full explanation of behavior. The tendency toward stability is further defined by the economy principle, the principle of inertia: organisms tend to perform their necessary functions, and to perpetuate constant conditions through a minimum discharge of energy. This energy-saving tendency keeps at a minimum the amount of force necessary for adjustment to the environment. However, the principle of inertia compels the organism to perpetuate automatic behavior that was satisfactory in the past but that may become no longer adequate. This "laziness" was called by Freud *fixation*. Alexander noticed that, under trying conditions and in the face of new and threatening situations, people tend to fall back on earlier patterns of behavior. This orderly retreat to the past, called *regression,* is one of the fundamental factors in psychopathology. Life is an ever-repeated struggle between the organism's tendency to retain old behavioral patterns according to the principle of inertia, and the challenge of growth and adjustment.

One of Freud's fundamental discoveries was that a child's playful exercises, along with the mature manifestation of sexuality, belong to the same category, which he called "erotic." (This was actually the rediscovery of a fact known to the ancients, for the Greek god Eros was the god of both love and play, and was represented by a child). Erotic phenomena do not follow the principle of inertia, but expend energy. They are creative, and serve as the motor power behind growth and reproduction. They do not represent automatic repetitions or adjustments, but lead the organism toward new ventures and new experiences. Thus, when impulses serve the survival of the organism and preserve energy, they are nonsexual. When they discharge surplus energy in play or love, they are sexual (Alexander, 1948; French).

WOLMAN'S INTERINDIVIDUAL CATHEXIS AND ARES

Research in and treatment of psychoses led to further modifications of psychoanalytic theory, especially in the direction of interindividual relations.

When Freud wrote about object-relations, it was about the individual who cathects and not about the cathected object. When A loves B, said Freud, A's libido is cathected. But what happens to B when A loves him? Or when love is mutual? Freud dealt only with the distribution of the libido *within* the individual. Narcissism is the cathexis of the libido in oneself, object-relation is the cathexis of libido in others. But what happens to those toward whom the cathected libido turns is a matter that requires further study (Wolman, 1966a).

The sociologically oriented neoanalytic schools of Karen Horney and H. S. Sullivan took up this issue. Horney devoted a great deal of attention to the *need to be loved*. When the child feels loved, accepted, and cared for, he develops the feeling of *safety*. When the child feels rejected, a *basic anxiety* develops. Human activities are guided by both pleasure and safety; people would renounce pleasure rather than safety, said Horney (p. 73). Instead of Freudian sexual or aim-inhibited love, she introduced an environmentalistic concept of protection and safety. Also, instead of Freud's active cathexis of libido or need to love, Horney emphasized the need to be loved (Wolman, 1954, p. 4).

Sullivan moved further away from Freud and emphasized interpersonal relations. "Personality can never be isolated from the complexity of interpersonal relations in which the person lives and has his being," he wrote. In psychiatric inquiry we study the interpersonal situation, not simply a person as *an isolated and self-contained entity.* Sullivan, without using the term cathexis, emphasized empathy, which he described as a kind of "emotional contagion or communion" between the child and the parental figures. He wrote, "The infant shows a curious relationship or connection with the significant adult, ordinarily the mother. If the mother . . . is seriously disturbed . . . around the time of feeding, then on that occasion, there will be feeding difficulty or the infant will have indigestion" (Sullivan, 1947, p. 7).

Horney and Sullivan added important aspects to the study of social relations. Horney emphasized the *receiving object;* Sullivan, the interpersonal involvement. Yet there is no need to reject Freud's model of personality and substitute for it the models introduced by Horney or Sullivan. The comparison between these three theories of personality (Wolman, 1960, Chapters 6 and 9) would show the superiority of the Freudian model of personality.

Freud's model of personality can be adapted to interindividual relations by a broadening of Freud's term cathexis (Wolman, 1960, pp. 302-303). While Freud dealt with the individual who cathects his libido in objects, I suggest the inclusion of the cathected objects in our study. Thus one can make full use of the important contributions of the neoanalytic schools without abandoning the Freudian system.

The concept of interindividual cathexis is a *theoretical construct.* There are no neurological or physiological counterparts to it. One may find some similarity to Pavlov's explanation of reflex. "An external stimulus," wrote Pavlov, is transformed into a nervous process and transmitted along a circuitous route (from the peripheral endings of the centripetal nerve, along its fibers to the apparatus of the central nervous system, and out along the centrifugal path until, reaching one or another organ, it excites its activity)" (p. 121). Pavlov's description can be explained in terms of cathexis of physical energy; the external stimulus somehow transmits a part of its energetic load in the peripheral endings of the centripetal nerve and thus cathects or charges this nerve ending and, through the circuitous route, cathects the nerve center also.

By analogy, and it is but an analogy, one may speculate about the interindividual cathexes of mental energy. It must be stated clearly, however, "that I neither have evidence nor know how to find it, that mental energy is cathected and that it follows the analogy with physical energy. Thus, I have to say that at the present time I use the term 'interindividual cathexis' as a theoretical construct and nothing else" (Wolman, 1966, pp. 25-26).

An additional modification involves Freud's concept of death instinct. Fenichel criticized Freud as follows:

> A death instinct would not be compatible with the approved biological concept of instinct. The thesis of an instinct source that makes the organism react ot stimuli with drives toward "instinct actions," which then change the source in an appropriate manner, cannot be applied to a death instinct. The dissimulation in the cells, an objective destruction, cannot be a "source" of a destructive instinct (p. 60).

Eros and Ares

A new concept was introduced, the concept of Ares, the god of war, instead of Freud's concept of Thanatos, god of death (*Ibid.,* pp. 20 ff). Death is the end of life, the zero point. There is no drive to die, and no instinctual force "promotes" death. There is, however, a desire to kill, to kill for survival.

One may hypothesize that there is but one general, universal drive, the *Lust for Life*. There is one general biochemical energy, but the energy can be transformed into mental energy in any fashion, and the discharge of energy can go in any direction: It can be Eros and libido, whenever it supports life, and libido can be cathected in self or others, in a sexual or a desexualized way. Whenever there is a threat to life, however, the self-directed Eros is accompanied by the object-directed *Ares*.

Ares is the name for the destructive aim of the general drive, Lust for Life and serves the purpose of survival served by Eros. Imagine an immortal and omnipotent creature whose life and wellbeing could never be threatened by anyone or anything. Apparently such a creature would be pure Eros; there would be neither need nor room for Ares.

But all animals, including human beings, live under threat of the inanimate and animate nature. To face this threat, Lust for Life turns not into Eros but Ares. Eros and Ares are two channels of the same drive of Lust for Life; activated in two different types of situations, they basically seek the same end—the survival of the individual and, in some situations, survival of the species.

It seems that Ares is not only the more primitive, the phylogenetically earlier drive than Eros, but as a rule it is more powerful than Eros. No dog can copulate when his skin is burned but Pavlov's dogs salivated when he burnt their skin (Pavlov, p. 228). According to Pavlov, the cortical food center is stronger than the skin center. Apparently the sex center is weaker than the skin center. When Pavlov tried to crush the dogs' bones, even salivation stopped. Obviously, hungry animals can bear hustle and tussle and minor wounds; but bone breaking means death, and faced by the threat of such injury, all energy must be mobilized in the defense of life.

Furthermore, hurt, hungry, thirsty, exhausted, sick, or wounded organisms act in an irritable, hostile, and destructive manner. It seems that whenever its store of libido is momentarily used up, the organism works on *destrudo* (destructive energy). The libido seems to be a "higher" fuel, the destrudo a "lower" one; when there is no threat to life, a balanced love for oneself and for others suffices for survival. In emergency and in exhaustion of libido, destrudo is, metaphorically speaking, plugged in. Men in great anger act as if they had received a new supply of energy—the universal latent destrudo is put to use.

Eros and Ares are the two arms of the struggle for survival and two forces that release mental energy. Freud called these forces *instincts*. The instinct Ares has, like Eros, an impetus, source, object, and aim. The impetus is the amount of destrudo that it may activate. Its source is a threat to one's own life. The aim of Ares is a complete or partial destruction of enemies. The object can be oneself, or any other organism.

Ares, the instinct of hostility, fits well into the definition of instinct given by Fenichel: "The instinct attempts to remove the somatic changes at the source of the instinct." The somatic changes in Ares include: accelerated heart beat, perspiration, trembling, contraction of muscles, baring of teeth, growling, and so on. The threat of annihilation is the main cause of such somatic changes. The hostile action, which is a discharge of destrudo aiming at the destruction of the threatening object, restores the inner balance (in analogy to the actions of Eros). The threat may be related to an inner stimulus of hunger or an outer stimulus that jeopardizes one's life, prevents satisfaction of hunger, prevents escape, or exists as any other combination of hostile stimuli (Wolman, *Eros and Ares,* in press).

PART TWO
The Practice of Psychoanalysis

11

The Mind that Set the Clock Back

They were called lunatics, in the belief that the light of the moon (*luna* in Latin) attracted them and made them sleepwalk. They were called madmen, for their behavior resembled that of men in a furious rage. They were called degenerates, because they were thought of as a negation of normal genetic development. They were treated as freaks of nature, outcasts, and scum of the earth. They were accused of malice and of intentional crimes against humanity in service of Satan, and therefore punished and tortured.

Medieval times excelled in cruelty to the mentally disturbed; and neither Judaism nor Christianity sought to alleviate their ill fate. Modern times, too, have witnessed the unabated inhumanity of men toward those whose minds were believed to be deranged, possessed by devils, and obsessed with madness.

As late as 1803, the throwing of mental patients into water and the firing of cannons was believed to be a fair treatment, calculated to bring them back to their senses. As a part of this "noninjurious torture" program, J. C. Reil suggested presenting the mental patients with a show with "judges, prosecutors, angels coming from Heaven, dead coming out of their graves which in accordance with the needs of various patients should be played to produce the illusion of verisimilitude" (quoted after Zilboorg and Henry, p. 287).

Pinel's Reforms

The man who broke through the walls of the mental asylum and brought hope to its inmates was Dr. Pinel. In September 1793, Dr.

137

Philippe Pinel addressed the Parisian City Council, the *Commune de Paris*. The political air was hot, and the ruins of the Bastille, where political prisoners had been held without trial, were still smoldering. Parisians opened the gates of the political jails, freed the prisoners and, in hopes of putting an end to man's injustice to man, destroyed the old fortress. But not too far from the Bastille stood Bicêtre, an old building where people were locked in chains without trial and flogged, but not for political reasons. They were tortured because they were declared to be madmen, lunatics, and possessed. Freedom, equality and brotherhood, the cry of the French Revolution, failed to pierce the walls of Bicêtre.

"These people are mentally sick," declared Dr. Pinel. They are "far from being guilty people deserving punishment." They are sick people "whose miserable state deserves all the consideration that is due to suffering humanity" (quoted after Zilboorg and Henry, p. 322 ff.). The head of the Commune, Citizen Couthon, decided to visit Bicêtre. He was greeted by the inmates with curses. Couthon asked Pinel: "Are you mad yourself that you want to unchain these animals?" Dr. Pinel replied: "These mentally ill are untreatable only because they are deprived of fresh air and personal freedom."

Pinel declared the inmates of mental asylums "sick" and some of the institutions were reformed, and transformed into mental hospitals. This in itself was a revolutionary step. The Judaeo-Christian tradition is one that is sympathetic toward ill people, and charity is a part of it. As "sick people," mentally disturbed individuals did not belong in an asylum. Medical science had to take care of them, and Pinel and scores of other physicians turned to research in mental disorders.

Early False Starts

Mason Cox (1762-1822) believed that an abundance of blood in the brain caused mental disorder, thus bloodletting was the proper method of treatment. Of course, this idea was rooted in past errors, but psychopathology, the science of mental disorder, had to go through its trial-and-error stages.

At the beginning there was plenty of error. In many cases physicians did not know what to do with mental patients. Disturbed patients were given drugs, forced to take hot and cold baths, advised to take vacations, or change their environment. Needless to say, in most cases no significant changes were produced. Quite often hysteria was treated surgically; in 1882 a Dr. Pean removed an ovary to cure a woman's hysteria. . . .

Temporary changes were brought about by direct suggestion. Esquirol (1772-1840) believed that mental disorders are caused by psychological factors, but Mirel (1809-1873) believed that biological degeneration was responsible.

The majority of research workers, however, believed in organic origins of the mental disorders. Maudsley (1835-1918) in England maintained that all mental disorders are diseases of the brain. According to Maudsley the main causes of mental disorders were infections, poisons, anemias, and other blood and circulatory disturbances. To Griesinger (1817-1868) in Germany, mental disorders were mere symptoms of a brain disease. The discovery of brain centers, and Wernicke's (1848-1905) studies of aphasias and amnesias, strengthened the belief that all mental disorders are ultimately diseases of the organism, and especially of the nervous and circulatory systems.

Freud's teachers shared these ideas. Theodor Meynert (1833-1892), Professor in the Viennese School of Medicine, believed that mental diseases are related to vasomotor disturbances combined with local brain dysfunction. According to Meynert, mania and melancholia were caused by pathological changes in blood vessels in the cortex and in the cortical cells themselves, while delusions and hallucinations were a product of disturbance in subcortical centers. Meynert was opposed to the term psychiatry; the so-called nervous diseases were, according to him, diseases of nerve cells and products of vasomotor pathology.

Yet this impressive body of research conducted by Meynert, Hughling-Jackson, Broca, Brücke, Ludwig, and others failed to answer questions related to the vast majority of mental disorders. Whatever was not clearly organic was called "functional," to indicate that though anatomical and histological studies did not discover any evidence of pathology, something had gone wrong with the "function" of the nervous system. Needless to say, all neurotic and most psychotic disorders were put in the category of "functional mental diseases."

Labeling of mental diseases did not contribute much toward their understanding, and no one knew how to treat nonorganic mental disorders. Kraepelin's classificatory system introduced some order into the multitude of symptoms, but not even the best classificatory system offers a magic cure. Small wonder that Abraham described the situation as follows:

> Although our results at present are incomplete, it is only psycho-analysis that will reveal the hidden structure of this large group of mental diseases. And moreover, its first therapeutic results in this sphere justify us in the expectation that it may be reserved for psycho-analysis to lead psychiatry out of the *impasse* of therapeutic nihilism (1911, p. 156).

REGRESSION

It took a great deal of moral courage for Freud to stand up against prevailing public opinion; but it might have been even more difficult to rebel against the authority of medical science and declare that mental disorder is not a degeneration, nor a deformation of nerve cells, nor a failure in their functioning. Even Charcot, who used hypnosis for eliciting and removing hysterical symptoms, explained his work in terms of neurology.

Freud said that mental disorder is a personality trouble.

It is a *regression* in one's mental development.

It is a failure to grow up and become an adult.

"Regression," Freud wrote as early as in 1900, "plays a no less important part in the theory of the formation of neurotic symptoms than it does in that of dreams" (1900, p. 548). Every human being goes through developmental stages from birth toward adulthood; those who did not grow up or who went back are mentally disturbed.

> Owing to the general tendency to variation in biological processes it must necessarily happen that not all these preparatory phases will be passed through and completely outgrown with the same degree of success; some parts of the function will be permanently arrested. The usual course of development can be disturbed and altered by current impressions from without (Freud, 1915-1917, p. 297).

Sometimes parts of the libido, or parts of its component impulses become arrested at an early phase of development. This arrest was called by Freud *fixation*. The fact that some portions of libido became fixated increases the danger that some day the entire libido may *re-*

gress to those points of fixation. The libido rarely progresses un-hampered from one phase to the next. Some fixations are formed, and partial regressions take place. Under trying circumstances the fixations may become substantial; and a weakened libido is less capable of over-coming external obstacles and proceeding smoothly. Regression to an early developmental stage of libido is the essence of neurosis.

There are two types of regressions of the libido: one is a regression to where early love objects are again of transcendent importance; the other is a regression to an early stage.

The danger of regression under stress depends on the strength of past fixations and the severity and duration of the stress. The fixation of libido is the predisposing factor, while frustration is the precipitating factor.

Not every stress, pain, and frustration is pathogenic, that is, produc-ing disorder. Everyday life is full of adverse, unpleasant, and threaten-ing events that do not affect a person's mental health and turn him into a neurotic.

ANXIETY

Apparently it is the psychological reaction to stress that has to be considered in this connection. The ego's reaction to external threats is *fear*. And when the ego is exposed to threats from within, that is, from the id or superego, the feeling of *anxiety* ensues. The term anxiety was used by Freud in more than one connotation. Originally Freud be-lieved that anxiety was the result of blocking of sexual needs. The com-bination of unsatisfied libido and undischarged excitation was supposed to cause anxiety-neuroses; the thwarted libido was transformed into a state of anxiety.

Having introduced the structural theory in 1923, Freud introduced a new theory of anxiety three years later. The new theory did not dis-card the old one, but reduced the scope of its meaning to some few special cases. According to the 1926 theory, anxiety originates from the infant's inability to master excitations. The neonate is exposed to more stimulation than he can possibly master. The abundant stimula-tion is traumatic, and creates the painful feeling of *primary anxiety*.

Birth-trauma is the prototype of all future anxiety states (cf. Rank 1929). Separation from mother is another anxiety-producing experience.

Castration fears, guilt feelings, fear of abandonment and rejection are the most frequently experienced anxiety-producing situations. The feeling of being helpless is one of the most frequent symptoms of neurotic disturbances; it is especially typical of traumatic neuroses. Also, the inability to control one's own excitation (whether aggressive or sexual) may create a state of anxiety.

The early theory of anxiety became incorporated in the new and more broadly conceived theory. Since the satisfaction of instinctual demands may create a dangerous situation, the ego must control the instinctual impulses. A strong ego accomplishes this task easily; but a weak ego has to invest more energies in an anticathectic effort to ward off the unconscious impulses.

Anxiety is "a specific state of unpleasure accompanied by motor discharge along definite pathways," Freud wrote in 1926. Thus the three types of anxiety-producing situations in childhood can be reduced to one fundamental cause. Being left alone, being in the dark, and finding a strange person in place of the mother are the main anxiety-producing situations which reflect the *feeling of loss of the loved person*. Anxiety is a reaction to the absence of, or of separation from the loved object. Such a feeling is experienced in the birth-trauma, in weaning, and later on in castration fear. In all these situations, loss of support causes increased tension, and an economic disturbance demanding some discharge of energy.

If the infant longs for the sight of the mother, it does so surely, only because it already knows from experience that she gratifies all its needs without delay. The situation which the infant appraises as "danger" and against which it desires reassurance, is therefore, one of not being gratified, of an *increase of tension arising from non-gratification of its needs*—a situation against which it is powerless (Freud, 1926, p. 156).

A strong ego weathers dangers; thus anxiety is a sign of the ego's weakness. When the ego is threatened by external reality, it develops *reality-anxiety*. When the superego attacks the ego, a feeling of quiet and inferiority called *moral anxiety* ensues. When the id's pressures threaten to break through the ego controls, a *neurotic* anxiety develops.

Reality-anxiety is a reaction to a danger from without. Anxiety-preparedness may develop in one of the two following manners: either an old danger-signaling experience called "anxiety development" is re-experienced, or a past danger, having a paralyzing effect on the individual, is re-experienced.

Neurotic anxiety manifests itself in three ways. The first is anxiety neurosis, usually felt as some sort of over-all apprehension and a sense of oncoming doom. Anxiety neurosis is usually caused by the existence of undischarged excitation when blocked libido energy is transformed into an anxiety state.

Another type of neurotic anxiety is manifested in hysteria, and in some other neuroses. Certain ideas attached to libido become repressed and distorted, and the energy, whether libidinal or destructive, turns into anxiety.

The earliest childhood neuroses are phobias and obsessions. The fear of one's own libidinal destructive impulses is externalized and transformed into a fear of threats from without: neurotic anxiety is experienced as objective reality-anxiety, and viewed as a fear of an external threat. The neurotic disguises the fear of his own libido or his death instinct from which there is no flight, and substitutes for it an alleged external danger that can, supposedly, be warded off by obsessive behavior.

Moral anxiety is a reaction to pressure exercised by the superego. It is experienced as feelings of guilt, or a sense of shame, or a feeling of inferiority and inadequacy. A real threat to the organism does not necessarily produce anxiety; but anxiety can easily be produced by inner tension that is experienced as a threat from without. Thus, Freud explained, it is not the external danger itself that causes anxiety:

> What is it that is actually dangerous and actually feared in such a danger situation? It is clearly not the objective injury which need have absolutely no importance psychologically, but it is something which is set up in the mind by it. Birth, for example, our prototype for the state of anxiety, can hardly in itself be regarded as an injury, although it may involve a risk of injury. The fundamental thing about birth as about every danger situation, is that it evokes in mental experience a condition of tense excitation which is felt as pain and which cannot be mastered by discharge. . . . The operation of the pleasure principle does not guarantee us against objective injury but only against a particular injury to our mental economy. . . . The magnitude of the excitation turns an impression into a traumatic factor which paralyzes the

operation of the pleasure principle and gives significance to the danger situation (Freud, 1932, p. 130).

DEFENSE MECHANISMS

The term *defense mechanism* was introduced by Freud in 1894. Freud did not use it for thirty years, and in 1936 Anna Freud described the mechanisms in detail. Defense mechanisms are techniques used by the ego in warding off the instinctual demands of the id and the pressures of the superego. A strong ego does not need defenses; but when the ego is unable to cope with inner pressures, it erects defenses. All defense mechanisms except sublimation indicate an inner conflict and a state of anxiety.

The main defense mechanism is *repression*. Repression is an unconscious exclusion from the consciousness of objectionable impulses, memories, and ideas. The ego, as it were, pushes the objectionable material down into the unconscious, and acts as if the objectionable material were nonexistent.

The ego uses a good deal of its energy (anticathexes) to keep whatever it has repressed repressed forever. Whenever a repressed wish or idea comes close to the surface and attempts to re-enter the unconscious, the ego's chief defense mechanism is activated to push the undesirable wish down, back into the unconscious. Powerful anticathexes prevent the repressed material from becoming conscious again. These anticathexes are the forces that caused repression, and they keep the repressed material under close guard. The action of the ego that prevents the unconscious from becoming conscious is called *resistance*.

The mechanism of repression is applied to fight off Oedipal desires and castration fears. Whenever the ego applies the mechanism of repression, the genital organization of the phallic stage is wholly or partially pushed back to the earlier anal-sadistic stage, or even further back. Regression is always related to past fixations; it may be limited to a certain erotogenic zone (such as a regression to orality), or it may be an over-all regression to primary narcissism.

A successful and normal defense against objectionable instinctual wishes is called *sublimation*. Sublimation is a cathexis of instinctual energy into a substitute aim or object or both; it is a channeling of the instinctual demands into a new and desexualized desire or idea.

Another important defense mechanism is *rationalization*. Rationalization is an effort to distort reality to protect one's self-esteem. In its attempt to mediate between the id and reality, the weak ego ascribes rationality to the irrational demands of the id. The ego displays a "pretended regard" for reality, while the id has actually distorted it. Rationalization is fallacious reasoning that misrepresents irrational motivation in an effort to make it appear rational. A strong ego can accept defeat; but a weak ego would rather distort the truth than admit defeat. Rationalization is used as a coverup for mistakes, misjudgments, and failures: it tries to justify our behavior by reasons that are made to sound rational.

One frequently encountered rationalization is known as "sour grapes," after the fox in the fable who couldn't get the grapes he desired and consoled himself by calling them sour. People rationalize in the same way; it takes a mature personality with a strong ego to admit that not all desirable grapes are also attainable. A neurotic would rather make himself believe that sweet grapes were sour than admit that his efforts to get them were unsuccessful.

The defense mechanism of *undoing* represents a far-reaching loss of contact with reality. Undoing is a fallacious belief that one can undo or nullify previous actions that make him feel guilty. A strong ego admits past blunders, and a mature individual assumes responsibility for his behavior. A weak ego fears superego's reproaches and acts in accordance with a belief that wishing to nullify the past deeds can effect such nullifications. The mechanism of undoing is a patent distortion of truth; it is a kind of magic. Freud pictured the ego as trying to "blow away" not only the consequences of an event, but the fact that the event itself ever took place.

Sometimes the weak ego rejects not the past but the present; the defense mechanism involved in such a rejection is called *denial*. When its actual current life becomes too painful to accept, or too difficult to cope with, the infantile ego withdraws from reality, breaking away from the truth, and refusing to acknowledge the existence of painful facts. Memory and perceptions prevent an unlimited escape from reality; but in some pathological cases the hard-pressed ego gives up reality-testing and simply denies facts. Some persons deny the loss of beloved ones and act as if the latter were still around.

Introjection is a defense mechanism rooted in the oral phase of libido development. It is the desire to swallow the love object and thus to identify with it. Introjection expresses the primitive and ambivalent attitude that combines love and destruction in a cannibalistic incorporation of the love object, and in identification with the object incorporated. When some adults are unable to develop more mature object relationships, their weak egos regress to the oral defense mechanism of introjection. Neurotic identification with the love object becomes the only possible object relationship.

Projection is the opposite of introjection. Projection leads to paranoid distortion of reality. The archaic ego draws a line between "something to be swallowed" which is pleasurable and "something to be spit out" which is unpleasurable. What is inside belongs to the ego, and what was spit out becomes an alien body.

When the weak ego harbors feelings that invite the superego's harsh criticism, the ego may try to ascribe them to the outer world. Forbidden homosexual impulses are a case in point. Some homosexuals "project" their homosexual urges and believe that other people of the same sex desire them. Some neurotic and psychotic individuals cannot admit their own hostility, and so ascribe it to others in delusions of persecution.

A strong ego can handle the id. Some of the id impulses are gratified, some postponed or modified, and some flatly rejected and suppressed. A weak ego needs artificial defenses against impulses, and one of them is the developing of an extreme attitude opposed to the id desires. For instance, an individual with strong homosexual impulses may crusade against homosexuality. An individual who hates his father and is very unhappy about it may develop a ritual of affection directed toward his father; an individual torn by an impulse to be dirty may develop compulsive cleanliness. This formation of opposite attitudes aimed at warding of the id impulses is called *reaction formation*.

Isolation consists of an "interposition" of a refractory period in which nothing more is allowed to happen, no perception registered, and no action performed. It usually takes place after an unpleasant experience, when the ego, unable to face pain or humiliation, stops functioning for a while.

Isolation is often present in compulsion neuroses. This defense mechanism separates an emotional content from the idea into which the emotion was cathected, thus splitting an emotional experience into two separate parts. In cases of "split ego" or "duel personality," part of an experience is kept separate from the rest of one's ego.

In *displacement* there is a shift of emotion, symbolic meaning, or fantasy from the person or object toward which it was originally directed to another person or object. It involves the discharge of aroused emotions toward neutral or less dangerous objects. A child who has been spanked may kick another child or break his toys. Sometimes a minor situation may act as a trigger that releases pent-up emotions in a flurry of (displaced) anger that is all out of proportion to the immediate incident.

Displacement is of adjustive value because it enables the individual to discharge dangerous emotional tensions without recognizing the person at whom such feelings were originally directed, thereby avoiding the risk of loss of love and possible retaliation.

Through the process of symbolic association or spread, displacement may become extremely complex and deviant. Destructive criticism and gossip are frequently disguised methods of expressing hostility.

THE NATURE OF NEUROSIS

According to Freud, mental health is a precarious balance between the id, ego, and superego, and between the total personality and the outer world. This balance can be easily upset, and "there is scarcely any condition generally recognized as normal in which it would not be possible to demonstrate neurotic traits" (Freud, 1938, p. 81).

Neurosis is a *quantitative disharmony* between the various parts, forces, and areas of personality. Neurosis is always a disorder of the ego. The weak or poorly organized ego is unable to cope with inner and outer pressures. The precipitating cause is either that reality has become "intolerably painful," or that the instinctual pressure of the id has become unusually intensified.

The infantile ego struggles through difficult situations, warding off some of the instinctual demands by *repression,* and some of the demands of external reality by *denial.* Both defense mechanisms are usually unsuccessful. Actually, the ego is called upon to master the sexual excitations before it has grown sufficiently to be able to do so. When the ego's development has lagged behind the development of the libido, or when the libido has not safely passed the developmental phases, or when the superego is either underdeveloped or overgrown, the stage is set for a mental disorder.

Freud's neurological training and practice led him to believe that there are, really, two types of neurosis: the "actual" neuroses and the psychoneuroses. The actual neuroses, such as hypochondria, anxiety neurosis, and neurasthenia are caused by physiological aspects of abnormal sexual life, while psychoneuroses such as conversion hysteria, paranoia, obsessions, phobias, and hallucinations are caused by repressed memories of traumatic sexual experiences in the past (Freud, 1894; 1895; 1896; 1898).

In the early stage of his work Freud stressed the importance of organic factors. For example, the main difference between anxiety neurosis and neurasthenia was related to the "accumulation of excitation" in the former, and "impoverishment of excitation" in the latter (Freud, 1895, p. 114). Freud believed that sexual abstention causing "accumulation of excitation" was the source of anxiety. Blocked sexual energy turned into anxiety states. On the other hand, excessive masturbation caused "impoverishment of excitation" and led to neurasthenia experienced as lack of zest, lack of ambition, and general fatigue.

Freud pointed to the fact that some mental disorders are of a purely psychological origin. In these disorders, called *psychoneuroses,* the symptoms "arose through the psychical mechanism of (unconscious) defense, that is, in an attempt to repress an incompatible idea . . . in distressing opposition to the patient's ego" (1896, p. 162). Thus, for example, obsession is caused by a trauma connected with active sexual behavior in childhood; obsessions aim at substituting irrelevant thoughts for painful memories of past transgressions. "The ego," wrote Freud, "breaks away from the incompatible ideas." A passive participation in forbidden sexual activities may lead to *conversion hysteria,* a neurosis in which past traumas are converted into a "bodily form of expression."

Much later, in his two Encyclopedia articles (1923a), Freud restated his distinction between actual neuroses caused by abnormalities in present sexual behavior, and psychoneuroses caused by past traumatic events.

> The neurotic is incapable of enjoyment or of achievement—the first because his libido is attached to no real object, the last because so much of the energy which would otherwise be at his disposal is expended in maintaining the libido under repression, and in warding off

its attempts to assert itself. He would be well if the conflict between his ego and his libido came to an end, and if his ego again had the libido at its disposal (Freud 1915-1917, pp. 394-395).

Every neurosis offers, as it were, a certain gain. Some neurotic symptoms offer a *primary gain,* that is, an alleviation of the state of anxiety. Anxiety, being a state of tension between the ego and the id or the ego and the superego, is painfully experienced as apprehension, as feelings of inadequacy, fatigue, and depression—general and often diffuse feelings that accompany almost every neurosis.

Neurotic symptoms are a morbid way of escape from the painful anxiety state. A splitting headache that imitates physical illness is one way out; it is easier to assume that one is physically ill than to be torn by an inner conflict that demands making a decision. The physical symptom, called by Freud *conversion,* may alleviate the patient's guilt

ABRAHAM'S TIME TABLE

Stages of Libidinal Organization	*Stages in Development of Object Love*	*Dominant Point of Fixation*
1. Early oral (sucking) stage	Autoeroticism (no object, preambivalent)	Certain types of schizophrenia (stupor)
2. Late oral-sadistic (cannibalistic) stage	Narcissism: total incorporation of the object	Manic-depressive disorders (addiction, morbid impulses)
3. Early anal-sadistic stage	Partial love with incorporation	Paranoia, certain pregenital conversion neuroses
4. Late anal-sadistic stage	Partial love	Compulsion neurosis, other pregenital conversion neuroses
5. Early genital (phallic) stage	Object love, limited by the predominant castration complex	Hysteria
6. Final genital stage	Love (postambivalent)	Normality

* The table follows Fenichel's modifications (Fenichel, 1945, p. 101).

feeling and justify his procrastination. In such a case this conversion or psychosomatic symptom serves as a primary gain; it is, indeed, an escape from the frying pan into the fire.

Sometimes neurotic symptoms procure *secondary gain* that is helpful in avoiding the condemnation of others; in many cases—splitting headaches, loss of memory, morose moods, or self-inflicted pain—their aim is the winning of sympathy. All mental disorder representing regression into an early developmental stage, secondary gain symptoms can provide a sort of escape into illness, a means of avoiding responsibility.

Freud believed that the time and nature of fixation determine the nature of a given mental disorder. Accordingly, Abraham in his *Short Study of the Development of Libido* . . . (1924) suggested the preceding timetable of libido development and pathogenesis.

Traumatic Neuroses

Freud was never too systematic in his writings. On a few occasions, when he modified his theory, he did not discard the former ideas but simply added a new idea to the old one (Holt, 1965). Certainly such a method did not increase clarity.

The man who systematically described Freud's theory of mental disorder was Otto Fenichel. His seven hundred page volume *The Psychoanalytic Theory of Neurosis* brings together in a well-organized fashion the psychoanalytic interpretation of mental disorder. Fenichel grouped all disorders into traumatic neuroses (psychoneuroses) such as anxiety hysteria, conversion hysteria, organ neuroses, obsessive-compulsive neuroses, perversions, character neuroses, manic-depressive psychoses, and schizophrenia.

Traumatic neuroses are usually caused by an overwhelming, overpowering excitation that the ego is unable to master. Then the ego regresses, and the behavior of the patient becomes infantile. Patients are like helpless infants who act as if they expect some omnipotent parental figure to take care of them. Traumatized soldiers in wartime regress into infantilism, use baby-talk, display infantile modes of eating, and lose control of bowels and bladder. Some of them develop childish temper tantrums and states of panic, forgetting their adult status, age, and in some cases even name and identity, as if regressing into pre-verbal or even prenatal behavior.

Like all other neuroses, traumatic neurosis, is an act of regression.

In traumatic and war neuroses the human ego is defending itself from a danger which threatens it from without or which is embodied in a shape assumed by the ego itself. In the transference neuroses of peace, the enemy from which the ego is defending itself is actually the libido, whose demands seem to it to be menacing. In both cases the ego is afraid of being damaged—in the latter case by the libido and in the former by external violence. It might, indeed, be said that in the case of the war neuroses, in contrast to the pure traumatic neuroses and in approximation to the transference neuroses, what is feared is nevertheless an internal enemy. The theoretical difficulties standing in the way of a unifying hypothesis of this kind do not seem in-superable: it would after all be right and proper to describe repression, which lies at the basis of every neurosis, as a reaction to a trauma— as an elementary traumatic neurosis (Freud, 1919, p. 87).

Anxiety Hysteria

The mechanism of symptom-formation is always a product of re-pression of an instinctual wish. Whenever a wish or an impulse in the id creates a threatening situation in reality or a rebuff from the super-ego, the ego excludes the wish from consciousness. The ego has no intrinsic source of power in dealing with the id, for the ego itself is merely a part of the id and is differentiated therefrom through its con-tact with consciousness and the outer world. The ego is that part of the id which is conscious of reality, as distinguished from the instinct-ual drives of the id that operate on the pleasure principle without be-ing concerned with reality. The ego can control instinctual drives by affecting the id's pleasure-pain balance.

A symptom is a substitute gratification for a repressed impulse. Hav-ing been barred from entrance into the conscious and externally di-rected action, an impulse may set up a system of gratification inde-pendent of the ego. In doing so, the impulse brings about something different from its initial aim: the repressing ego cannot do away with the impulse, but it can accept a degraded gratification that denies the true nature of the desire in the id. Having allowed thus the establishment of a symptom, the ego must continue its processes of repression against this symptom in order to maintain the degraded status thereof. If the ego were to relax its defenses, the impulse would break through and resume its true course. Freud termed this repression against the symptom *secondary repression*. The strength of the ego depends, to a large extent, on its ability to organize mental activity. Thus the ego, while maintaining action against the symptom, comes to terms with it, because the removal of a symptom would set free the forbidden impulse. Anxiety hysteria is a case in point, for it uses a variety of the abovementioned forbid devices.

According to Freud anxiety hysteria, also often called neurasthenia, is characterized by a variety of symptoms including phobias, hypochondriac fears, headaches, restlessness, severe anxiety states, and general irritability. The choice defense mechanism is displacement. Hypochondriac fears are often displaced fears of castration. Feminine masochistic wishes can be displaced by a fear of falling down from high places or being run over.

The mechanism of displacement is most frequently used in phobias. Freud described a case of a morbid fear of horses in the story of the little Hans (1909), where the feared horse represented the little boy's father. Anxiety related to being bitten or eaten is related to castration. Fear of open places (agoraphobia) is most often related to fear of voyeurism. Fear of being locked in (claustrophobia) reflects the fear of being unable to escape one's own sexual excitement. The same also applies to the fear of injections, of seasickness, of dizziness, of losing consciousness, and any other situation that the patient may not be able to control.

Anxiety hysteria leads to overprotective attitudes. Usually, patients apply reaction formation mechanisms to ward off their hostile impulses, substituting opposite attitudes for the true impulses.

Freud used the famous case of little Hans to explain the mechanisms of phobias, displacement, and reaction formation. Hans's zoöphobia was related to the child's ambivalent attitude toward his father inherent in the Oedipal situation. In the case of a male child, affectionate and aggressive desires toward the father coincide with affection for the mother. In most cases of zoöphobia, it is the aggressive attitude toward the father that must undergo repression. The mechanism applied in zoöphobia is displacement. By externalizing the aggressive element and displacing it onto an animal which symbolizes the father, the boy denies his hostility toward the father. By making the animal the aggressor rather than himself, the child conceals the true nature of his aggressiveness. The fear of being bitten or even eaten represents an oral regression. Freud related zoöphobia to the fear of castration, for the little boy fears the father's retaliation in the form of castration. Where affection toward the father is too strong, the boy fears becoming like the mother, which again means castration. Anxiety created in the ego in view of the threat of castration leads to the repression of the id impulse.

Obsessive-Compulsive Neurosis

The obsessional neurotic's mind is "occupied with thoughts that do not really interest him, he feels impulses which seem alien to him, and he is impelled to perform actions which not only afford him no pleasure but from which he is powerless to desist" (Freud, 1915-1917, p. 235). The patient is obsessed with terrifying impulses and temptations to commit crimes of a sexual and aggressive nature. The patient is aware of his condition but cannot help himself.

Freud noticed (1913c) a certain affinity between anxiety hysteria and the obsessive-compulsive neurosis. In one instance an anxiety hysteria suddenly changed into a severe obsessional neurosis, as if the two neuroses were expressing "an identical content in different languages." Phobias are easily transformed into obsessions. The role of anal-sadistic impulses in the etiology of the obsessional (also obsessive-compulsive) neurosis was stressed by Freud and several of his associates.

Obsessive ideas lead to compulsive actions. Obsessions are usually a carryover from forbidden impulses, and compulsive behavior is a morbid way of preventing these impulses from breaking through. An individual with strong inclinations for playing with feces may develop exaggerated cleanliness and may compulsively wash his hands.

According to Freud the roots of the obsessive-compulsive neurosis lie in the Oedipal situation; the motive force is likewise castration-anxiety. However, in obsessional neurosis there is a regression to the anal-sadistic stage of development. A punitive and revengeful superego is typical of the obsessional neurosis. The threat of castration has been internalized in the superego and the obsessional neurotic is tormented by a feeling of guilt. The tension between this exaggerated superego demand and the anal-sadistic impulses is excruciating. The ambivalence of the Oedipal conflict leads to regression and reaction formation, rather than to displacement, as in phobias. Extreme cleanliness, derived from the anal-sadistic stage, is elevated to the status of a compulsion. In the acute conflict between the superego and the id in the obsessional neurosis, compulsive behavior preserves stability and prevents a vehement acting out. Needless to say, the ego in the obsessive-compulsive neurotic state is much constricted.

The mechanisms of undoing and isolation are frequently applied to assist repression in obsessive-compulsive neuroses. Undoing is the expression of a desire to do away with some experience or impulse; it is an irrational attempt to deny the existence of such unpleasantness. Undoing plays a significant role in the symptom-formation of the obsessive-compulsive neurosis. Sometimes it comes in the shape of symptoms designed to nullify or contradict one another, sometimes as a compulsive repetition of an act aimed at the denial of a previous experience. The defense mechanism of isolation attempts to keep an unwanted impulse repressed by means of separating the actuality of symptom-gratification from the rest of conscious mental life. The isolation mechanism requires that other mental activity be suspended in the interest of the compulsive act, thus preventing the uncovering of the true nature of the symptoms. The symptoms become separate and even isolated occurrences, void of any conscious meaning and not overtly related to their repressed content. Isolation serves resistance, and is an obstacle in the free-association process in psychoanalytic treatment.

Conversion Hysteria

Every neurosis contains sexual elements, and most symptoms reflect unfulfilled sexual desires. This statement applies especially to conversion hysteria. Conversion means transformation of mental energy into physical energy or, to put it in Freud's words, it is a retranslation of somatic energy from its psychological expression into the original somatic language.

Mental life originates in the organism and physical energy is the arch-source of all mental energies. When the outlets for mental energies are blocked, some amounts of these energies are discharged along physical paths: crying spells, temper tantrums, hysterical laughing and screaming, fainting, diarrhea, throwing up, and so on (Breuer and Freud 1895).

Conversion hysteria can imitate almost any physical disease and handicap. Many a hysteric develops a complete loss of desire to eat, to have sexual relations, or to do anything at all. Conversion symptoms include hysterical blindness, hysterical heart attacks, and even simulated pregnancy. Hysterics may experience the most severe pain in practically every part of the organism; disturbance of talking and walking, partial or complete motor paralysis, sleep talking and sleepwalking, tonic and clonic spasms belong to the galaxy of conversion symptoms.

The mental symptoms of hysteria are no less spectacular. Conversion hysterics are prone to exaggerate; they are carried away by true or imaginary victories and defeats. Hysterics occasionally experience hallucinations and delusions; discontinuity of awareness of oneself, the so-called "split personality," is one of the classic symptoms of conversion hysteria.

Such a split in the ego may take place when the ego is exposed to powerful and mutually exclusive demands made by external reality and the id. The ego can serve these two lords when it is itself strong enough to control the excessive demands of the id and to manipulate the external world. Weak egos, however, may not be able to do so. Sometimes two mental attitudes may develop and exist alongside each other: one attitude is related to reality, the other one (psychosis) is influenced by instincts, and detaches the ego from reality. Yet the personality split in hysteria never goes as deep as it does in psychosis, nor is it as lasting. In all neuroses two attitudes develop which are contrary to each other and independent of each other. One of them represents the reality-oriented ego and the other the repressed material of the id.

The Oedipus complex is at the core of conversion hysteria. The unresolved Oedipal conflict leads most often to urethral eroticism with the prevalence of masturbatory practices and bedwetting. Bedwetting in boys serves sexual gratification in a passive way; it symbolizes ejaculation without active effort. Bedwetting in girls symbolizes unresolved penis envy; retention of urine in girls often gives sexual pleasure analogous to anal retention.

Sexual disturbances (especially too early an ejaculation and other forms of impotence in men, and frigidity in women) are frequent in conversion hysterics. Regression to masturbatory fantasies and activities is one of the more common symptoms in conversion hysteria.

SEXUAL PATHOLOGY

The normal adult sexual source is the genitals; the object—an adult person of the opposite sex; the aim—heterosexual intercourse. The normal individual passes through developmental stages and, should he retain some of the characteristics of an earlier stage, that is, should he remain fixated, his sexual life will be abnormal. The infant is a "polymorphous pervert," and a sexually abnormal individual is a sexually retarded individual.

Some elements of early sexuality, such as touching, looking, embracing, and so on, are considered normal if they precede intercourse and increase the pleasure of intercourse. They are a sort of "appetite builder." According to Freud, a person becomes sexually abnormal when his sexual object becomes distorted and the whole body becomes the goal of the sexual impulse, thus preventing concentration on the genitalia. It is also abnormal, Freud wrote, for the anal opening to be used instead of the vagina, or for certain nongenital parts of the body, e.g., the mucous membrane of the mouth and anus to be treated as genitals.

In some pathological cases, a nongenital quantity is substituted for the sexual object. Usually unfit for the normal sexual aim, this substituted object may be hair, clothing, a foot, and so on.

Anything that can impede the attainment of the normal sexual aim, such as impotence or fear of the sex act, strengthens the inclination to linger at the preparatory acts and to transform them into sexual aims.

Touching and onlooking may become perverse if such action limits itself to the genitals or takes the form of voyeurism, and when it suppresses the normal sexual aim instead of preparing for it.

Abnormal sexuality is sometimes a fusion of Eros and Thanatos. Sadism is an attachment of sexual gratification to the hurting of the love object, while masochism is sexual gratification obtained through physical or mental pain.

Deviations in regard to the sexual object can be described as follows:

1. Absolutely inverted—homosexuals whose sexual objects are people of the same sex, while the opposite sex can never be an object of sexual longing

2. Psychosexually hermaphroditic—those whose sexual objects may be of either sex

3. Occasionally inverted or partly homosexual—under conditions of inaccessability of a partner of the opposite sex, a person of the same sex may be taken as a sexual object

The inverted are different in their attitude toward the peculiarities of their sexual impulse. Some have no desire to change; others, however, strive against their inversion and perceive in it a morbid compulsion.

The sexual aims of the invert are not uniform. Intercourse per anum, masturbation, and mucous membrane contact are all examples of perverted sexual aim.

In reply to claims made by some homosexuals about their alleged superiority, Freud wrote:

> The claim made by homosexuals or inverts that they constitute a select class of mankind falls at once to the ground when we discover that in every single neurotic evidence of homosexual tendencies is forthcoming and that a large proportion of the symptoms are expressions of this latent inversion. Those who openly call themselves homosexuals are merely those in whom the inversion is conscious and manifest; their number is negligible compared with those in whom it is latent. We are bound, in fact, to regard the choice of an object of the same sex as a regular type or offshoot of the capacity to love, and are learning every day more and more to recognize it as especially important. . . . One particular mental disorder, paranoia, no longer to be reckoned among the transference neuroses, invariably arises from an attempt to subdue unduly powerful homosexual tendencies (1915-1917, p. 270).

Homosexuality is associated with the negative Oedipus complex where the child identifies with the parent of the opposite sex and desires the parent of the same sex. Most male homosexuals fear being castrated by "the terrible phallic women" whose sexual organs carry the threat of castration. Weak and impotent persons often develop craving for children, called pedophilia; little children are less threatening to them than adults of the opposite sex.

Female sexuality is related to the castration complex and desire to be a man (penis envy), and the usual attraction for mother. Masculinity in females usually results from the process of identification with the figure of the father or another male relative.

Fetishism—sexual desire for certain objects such as hair or stockings or shoes—uses the mechanism of *disavowal* (also called denial). It reflects the fact that some men refuse to accept the fact that women do not possess penises. The fetish to a penis substitute—kleptomania or impulsive stealing of objects that have symbolic meaning—is usually of a sexual nature. Kleptomania is more frequent among women than among men, and kleptomanic women usually steal objects that symbolize penises. Pyromania, or setting fires, reflects pathological sexual excitement, usually orgasm, and is often associated with sadistic impulses. Sadism and masochism, as explained above, are products of a morbid fusion of Eros and Thanatos. Impotence in males and frigidity in females are, as a rule, associated with unresolved Oedipal attachment to parents.

There are hosts of perversions related to partial or complete fixations in oral, anal, urethral, and phallic developmental phases. We recall Freud's observation that the neonate is, polymorphously perverse, and may develop normally or retain some of the early sexual zones, objects, and aims.

Freud believed that perversions are a sort of negative neurosis. They represent the victory of pathological tendencies, and the ego's acceptance of defeat. Perverts and inverts regress to infantile sexuality because they fear adult sexuality. Some of them, the exhibitionists, expose themselves as if trying to prove that they *are* males, and their penises were not castrated. Some are afraid of (castrating) female sexual organs and stay impotent. Some fear incest whenever they approach a person of the opposite sex. In all perversions, "Adult sexuality is supplanted by infantile sexuality. Something must be repulsive in adult sexuality, and something especially attractive in infantile sexuality. While the latter factor is variable, the former is constant; it is always the castration complex that interferes with the capacity for enjoying fully genital sexuality. Actually the difference in the male and in the female castration complex directly corresponds to the differences between male and female perversions" (Fenichel, 1945, p. 326).

SYMPTOM-FORMATION

The maintenance of certain internal barriers or controls is a *sine qua non* of normality. Lowering of these barriers with a subsequent pressing forward of unconscious material takes place in sleep and is a necessary precondition for the formation of dreams. In dreams all of us behave like psychotics. But if, in the waking state, unconscious becomes conscious and thinking, speaking, and acting processes are seriously regressed to include condensations, displacements, secondary elaborations, and other unconscious elements, then the individual has regressed into psychosis.

All neuroses start with a frustration in early childhood, but the external frustration may be internalized and incorporated by the superego. Freud often used the term neurosis to describe both neuroses and psychoses. In 1924 Freud drew a clear-cut line between neurosis and psychosis. He wrote:

> *Neurosis is the result of a conflict between the ego and its id, whereas psychosis is the analogous outcome of a similar disturbance in the relation between the ego and its environment (outer world). . . .*
> The transference neuroses originate from the ego's refusing to accept a powerful instinctual impulse existing in its *id,* and denying its motor discharge, or disputing the object toward which it is aimed. The ego then defends itself against the impulse by the mechanism of repression; the repressed impulse struggles against this fate, and finds ways which the ego cannot control to create for itself substitutive gratification (a symptom), which is forced upon the ego in the form of a compromise; the ego finds its unity menaced and injured by this interloper, pursues against the symptom the impulse, and all this together produces the clinical picture of a neurosis . . . (Freud, 1924, pp. 251 ff.).

Schizophrenia

Freud distinguished two stages in schizophrenia. First, loss of reality: the ego has lost its object cathexis. The second is restitution, or striving toward recapturing reality. In neurosis reality is circumvented by a fantasy; in psychosis it is replaced by delusion and hallucination.

The manic-depressive psychotic oscillates between the joy and happiness resulting from the all-approving superego and the tortures of guilt feeling and depression that appear when the superego becomes sadistic. The superego

> becomes over-severe, abuses, humiliates, and ill-treats his unfortunate ego, threatens it with the severest punishments, reproaches it for long-forgotten actions which were at the time regarded quite lightly, and behaves as though it had spent the whole interval in amassing complaints and was only waiting for its present increase in strength to bring them forward and to condemn the ego on their account. The superego has the ego at its mercy and applies the most severe moral standards to it; indeed it represents the whole demands of morality and we see all at once that our moral sense of guilt is the expression of the tension between the ego and superego (Freud, 1932, pp. 87-88).

In latent schizophrenia, the ego is at the mercy of a severe and demanding superego. The introjected parental images assume a despotic control over the entire mental apparatus till the hard-pressed ego may give up the struggle and submerge in unconscious in a psychotic breakdown.

12

The Early Technique

On April 12, 1886, on Easter Sunday, the Viennese daily *Neue Freie Presse* published a little notice: *Herr Doctor* Sigmund Freud, *Privat-Dozent* (lecturer) in neurology at the Viennese University, returned to Vienna after six months in Paris and resides at Number Seven Rathaus Strasse. Sigmund Freud, M.D., was thirty years old, recently married and, after a brief academic and scientific career, had resigned to enter private practice.

Freud was not too eager nor too happy to open an office for private practice, but he felt he had no choice. His meager academic salary would not have allowed him to marry his beloved Martha Bernays.

Fresh from Paris, where he had been under the influence of Charcot's hypnotic method, Freud was glad to renew his friendship with Josef Breuer, a well-established Viennese physician who practiced hypnosis. Freud's first patients were hysterics, and at that time hysteria was treated with a variety of methods—such as hydrotherapy, electrotherapy, rest, massage, and so on. These methods were considered modern and progressive compared to earlier methods; for even at the end of the nineteenth century, hysteria in women was treated by hysterectomy.

Both Breuer and Charcot were innovators who treated hysteria with hypnosis. They applied, however, different methods. Charcot was more direct, removing symptoms by imposing his will on the patient's, while Breuer discovered that hypnotized patients would express their feelings spontaneously. Charcot ordered the hypnotized patients to renounce their symptoms, while Breuer ordered the patients to recall and re-enact, under hypnosis, the traumatic experiences that produced hysteria. This "abreacting" (*abreagieren* in German) was believed to help the patients to get rid of their symptoms. The method applied by Breuer was hypnotic suggestion; but the role of hypnotic suggestion was reduced to a tool aimed at release of tension and restoration of emotional balance. Small wonder that the method was called *cathartic,* from the Greek word for purification: *catharsis*. The blocked emotions were believed to find an outlet, bringing relief to the troubled individual.

When Freud began to work with Breuer, they treated patients by letting them recall past experiences under hypnosis. The reliving of a trauma was the cure of the neurosis.

The fundamental fact was that the symptoms of hysterical patients are founded upon highly significant but forgotten scenes in their past lives (traumas); the therapy founded upon this consisted in causing them to remember and reproduce these scenes in a state of hypnosis (catharsis); and the fragment of theory inferred from this was that these symptoms represented an abnormal form of discharge for quantities of excitation which had not been disposed of otherwise (conversion) (Freud, 1914a).

In 1895 Breuer and Freud published a volume entitled *Studies in Hysteria*. These studies reported successful treatment of hysterical symptoms by the cathartic method. The assumption was made that emotional conflicts may lead to a repression, that is, some quantity of energy together with its emotional content may slide down into the unconscious. If, however, the patient relives the conflict in free association, the road is open for discharge of the repressed energy with its emotional content. The mind clears off (catharts) the unconscious emotional load (often called a complex). This purgative or cathartic discharge of emotional energy constituted abreaction, as described above.

In the suggestive hypnotic method, as used, for instance, by Charcot, the therapist instructed the hypnotized patients and removed the symptoms using direct influence. The therapist might have said to a patient suffering from migraine headaches, "You have no more headache"; or, to an agoraphobic patient, "You will no longer be afraid of open places." Freud gave up this method after a short trial. As he explained this decision: "I gave up the suggestive technique and with it, hypnosis, so early in my practice because I despaired of making suggestions powerful and enduring enough to effect permanent cure" (1905d).

In the hypnocathartic method, the therapist hypnotized the patient and gave him no orders, except encouraging him to recall past events. When the patient recalled the traumatic events that caused his present troubles, he abreacted them in words, tears, and sobs. This recollection of the past and the ensuing vehement discharge of pent-up emotions was supposed to remove the symptoms and bring about the cure. On May 1, 1889, Freud applied this new method for the first time, calling it "hypnotic analysis" and "psychical analysis." Freud's patient is known as Mrs. Emmy von N.

For a while Freud had followed Breuer's hypnotic method but, not always a successful hypnotist, Freud gradually substituted "concentration" for hypnosis. He pressed his hand on the patient's head (the patient was reclining on a couch), and suggested that the patient try to recall past events that might be related to his present emotional problems. Freud soon noticed that there was no need for pressing the patient's head, nor for suggesting anything. Given a free rein, the patient's mind went wandering. This method of letting the patient say whatever came to his mind became the basic rule of psychoanalytic technique. The patient's *free association* led him to speak of whatever bothered him, and this inevitably hinged on past traumatic experiences.

In the paper entitled "Freud's Psychoanalytic Procedure" (1904), Freud explained why he had abandoned the cathartic method. The new method of free associations was not contradictory to catharsis; it did, however, offer a better opportunity of widening the therapist's access to the patient's unconscious mind.

Both the cathartic method and the free association method were based on the assumption that neurosis results from a conflict between unconscious libido impulses and conscious controls. The fundamental rule insisted on the expression of everything, whether it seemed important or trivial, pleasant or embarrassing.

The use of the couch prevented unnecessary interaction between the analyst and the patient. It protected the patient from being exposed to continuous observation by the analyst, and left him with his own meditations. It also protected the analyst from the searching looks of the patient, thus permitting a relaxed and "evenly hovering" attention.

In 1923, just before he published his structural theory in *The Ego and the Id* (1923b), Freud described his method in two brief Encyclopedia articles (1923a). Freud explained that his deterministic point of view had led him to substitute free association for hypnosis. In free association, the repressed memory of traumatic experiences comes to the surface. The unraveling of the unconscious and making it conscious removes the causes of the symptoms. Symptoms are the effects of the repressed traumas; the removal of causes should lead to the disappearance of effects. Thus adhering to free associations, the fundamental rule of psychoanalysis, does not contradict the cathartic method, but merely modifies it.

The method of free associations was a turning point in the treatment of mental disorders. All healing methods heretofore had been based on a clear-cut division of roles between the therapist and the patient. The therapist, be it a physician, a dentist, or a nurse "treats" the patient and the patient receives treatment. The therapist is active, the patient passive. The new method revolutionized the doctor-patient relationship. The psychoanalyst took on the role of a reserved listener whose undivided attention was given to the patient's free association. The patient's communication deviated from "reporting" his ills to the doctor. In free associations, the patient's mind jumped from one topic to another; he was not prohibited from including irrational thoughts and fantasies.

Free associations facilitate regression in the patient and the uncovering of unconscious processes. The analyst is supposed to restrain himself, and avoid giving any stimuli or any reality cues. The stimulus deprivation, the reclining position, and the dependent attitude of the analyst produce topographic and structural regression in the patient. In the artificial setting of the analyst's office, repressed unconscious thoughts come to the surface and lay bare the primary processes.

Freud did not fight against symptoms but began to unravel the causes of mental disorders. The causes are buried in the unconscious, and they must be brought up to the surface and resolved. The lowering of the ego defenses permits access to repressed material, and the re-experiencing of past traumas. One cannot fight an invisible enemy; obtaining insight into, and resolution of the unconscious conflicts became a guiding principle of psychoanalytic technique, and it has been incorporated by disciples and dissidents alike.

As noted above, at the beginning Freud tried to force the unconscious to become conscious using hypnosis and, later on, suggestive pressure to overcome amnesia and resistance. Some of the dissident schools still use these methods. Freud himself soon abandoned pressure; his keenly empirical approach to clinical data had made him aware of the spontaneous help offered by the patient's unconscious. Freud discovered that whatever had been repressed tended to recur, again and again. Unhealed wounds called for help and past traumas forced themselves outward again and again. The principle of *repetition compulsion* was a logical inference from Freud's strict determinism, and from the universal law of the preservation of energy, accepted by Freud. Nondischarged energy called for a discharge, and there was no need for an external pressure.

Having reached this point in his thinking, Freud could reject the cathartic method, and introduce the method of free associations that eventually became the fundamental rule of psychoanalytic treatment.

The cathartic method was based on an oversimplified interpretation of the law of preservation of energy: a momentary discharge of mental energy does not resolve inner conflicts. In accordance with Freud's monistic philosophy, mental energy is a derivative of physical energy. Whatever exists, exists in a certain quantity; mental processes are therefore quantitative processes of accumulation and discharge of energy.

The belief in the total efficacy of acting out was a childhood disease of psychoanalysis; but insight into the unconscious remained the cornerstone of the method.

The technique of using free association as a gate to the unconscious became the fundamental rule in psychoanalytic treatment, Freudian and non-Freudian. All schools of psychoanalytic thought have learned from Freud to look for the hidden causes of symptom-formation. Nothing posited in Adler's teleologism, or in C. G. Jung's syncronicity can obviate the indisputably deterministic nature of mental disorders. One may deviate from Freud's nosology, reject the Freud-Abraham timetable of etiology, introduce new stages and concepts concerning personality development; yet no one can deny the fact that mental disorders are a consequence of a cluster of unconscious causes.

Freud introduced the principle of overdetermination, and included the hereditary factors in the id; he stressed the biologically determined developmental stages that are dependent on interaction with the environment; he spread a broad net of phylogenetic and ontogenetic factors that interact with environmental forces shaping human personality. No wonder Freud himself, and later on his faithful disciples, and even ardent dissidents, went further on in their studies, stressing one aspect of Freud's work against the other factors.

13
Interpretation and Insight

Knowledge of oneself does not necessarily mean cure, but in most cases it is rather difficult to improve without knowing what has to be improved. Insight into the hidden motives of one's actions is a valuable and important step toward mental health.

Between the years 1900, when *The Interpretation of Dreams* was published, and 1923, the publication date of *The Ego and the Id,* Freud's psychoanalytic technique was based on the theory of libido and unconscious. In this technique the interpretation of unconscious material was aimed at reconstruction of the past, and abreaction of blocked energies tied up in past conflicts. Then, as we have seen, Freud shifted the emphasis from cathartic abreaction to offering insight to the patient. Insight was supposed to help abreaction and to facilitate its purgatory effect; catharsis was included in treatment, though it was pushed into the background. The interpretation of the unconscious became the main tool used in psychoanalytic treatment of neuroses.

One must keep in mind that Freud's early technique was a logical sequence to his topographic theory. The unconscious represented sexual drives pushing toward gratification at any price. The conscious censorship represented the forces of self-preservation originally called *ego impulses.* The conflict between sexual drives and self-preservation drives, and repression of sexual desires constituted the cause of neurosis. The task of the psychoanalytic method was to unrepress the repressed material and offer a rational solution of the conflict. Thus reconstruction of the past, and interpretation of it, were supposed to offer a resolution of infantile conflicts and a better integration of personality.

167

RECONSTRUCTION

From this point of view the purpose of reconstruction and interpretation was gradually redirected from facilitating abreaction toward substituting *recollection* for acting out. In the initial stage of his practice, Freud believed that a dramatic re-enactment of past emotional conflicts led to their dissolution. Catharsis, viewed as a discharge of energy, was supposed to remove the symptoms. Clinical experience, and the subsequent discovery of the constancy principle and the phenomenon of repetition compulsion, put the issue of abreaction in a different light. All patients tend to repeat past errors, and just acting out or repeating past experiences cannot have much therapeutic effect. Thus, acting out, especially outside therapeutic sessions, has to be forbidden by the analyst, for it merely aggravates the patient's conflict with his environment and complicates his inner life.

Repetition compulsion in psychoanalytic sessions is transference. Even in transference acting out will lead nowhere; but, as will be discussed later, recollection of past experiences in transference situations gives better chances for interpretation.

The interpretation of the unconscious was originally based on the assumption that unconscious material, brought to the conscious surface and properly interpreted, must lose its cathexes, that is, the energetic load; then, the patient's boiling desire would cause this material to become sheer memory.

Psychoanalytic interpretation deals with the content of the infantile conflict. Interpretation removes the amnestic repression, restores conscious memory of the traumatic experiences, and reconstructs the conflict.

> [The work of reconstruction] resembles to a great extent an archaeologist's excavation of some dwelling-place that has been destroyed and buried, or of some ancient edifice. The two processes are in fact identical, except that the analyst works under better conditions and has more material at his command to assist him, since what he is dealing with is not something destroyed, but something that is still alive. . . . But just as the archaeologist builds up the walls of the building from the foundations that have remained standing, determines the number and position of the columns from the depressions in the floor and reconstructs the mural decorations and paintings from the remains

found in the debris, so does the analyst proceed when he draws his inferences from the fragments of memories, from the associations and from the behavior of the subject of analysis. (Freud, 1937, p. 259).

INTERPRETATION

The success of interpretation depends largely on *timing* (Freud, 1910b; 1910c; 1913b). Too early an interpretation may evoke the patient's resistance; in some instances it may be so revolting as to make him discontinue treatment altogether. In some other instances it may bring too early a relief, and reduce the patient's motivation for being cured. In still other cases, an early interpretation may be accepted by the patient on a purely intellectual level; it may arouse his curiosity, but have no effect on his emotional life.

The question of *what* to interpret was never answered by Freud in a final manner. Bernstein (1965, p. 1179) pointed to nine distinct areas of psychoanalytic interpretation: (1) the patient's dreams, (2) his free associations, (3) symptoms and symptomatic behavior, (4) behavior during the analytic sessions, (5) behavior outside the analytic sessions, (6) the patient's past experiences, (7) the patient's attitude toward the psychoanalyst, (8) the patient's past and present relations with other people, and (9) the patient's over-all style of life and personality makeup.

Apparently psychoanalytic interpretation plays a dual role. First, in regard to *topography,* interpretation brings unconscious elements into the open. By the unraveling of their hidden meaning, interpretation raises them to the level of conscious. In short, interpretation transforms unconscious into conscious and helps it to become integrated into the preconscious-conscious system (Freud, 1904, p. 252).

The second task of interpretation is economic, that is, pertaining to the balance of cathexes. Repressed material is, topographically speaking, unconscious; but at the same time it carries an emotional load of libido or destructive energy. Interpretation, using verbal symbols, may modify the direction of cathexes and neutralization of impulses. The ego operates with symbols, it is capable of binding and neutralizing great amounts of hitherto blind, id-seated energy. To talk about impulses and to understand them is a great step toward their neutralization and control. This aspect of interpretation was further developed with the so-called ego-psychology of Hartmann, Kris, and Loewenstein (see Chapter Ten).

Dora

In 1905 Freud published *A Fragment of Analysis of a Case of Hysteria*. In this case report Freud stressed that thorough knowledge of the theory of the dream, and the technique of dream interpretation is a necessary prerequisite for the treatment of neurotics. Thus, Freud stated, "whereas the practical aim of the treatment is to remove all possible symptoms and replace them by conscious thoughts, we may regard it as a second and theoretical aim to repair all the damages to the patient's memory" (1905c). The two goals, namely the reconstruction of the past and the substitution of unconscious symptoms by conscious and rational behavior, dominated the psychoanalytic work.

Dora is the case history of an eighteen year old hysteric who was greatly torn by conflicting heterosexual and homosexual desires. Several people in her life were involved in her illness: her father, with whom she was very much in love; her pedantic mother, with whom she competed; her governess, who used to attract her father's attention; and Herr K. and his wife, with both of whom Dora was involved. None of these people was intentionally responsible for Dora's troubles—"Case histories have no villains, only victims," Freud remarked.

Dora had a sick father who had a sick mistress, who had a sick husband, Herr K., who propositioned Dora. Dora's illness was a morbid effort to escape from this vicious circle.

Dora's neurotic symptoms started at the age of eight; at the age of sixteen she threatened her family with suicide. Her father did not take the threats too seriously; we believed that it was a concoction of an attempt at love-making on the part of Herr K.

According to Freud, Dora was in love with her father and wished to replace her mother. Her father, however, was in love with Frau K., Herr K.'s wife. Ostensibly on long trips because of his health, Dora's father actually spent considerable time with Frau K. Dora knew of the relationship, and was deeply jealous. Dora was in the grips of an unconscious homosexual crush on Frau K., and she also loved her father. Meanwhile Herr K., who was very fond of Dora, often bought her gifts. Once Dora accompanied her father on a visit to the K.'s summer home, where she slept in the room with Frau K. However, on the day that Herr K. propositioned her, she became very upset and left the K.'s summer house. Dora suspected that her father knew about Herr K.'s intentions and had virtually handed her over to Herr K. as the price for his toleration of the relations between Frau K. and Dora's father. In other circumstances Dora might have accepted Herr K. In fact, she probably had hoped that he would ask again; but since he didn't ask, Dora told her father the story in revenge, after a delay of two weeks.

Freud believed that, in the normal course of events, some elements of homosexual love are channeled into normal heterosexual development. Should this normal heterosexual development be blocked, homosexual feelings could be revived in adolescence. Freud believed that Dora may have felt resentment about having been "sacrificed" to Herr K. as the price for her father's illicit relations with Frau K.; but at the same time Dora desired to possess the woman who was her rival for her father's affections. According to Freud,

Dora "told herself incessantly that her father had sacrificed her to this woman. She concealed from herself the fact that she begrudged her father Frau K.'s love, and had not forgiven the woman she loved for the disillusionment she had been caused by her betrayal. The jealous emotions of a woman had been linked in her unconscious with a jealousy such as might have been more proper for a man to feel. These masculine, or, more properly speaking, gynaecophylic currents of feeling are to be regarded as typical of the unconscious erotic life of hysterical girls."

Freud called Dora's homosexual love "the strongest unconscious current in her mental life" because it was dominant while not being overt. Dora maintained that she detested Frau K.; however Freud showed her much evidence to the contrary and finally Dora no longer resisted Freud's interpretations.

Freud described the interpretation of highly significant dreams. The first dream was reported by Dora as follows:

My house was on fire. My father was standing beside my bed and woke me up. I dressed myself quickly. Mother wanted to stop and save her jewel case. Father said: "I refuse to let myself and my two children be burnt for the sake of your jewel case." We hurried downstairs and as soon as we got outside I woke up. (*Ibid.*)

Freud's interpretation related the dream to an episode in the K.'s summer house. One night Dora had awoken and found Herr K. standing over her. (In the dream she had seen her father standing over her.) Always afraid that Herr K. would come in at any moment, she had always dressed very quickly (as she had done in the dream). For the same reason, Dora had been afraid to sleep at the K.'s house. The jewel box represented the female genitals; the fire, which meant destruction, represented intercourse. In the dream her father had been very concerned about saving her, while in reality she would have blamed her father if she had yielded to Herr K. "Incapacity for meeting a real erotic demand is one of the most essential features of a neurosis. Neurotics are dominated by a conflict between reality and phantasy. If what they desire is given to them, they flee from it; they abandon themselves to their phantasies the most readily when they do not fear to see them realized."

Dora broke off the analysis before she was cured. Freud believed that the way he had acted might have influenced the fact that transference had not developed and that the patient had terminated the analysis. Freud concluded the description of Dora's case as follows:

. . . I knew Dora would not come back again. Her breaking off so unexpectedly, just when my hopes of a successful termination of the treatment were at their highest, and thus her bringing those hopes to nothing—this was an unmistakable act of vengeance on her part. Her purpose of self-injury also profited by this action. No one, who, like me, conjures up the most evil of those half-tamed demons of the human breast, and seeks to wrestle with them can expect to come through the struggle unscathed. Might I perhaps have kept the girl under my treatment if I myself had acted a part, if I had exaggerated the importance to me of her staying on, and had shown a personal interest in her—a course which, even after allowing for my position as her physician, would have been tantamount to providing her with a substitute for the affection she longed for? I do not know. Since in every case a part of the factors that are encountered under the form of resistance remains unknown, I have always avoided acting a part and have contented myself with practicing the humbler arts of psychology." (1905c, pp. 123-124).

Away from the Intellectual Bias

In the treatment of Dora, and in other cases, Freud believed that his task was to undo the repressions and to remove the lid of amnesia. Reconstruction of the past was supposed to stimulate abreaction of the conflict and removal of the symptoms. However, reconstruction did not always lead to abreaction; nor did abreaction always bring about a radical change in symptoms.

The idea that cure could be obtained through making the unconscious conscious suffered a severe setback. Sometimes even when the patient became convinced that his symptom was rooted in a certain past experience, and even when the interpretation of dreams and other unconscious material brought about correct reconstructing of the past, cure was not forthcoming. Some patients showed considerable intellectual grasp and comprehension of the psychoanalytic theory; but this did not make them well. Certainly insight into one's own mental state is of more help in treating mental health problems than is the understanding of one's teeth or gums in dental treatment; but ultimately something else is needed to produce both mental and dental cure.

As Freud moved away from intellectualistic bias, digging out the unconscious and making it conscious remained an integral part of his technique; its value, however, became dependent on emotional factors linked to the structural theory and to human interaction.

The shift away from interpretation came about gradually. In the years 1911 to 1915, Freud wrote six papers dealing with the psychoanalytic technique.

In the paper "The Handling of Dream Interpretation in Psychoanalysis" (1911c), Freud tried to cool the enthusiasm of his disciples for dream interpretation. Sometimes patients bring to the analytic sessions more dreams than could ever be interpreted. Some patients may even use their dreams as a resistance. Dreams are merely a part of the unconscious life: and there is no magic cure in their interpretation alone. The interpretation of dreams should follow the same rules as the interpretation of any other material brought by the patient; but it must be stressed that interpretations as such cannot singlehandedly effect a cure.

Telling the patient what he does not know because he has repressed it is only one of the necessary preliminaries in the therapy. If knowledge about his unconscious were as important for the patient as the inexperienced in psychoanalysis imagine, it would be sufficient to cure him for him to go to lectures or read books. Such measures, however, have as little effect on the symptoms of nervous disease as distributing menu cards in time of famine has on people's hunger (Freud, 1910c, p. 222).

Only for awhile did psychoanalysis suffer from a sort of intellectual bias; and only at the beginning did Freud fail to distinguish the patient's awareness of past experiences, regained in the process of free association, from the analyst's comprehension and interpretation of the repressed material. The concluding remarks to the case of Dora (quoted above) are, therefore, an important contribution to the understanding of the nature of psychoanalytic treatment.

Freud had to work through his entire psychological theory before he arrived at the conclusion that neither insight nor abreaction was crucial in psychoanalytic treatment. Ultimately dealing with transference and resistance became the cornerstone of the psychoanalytic method (Wolman, 1967c). Both ideas appear quite early in Freud's writing. Resistance was mentioned for the first time as early as 1890 (Breuer and Freud, p. 154). At about the same time, in 1892, the term transference was used (*Ibid.*, pp. 301-302), but the full impacts of these concepts took effect slowly.

Even before the introduction of the structural theory in 1923, transference and resistance had become the backbones of psychoanalytic technique. Interpretation and insight retained their usefulness, but only in conjunction with the treatment of transferences and resistances. Freud himself cautioned fellow analysts against too eager a pursuit of interpretation: intellectual insight and even some emotional abreaction cannot cure a patient.

14

Transference:
The Therapeutic Neurosis

Freud learned psychoanalytic technique the hard way: he learned it on himself. Self-analysis resembles self-surgery, and both are dangerous. Psychoanalysis involves digging into one's unconscious and unraveling hidden impulses and conflicts. Psychoanalysis may be compared to the dismantling of underground or underwater mines: only the skilled can do it without causing an explosion.

Psychoanalysis practiced by inadequately trained people may be exceedingly harmful. The half-trained practitioner may unleash forces that he is not able to control. Poorly trained people in any field are potentially dangerous; in psychoanalysis they are even more so.

Self-analysis is even more dangerous because no matter how skilled one is, lack of objectivity and lack of outside support may prove disastrous. The risks of mental collapse are great and the chances for success are slim. Even such a giant as Freud described his self-analysis as follows: "Inwardly, I am deeply impoverished. I have had to demolish all my castles in the air, and I have just plucked up enough courage to start rebuilding them" (1887-1902).

Freud's self-analysis took several years and is partially overtly reported in letters to Dr. Fliess (1887-1902), partly included in a veiled manner in *The Interpretation of Dreams,* and also reported in scattered form in a great many papers. His own analysis made it clear that one's present-day feelings are often a replica—and re-experience—of early childhood involvements. This re-experience of past emotions is not only applicable to psychoanalytic treatment, but may, in the psychoanalytic situation, often offer invaluable help.

Reconstruction and interpretation may leave the patient cold and produce little change in his personality. A patient may accept interpretations, or he may doubt their credibility. In either case, he may develop a purely intellectual attitude, and view psychoanalytic interpretation as mere news and commentary.

Profound conviction is needed to produce behavioral change. Such an authenticity of conviction can be procured only through actual experience. The reliving of past emotional involvements offers optimal chances for lifting of the repressive veil and resolution of past conflicts.

TRANSFERENCE

The psychoanalytic situation provides ideal conditions for reliving infantile emotions. The patient comes asking for help, and this fact puts him into a dependent, child-versus-parent relation with the analyst. The analyst's amiable, yet nonparticipative listening contributes to the patient's feeling of having found a friendly, benevolent, omniscient parental substitute. Free associations and the reclining position facilitate emotional regression. The patient lets his defenses down and, in a regressive mood, weaves emotional fantasies around the silent analyst (who represents, as indicated, a parental figure). Past feelings and conflicts re-emerge in the patient's mind and he relives the family drama as he experienced it in his childhood. The patient transfers his past emotional attachments to the psychoanalyst.

Transference does not follow the rules of the pleasure principle, but rather of the repetition compulsion principle. Whether the past was pleasant or painful, it comes to life again and is re-enacted in relation to the psychoanalyst.

The attitude that the patient Anna O. developed toward Dr. Breuer (Breuer & Freud, pp. 21-47), was quite spectacular. When Breuer became aware of the vehement feelings of this patient, he interrupted her treatment and gave up any therapeutic work that could facilitate transference. Freud courageously continued alone, being fully aware of the dangers of the method. However, it must be clearly stated that

Psychoanalytic treatment does not *create* transferences, it merely brings them to light, like so many other hidden psychical factors. The only difference is this—that spontaneously a patient will only call up affectionate and friendly transferences to help toward his recovery; if they cannot be called up, he feels the physician is "antipathetic" to him, and breaks away from him as fast as possible and without having been influenced by him. In psychoanalysis, on the other hand, since the play of motives is different, all the patient's tendencies, including hostile ones, are aroused; they are then turned to account for the purposes of the analysis by being made conscious, and in this way the transference is constantly being destroyed. Transference, which seems ordained to be the greatest obstacle to psychoanalysis, becomes its most powerful ally, if its presence can be detected each time and explained to the patient (Freud, 1905c, p. 117).

The case of Dora (1905c) and the paper "The Dynamics of Transference" (1912b) describe the problems of transference. The ultimate conclusion was simple. Freud realized that every emotional conflict was "played out in the phenomena of the transference."

What are transferences? They are new editions or facsimiles of the impulses and phantasies which are aroused and made conscious during the progress of the analysis; but they have this peculiarity, which is characteristic for their species, that they replace some earlier person by the person of the physician. To put it another way: a whole series of psychological experiences are revived, not as belonging to the past, but as applying to the person of the physician at the present moment. Some of these transferences have a content which differs from that of their model in no respect whatever except for the substitution. These then—to keep to the same metaphor—are merely new impressions or reprints. Others are more ingeniously constructed; their content has been subjected to a moderating influence—to *sublimation,* as I call it— and they may even become conscious, by cleverly taking advantage of some real peculiarity in the physician's person or circumstances and attaching themselves to that. These, then, will no longer be new impressions, but revised editions (Freud, 1905c, p. 116).

Transference is a process of cathexis in a state of regression. If it is a cathexis of libido, it is a "positive" transference; if it is a cathexis of destructive energy, it is a "negative" transference.

Transference becomes a neurosis, a neurosis in which the patient re-lives his past conflicts using the analyst as a target for libidinal cathexes and destructive assaults. The patient ascribes to the analyst personality traits actually belonging to the patient's parents. Becoming involved with his analyst, the patient becomes less concerned with his own problems. Love and hate for the analyst may reach considerable intensity and, unless treated properly, may impede the progress of psychoanalysis (1915c).

The psychoanalyst must neither ignore nor satisfy the transference:

> It is, therefore, just as disastrous for the analysis if the patient's craving for love prevails as if it is suppressed. The way the analyst must take is neither of these; it is one for which there is no prototype in real life. He must guard against ignoring the transference-love, scaring it away or making the patient disgusted with it; and just as resolutely must he withhold any response to it. He must face the transference-love boldly but treat it like something unreal, as a condition which must be gone through during the treatment and traced back to its unconscious origins, so that it shall assist in bringing to light all that is most hidden in the development of the patient's erotic life, and help her to learn to control it . . . . The patient, whose sexual repressions are of course not yet removed but merely pushed into the background, will then feel safe enough to allow all her conditions for loving, all the phantasies of her sexual desires, all the individual details of her way of being in love to come to light, and then will herself open up the way back from them to the infantile roots of her love (Freud, 1915c, p. 185).

Transference may get out of hand if and when, instead of being merely an emotional experience verbally expressed in the analyst's office, it leads to acting out.

Interpretation and Analysis

Therefore, the main task of the analyst is to keep transference as an expression of memories of past experiences, not as a here-and-now experience. At this point the most important method is *interpretation*. Interpretation of transference makes the patient aware of the fact that his infatuation with the analyst is not related to the analyst as a person, but it is simply a reflection of previous emotional entanglements. The analyst is only a substitute for a parental figure; and the love or hate toward the analyst is an act of repetition compulsion. The analyst, as a target for the patient's emotions, is merely a substitute for parental figures. Transferred emotions are real emotions, and the interpretation of transferences is an interpretation of the feeling. The interpretation of transferences has therefore the mark of authenticity necessary for modification of behavior.

Freud was fully aware of the fact that transference is an indispensable prerequisite for any progress in psychoanalytic treatment. The heat of transference, as it were, melts the defenses and enables the patient to reopen wounds suffered in early years. The patient re-experiences his infantile conflicts using the analyst as a target. The patient seems to overlook all his problems and concentrates on his attitude toward the analyst. Love, admiration, and adoration on one side, resentment, hatred, and disrespect on the other, dominate the psychoanalytic sessions. The patient acts like an unhappy child, voicing his feelings toward the omnipotent, yet permissive parent. The neurosis that brought the patient to the analyst's office recedes into the background, and the "transference neurosis" is played out instead. The interpretation of the transference brings to resolution the underlying infantile conflicts; and the cure of the transference neurosis leads to the cure of the neurosis proper.

Some psychoanalysts believe that the interpretation of transference is the only change-producing interpretation because it is related directly to the immediate psychoanalytic situation. The patient sees and experiences what is interpreted. Such an interpretation, called *mutative*, is capable of producing substantial alterations in personality (Strachey, 1934).

Transference is a universal phenomenon, for everyone carries within his memory residues of past feelings and experiences. Transference elements influence one's choice of colors, preferences in music and art, and choice of a love object. Transference elements color human ambitions and desires, for no one can completely get rid of his past.

Transference becomes morbid when the past beclouds the present and the individual acts as if he were still a child. In the psychoanalytic situation, regression to childhood is necessary for the resolution of conflicts rooted in the past.

Since the main neurotic conflict revolves around "the family romance" or the Oedipus complex, its resolution must come through a re-enactment of this romance. During his transference the patient runs the gamut of infantile and, most often, ambivalent feelings toward his parents. Reich (1945, p. 33 ff.) maintained that transference neurosis seems to unfold itself in an order that is the reverse of the arrangement of the true neurosis; and the analysis of transference must account for this reverse order. Transference usually starts as a resentment against the analyst viewed as the father-substitute, then turns into love for the analyst-father, then becomes identification with the mother, ascribing feminine traits to the analyst. This identification turns into hate for the mother-analyst, and then love for the mother represented by the analyst. The Oedipal love, if properly interpreted, yields ground to the ability to experience normal love for a woman. The transference-love for the analyst resolved, the patient is capable of entering into normal human relationships.

Loewenstein (1951) suggested proceeding not only in a regressive order (from present to past experiences), but, whenever necessary, from the past to a later stage. Infantile oral aggressive impulses revealed in transference might be related to their later occurrence in early adolescence and interpreted on that level. This "reconstruction upward" has added flexibility to the interpretation of transferences.

Transference as Resistance

Transference is both the greatest help and strongest hindrance in psychoanalytic treatment (Freud, 1912b). In accordance with the principle of repetition compulsion, recollection of past emotional involvements brings about a tendency to re-enact them. The patient's complex involvement with his parents in childhood comes to the fore in direct regard to the psychoanalyst. The patient tries to destroy the analyst's authority and convert him into a lover. Undue intensification of love and exaggerated readiness for a love affair complicate the psychoanalyst's work and prevent resolution of inner conflicts. Obviously, such an intensification of transference is, indeed, resistance (Freud, 1915c).

Negative transference is even more readily used as resistance. The patient puts forward irrational demands and accuses his analyst of all the injustices—true and imaginary—that he suffered from his parents.

COUNTERTRANSFERENCE

One of the greatest dangers is that the psychoanalyst himself may fall prey to the patient's feelings. The psychoanalyst "must recognize that the patient's falling in love is induced by the analytic situation and is not to be ascribed to the charms of his person," Freud wrote (*Ibid.*, p. 159).

It is not easy to maintain equanimity in the face of emotional on-slaughts. Expressions of love are flattering; expressions of hatred hurt and offend. The professional obligation of the psychoanalyst toward his patient is not to react to the patient's emotions but to interpret them. One could say that a good analyst gets involved with the patient's case without getting involved with the patient's person (Wolman, 1966a).

Freud warned the analyst that

> The analytic psychotherapist thus has a threefold battle to wage—in his own mind against the forces which would draw him down below the level of analysis; outside analysis against the opponents who dispute the importance he attaches to the sexual instinctual forces and hinder him from making use of them in his scientific method; and in the analysis against his patients, who at first behave like his critics but later on disclose the over-estimation of sexual life which has them in thrall, and who try to take him captive in the net of their socially ungovernable passions (1915c, pp. 171-173).

In order to help others, the analyst must be able to control his own impulses. Holding countertransference in check and preventing any personal involvement with the patient is an ethical and professional prerequisite for psychoanalytic practice (Spitz).

All people react to other people's emotions. Most people are sensitive to criticism and enjoy praise and admiration. It is not easy to be exposed to the nagging criticism of a patient in the throes of negative transference. Many young analysts, not sure of their competence and mastery of the situation, take criticism poorly and sometimes accuse themselves of failure. Fear of being hated looms as large in counter-transference phenomena as the need to be loved. The analyst's un-resolved emotional conflicts may seriously affect the process of treat-ment. If the analyst's personality is unbalanced, the fact may interfere with his work, making him sensitive to patients' positive and negative transferences, and disrupting the required objective and professional attitude. Thus, successful completion of personal analysis is a necessary prerequisite for the analyzying of other people. Today personal analysis of the future analyst is an integral part of the psychoanalytic training.

15

Resistance: The Fight Against Being Cured

People under emotional stress are usually aware of the fact that they need psychological help, yet they often procrastinate in seeking it. It is apparently much easier to ask for help for a physical ailment than for mental disorder, although mental anguish may be more severe and more difficult to bear than physical pain.

Even when a person decides to seek psychological help, he may soon find out that it is not easy to cooperate with the psychoanalyst. It is certainly much easier to sit in a dental chair and let the dentist do the job, or lie on the physician's examination table and let him do his work. The psychoanalytic couch apparently presents new and unpredicted difficulties. The analyst pronounces the fundamental rule of free associations in words like these: Please tell me everything that comes to your mind, pleasant or unpleasant, relevant or irrelevant, important or unimportant. Tell me everything that crosses your mind, and do not withhold anything at all.

Nothing seems easier than compliance with this simple rule—yet patients find it difficult and resist it. Freud compared resistance to a "demon" who refuses to come to light because to do so might mean his end; patients act as if they were afraid of letting their thoughts flow freely and, in most cases, they obstruct the process of treatment.

VARIETIES OF RESISTANCE

There are, all together, five types of resistance (Freud, 1912b; 1915c; Fenichel; Glover) namely:

1. Repression resistance
2. Transference resistance—repressed materials being re-enacted instead of being recollected
3. Resistance aiming at secondary, or epinosic, gain
4. Id resistance—dictated by repetition compulsion
5. Superego resistance that originates in the need to be punished

Repression Resistance

Obviously, the same forces that repressed undesirable and unacceptable wishes resist the reopening of the buried issues. They keep on repressing, resisting the unraveling of what has been repressed. The fear of the repressed material prevents its unrepressing.

Resistance can take on almost any form and shape. Failure to verbalize in free association, periods of prolonged silence, breaking appointments or coming late to them, acting out impulses, blocking memories, and antagonistic reaction to treatment are the most frequent signs of resistance. Patients resist by producing hosts of long, foggy, and involved dreams that belabor the same theme; by being drowsy and falling asleep on the couch; by discussing their problems with outsiders; by producing nonsensical associations; by being irritable and hostile to the analyst, and so on (Freud, 1919a).

Originally the concepts of repression and resistance were coated in terms of the topographic theory. The conscious was the repressing and resisting censor, while the unconscious pressed for discharge of the repressed material.

With the introduction of the structural theory, the ego itself became the repressing and resisting censor. Topographically, the ego belongs to all three strata, usually the conscious, preconscious and unconscious. The unconscious part of the ego is the repressing agency, and repression itself is an unconscious process (Freud, 1920a). The battle between the id forces pressing for repetition compulsion and the ego forces blocking the immediate discharge of energy is fought in the murky waters of the unconscious.

In repression resistance the patient may forget most recent events; he may be unable to free associate; his associations may go in every possible direction, preventing a continuous flow; he may accept the analyst's interpretation and apply it to everyone except himself. Some patients use the "fundamental rule" in a resistive way, repeating the same material again and again.

Resistance often uses defense mechanisms, especially projection, reaction formation, and displacement.

> They can be observed in operation alike in dreams, symptom-formations, and everyday life and, to the extent that they contribute under ordinary circumstances to harmonious adaptation, are difficult to reduce in analysis: although of course from the analyst's point of view they are easy enough to detect. Projection having originally functioned actively at a period before reality-proving is advanced is extremely hard to bring home to the patient, as in the obvious case of the paranoidal system. Reaction formation, being essentially a fixed form of anti-cathexis dealing with specific forms of repressed instinct, is easier to establish intellectually than emotionally; and displacement, though relatively easy for the patient to recognize and appreciate, is so continuously in operation in everyday life that its pathological and defensive forms can well be screened (Glover, 1955, p. 62).

Unresolved resistance may bring a stalemate in analysis. Obsessive-compulsive patients will continue to overelaborate insignificant details, while other types may ruminate interminably. Each clinical type—indeed each individual—displays a variety of resistive patterns related to the level of fixation, type of disorder, and patient's life history.

Transference Resistance

Transference is at once the greatest aid and greatest obstacle in psychoanalytic treatment. In negative transference the patient views the analyst as an unfair, unloving, rejecting parental figure and accuses him of all the actual parents' past injustices and rejections. With some exceptions, the sex and age of the psychoanalyst do not matter. The patient becomes irritable and hostile, looking for errors and unfairness in the psychoanalyst's behavior.

Positive transference, however, can also erect stumbling blocks in the road to cure. The enamored patient requests special attention and "tender loving care" from the analyst. Abstention being one of the rules of psychoanalytic procedure, the patient's emotional needs must not be gratified. However, at the peak of positive transference the patient is not interested in the treatment of his neurosis but in obtaining love from the analyst. Transference-love may be mild and easily controllable, but it may also become vehemently acted out.

The analyst's task is to prevent the use of transference as a resistance. The analyst must transform the acting out of past feelings into a recollection of them. However, should a patient frustrated in his infantile love persist in loving the analyst, then the latter may discontinue the treatment. In some cases, to the analyst's dismay, the patient may substantially deteriorate, as if to prove to the analyst how much he still needs help. Some patients refuse to improve, in order to be able to continue their visits to the beloved parental figure.

Epinosic Resistance

Mental disorder is most often an escape from the hardships of adult life into an imaginary haven of protected childhood. Neurosis is a regression to the role of a child and offers, thus, some morbid gains. These gains are either primary, that is, effecting an alleviation of inner tensions and anxiety, or secondary, that is, achieving social approval and sympathy.

Resistance may be epinosic and aim at the perpetuation of secondary gain. The patient may wish to stay neurotic and gain all the sympathy and consideration that can be wrung from the sick role. The patient may not like his headaches, nauseas, depressions, and other unpleasant symptoms; but the bittersweet taste of being pitied is not readily renounced.

There is no doubt that this type of resistance comes from the ego itself. It is as if the ego feared to give up its neurotic mechanisms and face a head-on collision with instinctual impulses. Epinosic resistance occurs most frequently at the beginning of the treatment, and in the final stage, when the patient is expected to grow up and to abandon infantile modes of emotional life.

Id Resistances

It was not always true "that it would be sufficient to treat [the resistances] like portions of the id and, by making them conscious, bring them into connection with the rest of the ego" (Freud, 1937). Apparently this is not enough because the ego itself resists the uncovering of resistances. The id blindly follows the constancy principle, and what has happened once tends to be recapitulated. Repetition compulsion is a form of resistance and a very stubborn one.

The stronger the resistance, the greater the inclination to repeat rather than recollect. Id resistances cannot be easily lifted because they hinge on the basic rules of unconscious behavior, namely the constancy and pleasure principles. A prolonged process of working through is needed. This process will be described in the following chapter.

Superego Resistance

Resistance may also come from the superego. The patient either accuses the analyst of being hypermoralistic, or "tests" him for allegedly biased opinions and prejudices. The patient perpetuates his symptoms, as if asking for punishment and rejoicing in misery.

Guilt-torn patients resist cure because, unconsciously, they wish to suffer. These patients feel that they do not deserve a better lot and passively surrender to what they believe is a well-deserved punishment. This pessimistic outlook on the self, and feeling of one's own worthlessness form serious stumbling blocks to treatment.

Quite often patients introject the true or imaginary superego of the analyst and identify with it. Glover, in *The Technique of Psychoanalysis,* maintains that this is one of the commonest causes of stalemate in analysis (1955, p. 65). The patient assumes that the analyst condemns him, and a silent resignation and acceptance of what the patient believes to be a justified rejection destroys the patient's motivation for being cured, and presents a formidable obstacle to psychoanalytic treatment.

RESOLUTION OF RESISTANCES

How can the analyst induce the patient to give up his resistances? Just telling a patient, "This is resistance," will not help. Nor can mere interpretation dislodge a well-entrenched resistance.

Transference is a prerequisite for the resolution of resistances. Positive transference is love, and one will do anything for whomever he loves. However, when transference goes too far, the patient may refuse to listen to interpretation, and analysis may become interminable.

Transference resistance involves both obedience and disobedience to the rules of psychoanalytic treatment, and in some cases renders progress impossible.

As a rule, patients are unaware of the fact that they are resisting. They came for analysis to be cured, and they cannot believe that by their behavior they intend to sabotage their treatment and recovery.

Thus, interpretation of resistances must come first, even before the interpretation of transference and the neurotic conflict proper. Unless resistance is overcome, interpretations will fall on deaf ears.

In interpreting the transference resistance, the analyst points to the fact that the patient's love or hate has been misaddressed. Neither the analyst's charm or lack of it has anything to do with the patient's feelings: these would have been the same with another analyst.

It must be stated clearly that no cure can be obtained without the resolution of resistance. Handling of resistances requires quasi-surgical skill and precision. Precision, tact, proper timing, and individualization distinguish analysts who are truly competent.

Not all resistances can be resolved in the same way. For instance, resistances coming from the id cannot be handled directly. The only way of handling them is through prolonged "working through" to be discussed later on. Repression, superego, and epinosic resistances can be resolved by lifting the lid of repression. This can be accomplished at the peak of resistance, when the patient's resistive behavior can be easily brought to his attention for recognition as such.

Technique in Dealing with Resistances

The skill of the psychoanalyst can be measured by his success in handling resistances. Poorly skilled analysts may become bogged down with what looks to them like insurmountable resistance, while a master takes the obstacles with grace and ease. Psychoanalysis is a process in which one individual uses his total personality to help another individual. Every analyst adds his personal touch to the treatment. Moreover, no analyst treats all his patients exactly the same way.

Freud was aware of the necessity of adjusting the technique to the type of disorder. In his critique of a "wild" analysis he wrote: "My impression was that the lady in question was suffering from anxiety-hysteria, and the whole value of such nosographical distinctions, one which quite justifies them, lies in the fact that they indicate a different etiology and a different therapy" (1910c).

Psychoanalytic technique developed mainly in the treatment of conversion hysterics. Hysterics, as a rule, oscillate between positive and negative transference attitudes toward the analyst. Both attitudes, encouraged by the passive-receptive attitude of the analyst, allow the patient to re-experience his neurotic conflict in the analytic situation. Resolution of resistances, reconstruction of the past, and the interpretation of the unconscious conflict relived in transference is the right method.

Obsessive-compulsive neurotics often use free associations as resistance. Therefore, in the paper "The Future Prospects of Psychoanalytic Therapy" Freud came to the

opinion that the analytic technique must undergo certain modifications according to the nature of the disease and the dominating instinctual trends in the patient. Our therapy was, in fact, first designed for conversion hysteria; in anxiety-hysteria (phobias) we must alter our procedure to some extent. The fact is that these patients cannot bring out the material necessary for resolving the phobia as long as they feel protected by retaining their phobic condition. . . . One cannot, of course, induce them to give up their protective measures and work under the influence of anxiety from the beginning of the treatment. One must therefore help them by interpreting their unconscious to them until they can make up their minds to do without the protection of their phobia and expose themselves to a now comparatively moderate degree of anxiety. Only when they have done so does the material necessary for achieving solution of the phobia become accessible. Other modifications of technique which seem to me not yet ready for discussion will be required in the treatment of obsessional neurosis. (1910b).

Freud was even more outspoken in his address, "Turnings in the Ways of Psychoanalytic Therapy" read before the Fifth International Psychoanalytic Congress in 1918 in Budapest.

Freud wrote about phobias as follows:

Take the example of agoraphobia; there are two classes of it, one slight and the other severe. Patients belonging to the first indeed suffer from anxiety when they go about alone, but they have not yet given up going out alone on that account; the others protect themselves from the anxiety by altogether giving up going about alone. With these last one succeeds only when one can induce them through the influence of the analysis to behave like the first class, that is, to go about alone and to struggle with their anxiety while they make the attempt. . . .

In severe cases of obsessive acts a passive waiting attitude seems even less well adapted; indeed in general these cases incline to favor an asymptomatic process of cure, an interminable protraction of the treatment; in their analysis there is always the danger of a great deal coming to light without its effecting any change in them. I think there is little doubt that here the correct technique can only be to wait until the treatment itself has become a compulsion, and then with this countercompulsion, forcibly to suppress the compulsion of the disease (Freud, 1919a).

In other words, phobic patients must be forced to face precisely what they fear most. Such an experience may prove invaluable in overcoming resistances.

In some cases resistance leads to acting out and demands immediate gratification of emotional needs. Psychoanalytic treatment requires abstention: patients' demands must not be satisfied, and, under no circumstances by the analyst. Sometimes acting out takes place outside the analytic sessions, and some patients act under momentary impulses. A radical change in the life situation of a person under analysis is rather inadvisable; for crucial decisions should be avoided while the whole motivational system is undergoing far-reaching changes. Marriage, divorce, change of occupation, and so on should be delayed until a time when the patient's personality has reached a more stable balance. Rush decisions may be just an acting out of infantile impulses and, as such, may represent resistance. The analyst's task in such a case is not to sit idly and watch, but to invoke the rule of abstentia. Contemporary psychoanalysts are, as a rule, more flexible, and use their judgment; instead of rigid restrictions they offer insight and, in trying situations, even guidance. But more about this in Chapter Seventeen.

16
Working Through and the Final Phase

According to Freud, not everyone can be analyzed:

> [To be analyzable, one] must be capable of a psychically normal condition; during periods of confusion or melancholic depression nothing can be accomplished even in cases of hysteria. Furthermore, a certain measure of natural intelligence and ethical development are to be required of him; if the physician has to deal with a worthless character, he soon loses the interest which make it possible for him to enter profoundly into the patient's mental life. Deep-rooted malformations of character, traits of an actually degenerate constitution, show themselves during treatment as sources of a resistance that scarcely can be overcome (Freud, 1904, p. 254).

Freud also believed in an age limit for psychoanalysis: he thought that around fifty "the ability to undo psychical processes begin to grow weaker." [*Ibid.*]

Whoever wishes to undergo analysis must accept the fundamental rule of free association, and a few additional rules such as those governing fixed appointment hours, fees, and so on. Since suffering is the main reason for undergoing analysis, psychoanalysis must not provide premature gratifications, for they would reduce the motivation for being cured. Thus psychoanalysis imposes the *rule of abstention,* preventing gratification as much as possible. Some amount of frustration is necessary for treatment, and psychoanalysts must avoid providing secondary (epinosic) gain.

It is a widespread misconception that psychoanalysis of an adult is a sort of after-education and, therefore, treatment of children must follow the same rules as the treatment of adults. In the preface to Aichhorn's *Wayward Youth* (1921) Freud wrote:

> The possibility of analytic influence rests on quite definite preconditions which can be summed up under the term "analytic situation"; it requires the development of certain psychical structures and a particular attitude to the analyst. Where these are lacking—as in the case of children, of juvenile delinquents and, as a rule, of impulsive criminals—something other than analysis must be employed though something which will be at one with analysis in its purpose.

THE CONCEPT OF CURE

With the introduction of the structural concepts, ego therapy became the focal task of psychoanalytic treatment. To transform unconscious into conscious, the topographic goal, was not dismissed but incorporated in the new over-all goal. "The business of analysis," Freud wrote, "is to secure the best possible conditions for the functioning of the ego; when this has been done, analysis has accomplished its task" (1937).

Thus, Freud's concept of cure hinges on the *struggle* of the ego, its ability to form new sublimation, to put all its energies to an efficient use, and to apply its resources for optimum success and enjoyment. Facing things as they are and making the best of them is tantamount to mental health.

The removal of symptoms reflects the negative part of the goal. When the patient is cured, the symptoms disappear. Thus, "the removal of symptoms of the illness is not specifically aimed at but is achieved, as it were, as a byproduct if the analysis is properly carried through" (Freud, 1923a).

On the positive side, the ability "to love and to work" are signs of mental health. Men have to work to survive and have to relate to other people. Not every patient can attain the same level of mental health and mental development. Freud cautioned analysts against superimposing their own ambitions on the patients and expecting the patients to attain goals that the latter are unable to attain.

In terms of psychoanalytic theory, mental health is a state of balance between the ego, the id, and the superego. The ego, holding a strong grip on reality, must control the total personality and guide behavior. The healthy ego does not struggle with the id and the superego. The ego meets the legitimate demands of the id and tries to satisfy them in a way that will not jeopardize the interests of the organism. The id is blind and presses for immediate gratifications (the "pleasure principle"); but the ego, while striving for gratification, tries to secure pleasure without taking unnecessary risks. The ego does not surrender to the superego either, but it takes into consideration the moral standards of society and complies with them in not too rigid a fashion.

WORKING THROUGH

Insight cannot be gained by mere interpretation of conscious behavior (often called *confrontation*), and interpretation of the unconscious. Psychoanalysis may become interminable unless resistances are overcome. Every victory in the struggle against resistances prepares the ground for the next victory. Thus, a prolonged process of working through must follow. The patient, still in transference, presents new and hitherto hidden defenses, exposes deeper layers of his infantile conflicts and gradually, step by step, resolves them.

Withdrawal of cathexes from infantile fixations enriches the patient's personality and puts at the disposal of his ego new emotional resources. The need for energy absorbing anticathexes subsides, and each step forward frees mental energies hitherto involved in inner strife. In the terminal phase, patients may tend to invest their abundant energy in a new adventure, seeking thus a somewhat premature gratification. Many a patient falls in love with the first new acquaintance and rushes into marriage. Here it is well to repeat that, in such a case, it is the analyst's task to invoke the rule of abstention, recommending a delay, and more time for making important decisions.

One could compare the patient in the final phase of analysis to a car whose power has been increased. An increase in the power of an automobile engine requires a proportional increase in the power of the brakes and the steering mechanism. Similarly, gradual resolution of mental conflicts frees mental energies; these energies must be put to rational use.

The ego represents both the brakes and the steering wheel of human personality. Through the entanglements of transference, the ego acquires a better balance between narcissistic and object-cathexes of libido, using the analyst as a target and a testing ground. The interaction with the analyst strengthens the ego's ability for reality-testing; and the unraveling of infantile conflicts increases the ego's control over emotions, impulses, and motility. The ego's grip on reality tightens and, freed from infantile and neurotic involvement, the ego is capable of engaging in a mature and constructive life.

A mature adult is capable of loving and working. Mature love involves adult sexual relationships combined with realistic appraisal of one's commitment, and respect and consideration for one's marital partner. In the terminal phase, the patient usually works through his relation with a person of the opposite sex. Such an adult readjustment of the ego may serve as a preparation for future marriage, or improvement of an existing one. The patient has learned, through his transference relations with the analyst, to renounce infantile demands and unrealistic hopes; he no longer plays the dual role of domineering parent and hurt child, nor does he expect his marital partner to be an idealized parental figure.

The readaptation of the ego leads to an improvement in the patient's ability to work, and to an increase in his efficiency and productivity. A self-defeating patient who had hoped to win love by suffering may learn through transference to give up this method of securing secondary gain. In fact, he may not need secondary gains any longer, and come to prefer realistic success to neurotic self-pity. Instead of infantile crying for help and neurotic complaining, he may use his resources in a rational and aggressive way to win a better socioeconomic status. Toward the end of treatment, many a patient seeks new job opportunities or even starts a new and better-suited occupation that had previously been avoided for neurotic reasons.

Better control of impulses is impossible without partial sublimation. In the heat of transference, some of the unsatisfied love and hate impulses turn into new channels. Some patients discover hobbies that serve as additional energy outlets; others turn to art, or seek other avenues for the sublimation of erotic and destructive impulses. No human being can have all his wishes fulfilled: in the final phase of treatment part of the patient's unrealized desires must become sublimated.

THE TERMINATION

A strong and realistic ego does not need supportive parental figures.
Transference is a self-terminating process. The patient leans on the
analyst while he is growing, but when the patient grows up he does not
need the analyst any longer. Transference dies a natural death and,
instead of an infantile submissiveness (positive transference) or infantile rebelliousness (negative transference), a friendly adult relationship develops. The need to depend on the analyst subsides, and stormy
feelings toward him gradually disappear.

In some cases, on the eve of termination or immediately thereafter,
there is a resurgence of neurotic symptoms. Such a "miniature neurosis," provoked by the threat of separation or by separation proper, is
nothing more than a temporary revival of transference feelings. A
person who has used his analyst as a crutch may fear walking without
that crutch. Needless to say, the more thorough the working through,
the less the chance for a "miniature neurosis." A miniature neurosis
does not require a second analysis, but merely a few hours of additional
working through of transference problems.

17

Variations and Modifications

Adler, Jung, Horney, Sullivan, and others, leaning on Freud's findings, developed their own treatment methods. The collective volume *Psychoanalytic Techniques: A Handbook for the Practicing Psychoanalyst* describes their methods under the heading "Non-Freudian Techniques" (Wolman, 1967c).

Several prominent psychoanalysts, however, have adhered to Freud's theories and the rationale of Freud's treatment, but they have introduced certain modifications in the master technique. This chapter describes some of these post-Freudian or neo-Freudian techniques. As Fenichel (1945) put it, "Whether the patient lies down or sits, whether or not certain rituals of procedure are used does not matter." In some cases, when the "classical" procedure is inapplicable, a non-classical technique "remains psychoanalysis." Thus, again, one must quote Fenichel, who has noted that "there are many ways to treat neuroses but only one way to understand them."

FREUD'S MODIFICATIONS

The foundations for modifications in the technique were set down in Freud's structural theory (1923b) and its implications. Prior to 1923, psychoanalytic treatment had emphasized the struggle between the unconscious and the conscious. After 1923 the emphasis gradually shifted to the ego and its defensive and adaptive function.

Some modifications were suggested by Freud himself. For instance, when a hysteric regressed into a severe depressive state, the usual technique was not applicable. Abraham, in his paper on treatment of manic-depressive disorders, suggested starting analysis when the patient is comparatively free from depression. Abraham repeated Freud's advice to start psychoanalysis of "melancholiacs" at a time "when they are just coming out of a depressive state and entering upon a free interval."

While the usual technique aims at the removal of defense mechanisms, in a paper presented to the Nuremberg Congress Freud advocated the support of the denial mechanisms in the hypomanic states (1910b). Freud wrote in the *General Introduction to Psychoanalysis:*

> Many attempts at treatment made in the beginning of psychoanalysis were failures because they were undertaken with cases altogether unsuited to the procedure, which nowadays we should exclude by following certain indications. These indications, however, could only be discovered by trying. In the beginning we did not know that paranoia and dementia praecox, when fully developed, are not amenable to analysis; we were still justified in trying the method on all kinds of disorders (p. 399).

Definite modifications in psychoanalytic technique are necessary in the treatment of obsessive-compulsives, and phobic patients (the so-called anxiety hysterics). As early as 1894, Freud observed the tendency of obsessive-compulsives to use free associations as resistance.

Schizophrenic patients reacted unfavorably to the reclining position and to the analyst's silence. Freud believed schizophrenia to be a narcissistic nontransference disorder.

> If the patient's ego is to be a useful ally in our common work, it must, however hard it may be pressed by the hostile powers, have retained a certain degree of coherence, a fragment at least of understanding for the demands of reality. But this is not to be expected from the ego of a psychotic; it cannot carry out a pact of this sort, indeed it can scarcely engage in it. It will very soon toss us away and the help we offer it, to join the portions of the external world that no longer mean anything to it. Thus we learn that we must renounce the idea of trying our plan of cure upon psychotics—renounce it forever, perhaps, or only for the moment, until we have discovered some other plan better suited for that purpose (Freud, 1938).

According to Freud, psychoanalysis is indicated for transference neuroses, namely the hysterias, phobias, obsessional neuroses, and character disorders. Patients' behavior outside the analytic hours should be as normal as possible, and should abreact the transference that took place in psychoanalytic session. However, psychoanalysis is not the choice method for the treatment of psychotics because of (1) their inability to develop transference, (2) their inability to adhere to the "analytic pact." While Freud believed schizophrenia to be a non-transference disorder, some contemporary analysts described later in this chapter have contested his notion of schizophrenia.

Neither was Freud overly optimistic about psychoanalysis of homosexuals. Because homosexuals do not suffer, it is not easy to transform an active, adult homosexual into a heterosexual. Freud believed that psychoanalysis can make heterosexuality accessible to the patient, but after that, "it lay with [the patient] to choose whether he wished to abandon the path that is banned by society, and in some cases he has done so" (Freud, 1920b). In the paper, "The Psychogenesis of a Case of Homosexuality in a Woman," Freud wrote:

> The ideal situation for analysis is when someone who is otherwise his own master is suffering from an inner conflict which he is unable to resolve alone so that he brings his trouble to the analyst and begs for his help (*Ibid.*).

Psychoanalysts form an alliance with one part of the patient's personality against the other part.

REICH'S CRACKING OF ARMOR

One modification of Freudian technique was introduced by Wilhelm Reich in 1933. Reich was critical of premature and unsystematic interpretations. He suggested starting from the interpretation of resistances, whether they were apparent or "latent," that is, not expressed verbally, but implied only.

Reich pointed to the necessity for paying attention to the over-all behavior of the patient that reflects the patient's character. Character, as explained in Chapter Seven, means the way a person faces life. Neurotic character is defensive, and psychoanalysis must crack its defenses. These defenses form the core of resistance and, unless they are cracked, analysis cannot succeed. However, while Abraham stressed the libidinal organization, Reich's concept of character is basically a description of defenses. It is the way the ego wards off libidinal and aggressive impulses from within, and dangerous stimuli from without.

Thus, according to Reich (1933) character resembles a rather rigid protective shell, a sort of *armor*. This armor reflects itself also in non-verbal aspects of behavior during psychoanalytic hours. The way the patient talks, looks, moves around, and so on is indicative of his narcissistic defensive armor.

The character [Reich wrote in 1933—the 1948 edition repeats it verbatim] consists in a *chronic* alteration of the ego which one might describe as a rigidity. It is the basis of the becoming chronic of a person's characteristic mode of reaction. Its meaning is the protection of the ego against external and internal dangers. As a protection mechanism which has become chronic it can rightly be called an *armor*. This armor inevitably means a reduction of the total psychic mobility. This reduction is alleviated by relationships with the outer world which are not conditioned by the character and thus are atypical. There are "gaps" in the armor through which libidinal and other interests are put out and pulled back like pseudopodia. The armor, however, is to be thought of as mobile. It operates according to the pleasure-unpleasure principle. In unpleasurable situations the armoring increases, in pleasurable situations it decreases. The degree of character mobility, the ability to open up to a situation or to close up against it, constitutes the difference between the healthy and the neurotic character structure. The prototypes of a pathologically rigid armoring are the affect-blocked compulsive character and schizophrenic autism which tend in the direction of catatonic rigidity.

The character armor developed as the chronic result of the conflict between instinctual demands and the frustrating outer world; the continuing actual conflicts between instinct and outer world give it its strength and continued reason for existence.

Reich suggested the following rules for character analysis:

1. Interpretation should proceed from the surface, manifest behavior and only gradually descend into deeper layers
2. Interpretation of resistances should come first, ahead of any other interpretation
3. Interpretation of resistances must wait until they are fully developed

In other words, the interpretation of unconscious impulses must come after interpretation of the defenses erected against these impulses.

FERENCZI'S ACTIVE TECHNIQUE

Ferenczi was one of Freud's most active coworkers. His psycho-analytic work can be divided into three stages (Balint) as follows:

1. Contributions to classical technique
2. The active technique
3. Pointers to future development

In his numerous papers that contributed to the classical technique, Ferenczi elucidated several fine theoretical and technical points. He certainly antedated Reich in drawing attention to such nonverbal expressions of patients as changes of voice pitch, salivation, giddiness, drowsiness, and so on. Ferenczi pointed out the factor of overdoing in free association; he also elaborated on necessary modification in the handling of transference, and control of countertransference.

The idea of "active technique" grew out of Ferenczi's observation that psychoanalysts are not as passive as they profess to be in their "evenly hovering attention." For instance, adherence to the rule of abstinence really brings about an active intervention in the patient's life. The analyst does regulate the patient's behavior by denying gratification, and insisting that the patient abstain from making far-reaching decisions while his motives and emotions are still in a state of flux.

In 1925 in the paper on the psychoanalysis of sexual habits, Ferenczi (1950) described his innovation. The term active technique applies primarily to the patient. The analyst's activity was delineated as friendly suggestion. Ferenczi's contention was that most patients suffered from harsh parental treatment; the psychoanalyst must, therefore, be definitely and clearly kind and considerate. This actively friendly attitude was suggested as appropriate toward the end of the treatment. Such a friendliness must resemble a mother-child relationship. In a later paper Ferenczi suggested muscular relaxation (1950).

Between 1927 and 1933 (when Ferenczi died), he wrote several papers (published together in English in 1955) pointing toward future developments. In some of these papers Ferenczi explained the limits of maternal empathy and forebearance in treatment, for even the most loving mother must set limits to her child's behavior. Ferenczi stressed the need for sincerity and frankness on the part of the analyst. In cases when the usual procedure and interpretations did not work, Ferenczi suggested that the analyst show genuine kindness and affection for the suffering patient.

PSYCHOANALYTIC PSYCHOTHERAPY

The future historian of culture will have to find out to what extent our therapeutic practices were a product of pragmatic thought and how much they owed to other factors. The famous psychoanalytic couch was instituted before psychoanalysis actually started; and the reclining position developed out of the hypnotic technique. When Freud realized the advantages of not having the patient and the analyst staring at one another, the reclining position became a convenient setting, facilitating free associations. Yet, Freud failed to notice that in severe anxiety states such as those experienced by schizophrenics, the reclining position was anything but ideal. The passive, evenly hovering attention of the analyst tended to increase anxiety in schizophrenic patients and, to some extent, furthered their regression (Wolman, 1965c). Small wonder that Freud arrived at the erroneous conclusion that schizophrenia is a narcissistic disorder and psychoanalysis was not indicated (cf. Wolman, 1967a).

Thus several adjustments were made for the treatment of psychotics. Outstanding psychoanalysts, such as Federn, Bychowski (1952), Eissler and others (in Brody and Redlich, 1952) have introduced substantial modifications in the master technique. Quite often the abandonment of the reclining position, curtailment of free association, and maintaining of flexibility in the number of sessions per week have been regarded as a renunciation of the psychoanalytic method and the modified treatment technique was called psychotherapy.

From a purely linguistic point of view, psychotherapy is a broader term in which psychoanalysis is included. Psychotherapy implies that all treatment methods are psychological, in contradistinction to physical and chemical methods. Psychoanalysis, individual psychology, hypnosis, conditioning, nondirective techniques, and so on are psychotherapeutic methods. Shock treatment, surgery, chemo-therapy, and so on are not.

In Freud's time the nonanalytic psychotherapies were so meager and so unsuccessful that Freud compared psychotherapy to "cheap alloy," while believing that psychoanalysis was "pure gold." However, several psychoanalysts, while faithful to Freud's rationale, modified and simplified the psychoanalytic technique. As mentioned above, some modifications have been necessary in the treatment of psychotics. The question of whether, in such cases, the term psychoanalysis or modified psychoanalysis should be used remains open: should one call these new techniques psychoanalytic psychotherapy, or psycho-analytically oriented psychotherapy? This issue, which may seem insignificant to outsiders, has created a good deal of controversy among psychoanalysts; and a prominent orthodox psychoanalyst, Tarachow, has elaborated a definite psychotherapeutic technique distinct from psychoanalysis proper (Tarachow and Stein 1967).

THE CORRECTIVE EMOTIONAL EXPERIENCE
OF ALEXANDER AND FRENCH

Two distinguished psychoanalysts associated with the Chicago Psychoanalytic Institute introduced far-reaching modifications in psychoanalytic technique. Franz Alexander and Thomas French believed that as long as a method of treatment is based on Freudian understanding of the dynamics of human nature, it is psychoanalytic. According to Alexander, "the various forms of psychotherapy as well as the classic psychoanalytic procedure [are] different applications of the universally valid principles of psychodynamics" (1956, p. 4). The basic principle of psychoanalysis is "to impart insight based on emotional experience" (*Ibid.,* p. 143).

Support and Insight

Alexander and French stressed two aspects of psychoanalytic treatment, namely support and insight. Insight is given to the patient through interpretation of unconscious conflicts. In free associations, in dreams, and so on the patient brings to the surface his repressed

wishes, and the fears of these wishes that caused repression. Analysis
of repressed material and repressing forces forms the core of insight.
The analyst and the patient explain the surface material (confrontation), and the deeper layers (interpretation).

However, as Freud and almost all Freudians have observed, a
purely intellectual approach to mental problems can hardly result in
their resolution. An emotional experience, called transference, emerges
in psychoanalytic sessions. This emotional factor is the main vehicle
of cure. Alexander and French didn't believe at all in the therapeutic
value of pure insight.

Transference

Needless to say, up to this point Alexander and French did not deviate much from Freud's teaching. They did deviate, however, in
the "handling" of transferences. The very idea that transference must
be handled, and not just allowed to develop, was a new one.

Alexander and French believed treatment is a profound emotional
experience, and that what occurs during its course is more than transference and, as such, must not be left to coincidental developments.
Though the patient relives in transference emotional involvements of
his childhood, the mere reliving cannot be healing. Past emotions
must be re-experienced in a setting that could enable their correction.
Thus "corrective emotional experience" must be offered to the patient.

This experience must be geared to the patient's needs—a rigid
every-day schedule may not be appropriate for some patients. Alexander
maintains that, in many cases, less frequent interviews are just as
productive as the classic procedure with daily sessions.

Alexander, French, Selesnick, and others experimented with less
frequent interviews and also with interruptions in treatment.

> At propitious moments the analyst may manipulate the frequency
> of analytic interviews or recommend a temporary interruption of
> treatment. In some cases, as for example, with acting-out patients, it
> may be necessary to increase the frequency of the interviews in order
> to develop a more intense transference relationship. This encourages a
> tendency toward identification with the analyst, who then has an
> opportunity to exert a restraining influence on the patient's impulses.
> Frequently, however, especially with those patients who use analysis

as a substitute for life experiences, it is better to reduce the frequency of the interviews or to set a tentative termination date for the analysis. Owing to these experimental manipulations, dependency on the analytic situation becomes a focal issue. The patient may discover that he can manage quite well without the analyst, and soon a more permanent separation may be recommended. Preparatory interruptions were found to be an excellent means of gauging the proper time for terminating the treatment. Alexander, French, and some of their colleagues at the Chicago Psychoanalytic Institute learned that the emotional reaction to previous interruptions is a more important clue than such criteria as recollection of infantile memories or the depth of intellectual insight. In cases when, during interruptions or reductions in frequency, feelings of yearning for the analyst become more intense upon returning to the analysis or upon increasing the frequency of the interviews, the patient may be able now to verbalize those feelings and thus gain greater insight into the nature of his dependent strivings. It is insight based on emotional experience, especially with regard to the transference, that is the aim of these stratagems (Selesnick, 1967).

Alexander believed that interruptions in treatment may have therapeutic value insofar as they show the degree of the patient's dependence on the analyst. By increasing or decreasing the number of sessions per week, the analyst may intensify or dilute the transference, according to the emotional needs of the patient and the treatment strategy.

Present and Past

Corrective emotional experience implies flexibility in the analyst's attitude toward the patient. A patient whose parents were discouraging, hypercritical, and derogatory needs a corrective emotional experience with an encouraging, noncritical, and respecting analyst. As previously indicated, the analyst must somehow convey to the patient a friendly, encouraging, and respectful attitude, offering not only insight but also *support* to the patient's emerging ego. He must enable the patient to relive the past in a new and corrective setting so that there is no reason to seek secondary gain and escape into neurosis. This is not promoting countertransference; it is giving the patient a chance to develop a more mature attitude toward life.

Corrective experience cannot be simply a replica of childhood, nor should it be a mere recollection and reconstruction of the past. Alexander and French (1946) stressed the importance of the here-and-now, real life situation of the patient. What's the use of digging out of the past if the patient still fails to adjust to his present life conditions? The discovery of the past should be geared toward the understanding of the current situation. The unraveling of childhood experiences offers clues to the present; the interpretation of the past is not a goal in itself, but a means toward the goal, and the goal is rational adjustment to mature, adult life. The present situation is, to some extent, enacted in the analyst's office. Here the patient has the opportunity to learn about himself and his own behavioral patterns.

Alexander did not approve of the passive attitude of the analyst. The analyst must convey to the patient his own self-confidence, and faith in the success of the treatment. The evenly hovering attention of the analyst who refrains from expressing his feelings may be of little therapeutic value. Alexander believed that the patient must *feel* the difference between the primitive, unstable, and rejecting parents and the present relation with the friendly and mature analyst. This new relation is the bedrock of the corrective and healing experience.

The main task of psychoanalytic therapy is to help the ego to assume its adaptive functions and to relate in a rational way to the tasks and challenges of adult life.

Dream Interpretation

According to French, a dream is like the famous Rosetta Stone, the deciphering of whose hieroglyphs was the starting point in the discovery of the language of ancient Egypt. A dream conveys the language of the patient's unconscious and this must be translated into the language of the conscious. The analyst must re-create the atmosphere of the dream in order to fully understand it and make it meaningful.

Dreams are usually too complicated to be encompassed by the analyst's "integrative ego" right at the beginning of the interpretation process. The process starts with scanning the material presented; the analyst must take time to think about the dream, study it, and fully digest its content. The analyst's thoughts sweep over the patient's dream material, the free associations, and also the preceding hours.

The nature of the clues determines which particular method of interpretation the analyst should follow. The manner of approach may be dictated by the dream itself, or by certain factors inherent in the personality of the analyst. The mental and somatic states of an individual determine whether and how he perceives an objective stimulus or problem. Furthermore, the fact that each analyst may have his own particular mode of working may cause him to prefer one interpretation method over another.

There is but one truly correct focal conflict interpretation for every dream, but there are many ways to arrive at it. Sometimes the analyst may be unwilling to evaluate critically his interpretative hunches. He may resist abandoning a hypothesis he has made earlier, or he may become sidetracked on a subfocal conflict.

The interpretation of dreams is successful if it explains why each part of the dream and the associations given to it are parts of the dreamer's total response to his present emotional situation.

There are two methods of checking the interpretation, namely the scientific check and the artistic (esthetic experience) check. The interpretation of a dream is scientifically sound if all the material fits in. The interpretation is esthetically correct if the analyst and the patient find an esthetic experience in it.

WOLMAN'S INTERACTIONAL TECHNIQUE

In 1931 Freud described three "libidinal types": *erotic, obsessive,* and *narcissistic.*

> Erotics are persons whose main interest—the relatively largest amount of their libido—is focused on love. Loving, but above all being loved, is for them the most important thing in life. They are governed by the dread of loss of love, and this makes them peculiarly dependent on those who may withhold their love from them. . . .
> [the obsessional's] distinctive characteristic is the supremacy exercised by the superego. . . . Persons of this type are governed by anxiety of conscience instead of by the dread of losing love; they exhibit, we might say, an inner instead of an outer dependence. . . .
> [In the narcissistic type] there is no tension between ego and superego—indeed, starting from this type one would hardly have arrived at

the notion of a superego . . . the main interest is focused on self-preservation. . . . The ego has a considerable amount of aggression available (Freud, 1931, pp. 248-249).

All mental disorders exclusive of the inherited (*geno-somatogenic*) ones are a product of interaction between the organism and the environment. If this interaction is physical or chemical, the disorder is called *eco-somatogenic*. If it is neither physical nor chemical, it should be called *sociogenic*. Thus all mental disorders fall into one of the three classes: geno-somatogenic, eco-somatogenic, or sociogenic. The so-called psychogenic mental disorders are a product of interaction with the social environment. They are caused either by cathexes, or by *conditioning*. In either case, the sociogenic mental disorders are produced by harmful influences of environmental factors.

These environmental factors affect the intra-individual balance of cathexes. The infant is prone to go through the oral, anal, urethral, and phallic stages. The very fact of the developmental stages is biologically determined. Moreover, the *way* the individual infant will go through them is determined by sociocultural factors. The level and severity of fixations and regressions largely depends on the *interaction* between the infant and his home environment. Parent-child interaction may facilitate or prevent growth, may encourage object relations or foster secondary narcissism, may block or speed up discharges of libido and destrudo. The formation of ego and superego is largely a product of interaction between the individual and his environment.

Pathogenesis of mutual disorders is, to a great extent, the story of parent-child relations and their impact on child development and personality formation. There is no doubt that the same pathogenic patterns are reflected in transference. The family drama is re-enacted by the patients who, as we have learned, ascribe to the analyst the actions, motives, and personality traits of their parents.

One can distinguish three interactional patterns, depending on whether the main purpose of the interaction is the satisfaction of the individual's needs (*instrumental*), or his partner's needs (*vectorial*), or both (*mutual* or *mutual acceptance*) (Wolman, 1957; 1960).

When people enter a social relationship in order to have their needs satisfied, when their purpose is to take and not to give, it is an *instrumental* relationship. Each individual regards others as tools or instruments to be used for his well-being. The life of an infant starts as a parasitic process in which the infant must be given all that is necessary for his survival. The relation of an infant to his mother is the prototype of instrumentalism.

Mutual or mutual acceptance relations develop gradually through motivation and learning. Already in the nursery school or playground, the child is presented with the opposition of other children to his instrumentalism. Gradually he learns to share, to take turns, to trade toys; acceptance, giving, and taking become viable bases for interaction.

Mutuality achieves its peak in friendship and marriage. Each partner desires to make his partner happy and expects that the feeling is reciprocated. Successful marriage is based on mutuality; each marital partner is determined to do his best for the well-being of his or her spouse, and expects the same from the other person.

Parenthood is the prototype of *vectorialism*. Parents give life, protect and care for it, irrespective of their child's looks, health, I.Q., disposition, or success. The more the infant needs their help, the more sympathy he elicits.

A normal or well-adjusted individual is balanced in social interaction. He is instrumental in the struggle for survival, mutual in relations with friends and in marriage, and vectorial in regard to children and to those who need help. He is reasonably selfish (instrumental), reasonably mutual, and reasonably vectorial.

Mentally disturbed individuals cannot preserve this balance. They are *hyperinstrumental,* displaying infantile selfishness and parasitism; or they neglect themselves and worry constantly about others in a morbid *hypervectorialism;* or they exaggerate in giving and in taking, in shifting moods of *paramutualism.*

Needless to say, these three types correspond to three types of libido balances. In hyperinstrumental types, e.g., psychopaths, the libido is self-hypercathected and object-hypocathected; destrudo is loosely object-cathected. In hypervectorial types, the libido is self-hypocathected and object-hypercathected. The destrudo is kept under rigid control, but breaks through in psychotic deterioration. Obsessions, phobias, neurasthenias, and schizophrenic psychoses belong to this category. In paramutual types, libido and destrudo easily shift back and forth from self- to object-cathexis. Conversion hysteria dissociative reactions, and manic-depressive disorders fall into this classification. The hyper-

CLASSIFICATION OF MENTAL DISORDERS

Types / Levels	Hyperinstrumentalism I	Paramutualism M	Hypervectorialism V
Neurosis	HYPERINSTRUMENTAL NEUROSIS (Certain anxiety and depressive reactions)	PARAMUTUAL NEUROSIS (Dissociative and conversion reactions)	HYPERVECTORIAL NEUROSIS (Obsessional, phobic, and neurasthenic reactions)
Character Neurosis	HYPERINSTRUMENTAL CHARACTER NEUROSIS (Sociopathic or psychopathic personality)	PARAMUTUAL CHARACTER NEUROSIS (Cyclothymic and passive-aggressive personality)	HYPERVECTORIAL CHARACTER NEUROSIS (Schizoid and compulsive personality)
Latent Psychosis	LATENT HYPERINSTRUMENTAL PSYCHOSIS (Psychopathic reactions bordering on psychosis)	LATENT PARAMUTUAL PSYCHOSIS (Borderline manic-depressive psychosis)	LATENT VECTORIASIS PRAECOX (Borderline and latent schizophrenia)
Manifest Psychosis	HYPERINSTRUMENTAL PSYCHOSIS (Psychotic psychopathy and moral insanity)	PARAMUTUAL PSYCHOSIS (Manifest manic-depressive psychosis)	VECTORIASIS PRAECOX (Manifest schizophrenia)
Dementia	Collapse of Personality Structure		

instrumental type comes close to Freud's narcissist; the hypervectorial resembles the obsessive; and the paramutual personality comes close to Freud's erotic type. Each type can be subdivided in five levels indicative of the severity of the disorder, namely (1) neurosis, (2) character neurosis, and (3) latent, (4) manifest, and (5) dementive psychosis.

Transference

Both transference and resistance are parts of here-and-now behavior. The patient relates to the analyst partially on the basis of past experiences; but partially he reacts to the real situation. His demands for instinctual gratification are mainly transference, representing a reactivation of his infantile wishes. But the adult patient is not an infant. He is an adult who pays for therapeutic services and his demands —rational or irrational—are a part of the here-and-now situation.

In the process of treatment the analyst is never passive. His very presence, his age, sex, looks, manner of speech, and certainly his sparse comments are interactional phenomena. They are powerful factors in shaping the patient's feelings, thoughts, and actions, partially in transference and surely in the realistic part of the patient's attitudes.

Whatever goes on between the analyst and his patient is an interaction. It is always an *exchange of cathexes,* correctly perceived or misinterpreted by the patient (and often by the analyst). The silent analyst may be perceived by his patients as a taciturn or unfriendly individual who is, or pretends to be, or tries to give the impression of being an omnipotent figure. If the analyst really tries to impress, it is his countertransference blunder. But whatever he tries to do and whatever he says or does, always constitutes interaction.

Every psychoanalytic treatment is, as Fenichel put it, "based on the analyst's influence on the patient" (p. 447). For no matter what the analyst's point of view is, he *always regulates transference.* He regulates it by imposing the fundamental rule, by suggesting the reclining position, by saying or not saying, "How are you?" by smiling or by not smiling, and so on.

Freud's difficulty with schizophrenics as compared with Federn's success with them is a case in point. The insistence on a reclining position facilitates topographic regression; regression is promoted even more by the fundamental rule of free association; the analyst's remoteness and silence tend to contribute to the schizophrenic's tension and withdrawal. No wonder Freud, who experienced these things in his practice, believed schizophrenia to be a nontransference disorder. Federn admitted schizophrenics to his home and witnessed most profound transference (1952). In my own work with schizophrenics described in a recent monograph (Wolman, 1966a) I developed the rule of *getting involved* with the patient's cause *without getting involved* with the patient in a personal way (avoidance of countertransference).

The analyst's role in shaping the patient's transference is only a part of the truth. In transference, the patient re-enacts the pathogenesis of neurosis. Freud was always aware of the differences in the types of transference, and I have tried to make this awareness more explicit, and explain it in terms of the three abovementioned sociopsychological types of overt behavior.

The Paramutuals

Freud's description of transference given in 1920 in *Beyond the Pleasure Principle* fits the paramutual type of neurosis (conversion hysteria, etc.).

> Loss of love and failure leave behind them a permanent injury to self-assurance in the form of a narcissistic scar, which . . . contributes more than anything to the "sense of inferiority." The tie of affection, which binds the child as a rule to the parent of the opposite sex, succumbs to disappointment. . . .
> Patients repeat all of these invented situations and painful emotions in the transference and revive them with the greatest ingenuity. They seek to bring about the interruption of the treatment while it is still incomplete; they contrive once more to feel themselves scorned. . . . But no lesson has been learned from the old experience of these activities, having led instead only to unpleasure (1920a).

The paramutual neurotic quickly develops positive transference. He or she falls in love with the allegedly omnipotent and benevolent parental figure. The analyst's attentive attitude is perceived as a keen interest in the patient, who, in turn, responds with glowing love to the meager signs of approval. The analyst represents the benevolent superego that does not criticize the patient, no matter what he says.

The true parents—especially the mother of the typical hysteric—were highly critical, and only on those occasions when the patient was very ill, or in great danger, did they show affection. The paramutual dreams of the "lost paradise" when he was one with his mother and tries to recapture it by self-defeat. As long as he believes he is loved, he re-enacts in transference his oral love for himself, the analyst, and everyone else.

Paramutuals easily swing from positive to negative transference. As long as they imagine that the analyst loves them, they are in a blissful euphoria. Most symptoms disappear and the analytic hours become, as one of my patients put it, "the happiest hours in my life."

In the transference process, the paramutual patient goes through the love-hate swings of his past experience.

Woe to the analyst who lets himself be drawn into the treadmill of the emotional ups and downs of a paramutual: the detached, objective, matter-of-fact treatment of transference, combined with an incisive interpretation of resistance (and transference used as a resistance) is the choice method. Let us remember that the treatment of paramutuals has been the bedrock of the classic psychoanalysis.

The Hypervectorials

The peculiar difficulty in working with hypervectorial neuroses (obsessions, phobias, neurasthenias, etc.) lies in the patient's excessive resistance. One of the motives of resistance is a strong need for punishment, associated with masochistic wishes. This unconscious need for punishment corresponds to aggressiveness which has been internalized and taken over by the superego.

> People in whom this unconscious guilt feeling is dominant, distinguish themselves under analytic treatment by exhibiting . . . a negative therapeutic reaction. In the normal course of events, if one gives a patient the solution of a symptom, at least the temporary disappearance of the symptom should result; with these patients, on the contrary, the effect is a momentary intensification of the symptom and the suffering that accompanies it. It often needs only a word of praise of their behavior during the cure, the utterance of a few words of hope as to the progress of analysis, to bring about an unmistakable aggravation of their condition. . . . Their behavior will appear as an expres-

sion of an unconscious sense of guilt, which favors illness with its attendant suffering and handicaps (Freud, 1932, pp. 150-151).

Freud himself recommended active interpretation and direct influence. As soon as transference is established, the analyst must induce the phobic patient to modify his overt phobic behavior; and this change must occur prior to the resolution of the underlying unconscious motives.

In the process of psychoanalytic treatment of hypervectorials, a passive, detached attitude on the part of the analyst will unduly prolong the treatment and, perhaps, make analysis interminable. The analyst must be vectorial, that is, genuinely friendly. He must not, however, transgress his professional role nor deviate from the ethical and professional rule of abstention, of frustrating the patient's instinctual demands. He must never fall into the trap of countertransference, and thus become a copy of the incestuous and seductive or seducible parent. A moderate aim-inhibited interest in the patient's well-being is necessary. Such an attitude of friendliness and respect for the patient will help to increase the patient's self-esteem and improve the intra-individual balance of libido cathexes.

The dictatorial, overdemanding, irrational superego of hypervectorials must be reshaped. Its irrationality must be exposed and the ensuing severe guilt feeling interpreted and worked through.

Profound transference may make analysis interminable. Many neurasthenic, phobic, and obsessive patients (the hypervectorials) may feel a sort of obligation toward the analyst as if he were their "poor" Mommy or Daddy. They may fear that he will die if abandoned.

It seems advisable to *prevent* too deep a transference in all hypervectorials, especially in the more severe cases. The more outspoken the analyst is, the smaller are the chances for a deep transference. When a hysteric showers the analyst with personal questions, the analyst either does not respond, or analyzes the patient's curiosity. But when a frightened obsessive or latent schizophrenic asks, "Are you married?" "Do you have children?" and so on, a frank and honest answer, matter-of-factly given, seems to be advisable. There is no reason to surrender to countertransference and confide to the patient, but a clear-cut answer keeps him close to reality and reduces the danger of too vehement a transference.

The Hyperinstrumentals

Hyperinstrumentals (psychopaths) on all five levels are not inclined to invest their libido in anyone; their transference, if any, stays shallow. While I have suggested avoidance of too deep a transference in hypervectorials, the crucial task with hyperinstrumentals is to foster as deep a transference as possible, and to mollify their negative transference. Needless to say, hyperinstrumentals hate whoever frustrates their wish for immediate impulse gratification.

Manipulation of transference in these cases is not an easy task. The hyperinstrumentals have learned in childhood to defend themselves against unfair and rejecting parents, or absentee, overindulgent parents. In either case, the pre-hyperinstrumental has never had the opportunity to identify with either of his parents. Most hyperinstrumentals are polymorphous perverts. Although they are very aggressive, they perceive themselves as defenseless, innocent children. This attitude colors their oral-aggressive transference.

Thus the analyst faces a complex task. His silent permissiveness may be misinterpreted as siding with the id. An expression of disapproval by the analyst is no good either, for this may lead to the inclusion of the analyst in the paranoid picture of world conspiracy against the poor, innocent patient. The analyst must take a stand and help in developing the patient's superego, but he must wait until the transference is sufficiently strong.

Treatment of Psychotics

The main modifications are dictated by the weakness of the ego. Every analytic treatment is interaction, classic or modified and, as such, must be geared to the patient's specific needs. I have not discussed in detail those aspects of technique that are general for all types of patients, such as dream interpretation and working through. In working with overt psychotics, dream interpretation is superfluous; with latent psychotics it may be dangerous. The removal of defense mechanisms is necessary in the treatment of neurotics; it is the main task in working with character neurotics. With psychotics, however, one may have to support the neurotic defenses (I have called them ego-protective symptoms, 1966a) against the danger of a total collapse of the ego.

In his "Recommendations" (1912a) Freud cautioned analysts against being overambitious, and recommended "tolerance for the patient's weakness." This advice must be strongly reiterated with regard to psychotics. The final stage of psychoanalysis is, as Glover put it, dedicated to *transference weaning* and *ego-re-adaptation* (p. 139). Treatment of psychotics is, from beginning to end, a re-adaptation of the ego. Supportive therapy is necessary for *all three types,* but it must be applied differently for each type. Testing reality, manipulating the superego, and even directive approach, may be necessary at the initial phase of treatment of the psychotic.

18

The Psychoanalyst and His Training

When two people analyzed by two different psychoanalysts compare notes, they will be astonished at the differences in the technique, even if both psychoanalysts belong to the same school. Only the initial steps of treatment can be predicted; everything else is highly individual and varied, though some general rules have been prescribed by Freud and other innovators (cf. Wolman's *Psychoanalytic Techniques: A Handbook for the Practicing Psychoanalyst,* 1967a).

Freud was fully aware of this fact and stated frankly that his technique is the only one suited to his individuality. He wrote, "I do not venture to deny that a physician quite differently constituted might find himself driven to adopt a different attitude to his patients and to the task before him" (1912a, p. 711). One must therefore keep in mind that not even the most orthodox psychoanalysts practiced psychoanalysis in exactly the same way that Freud did. Variations in psychoanalytic procedures are often a product of the personalities of analysts and patients.

Freud compared psychoanalysis to surgery, for both the surgeon and the analyst must keep their own feelings under strict control and concentrate on their task. This comparison is quite interesting, and one may compare psychoanalysis to highly complicated, bloodless surgery on a human personality. Although there are general rules of procedure, each surgery is individual, depending on the nature of the particular case and on the technique of the particular surgeon. The same operation could be performed in more than one way.

One surgeon may be forceful, dynamic, quick in making decisions; another surgeon may be more cautious, weighing every step, and acting in a compulsively meticulous manner. There are scores of psychological types, subtypes, and mixtures of types represented among successful surgeons; yet certain common traits exist that make one successful in the field.

Personality Traits

All other factors being equal, success in any field depends on three factors: aptitude, knowledge, and skill. A good surgeon, for instance, must have a special *talent* for surgery, must *know* thoroughly anatomy, physiology, pathology, and so on, and must develop a superb *skill* in performing his duties.

What are the specific aptitudes, gifts, and talents that enable one to become a good psychoanalyst?

For a few years I taught and supervised psychiatrists in a postdoctoral training program in a university hospital. For several months I sat in the wards observing human relations. Some psychiatrists talked down to patients, or talked at the patients instead of to them, carefully preserving their social status as doctors. They spoke to the patients or about them as if the patients were not individual human beings but some odd "mental cases." Some of these psychiatrists had obtained their degrees with honors at excellent universities, and they knew Freud by heart; yet they never became good therapists.

Not all psychiatrists acted in the same manner. Some psychiatrists related to the patients not on the physician-patient paradigm, but as people to people. They spoke to patients with the reverence due to age and the politeness due to everyone. They were friendly and indulged in small talk in the wards, creating a pleasant atmosphere. All other factors being equal, these psychiatrists proved to be successful in their work (Wolman, 1964b).

Apparently the tool that an analyst uses in his work is himself, his total personality. The analyst serves as a target for the patient's positive and negative emotions in transference; he constantly interacts with the depth of unconscious impulses and partakes in the growth of human minds from a morbid infantilism toward adult maturity.

Not everyone can relate well to other people and certainly not too many people can become good psychoanalysts. The ability to relate to people, to understand them, and to feel friendly toward them seem to me to be the main personality traits of a good analyst and, thus, the number one issue in any consideration of his professional aptitude. People who lack patience and compassion, people who don't like being with others, or have little tolerance for human weaknesses and little understanding for human frailty should stay away from the psychotherapeutic professions.

Mere friendliness and human interest will not suffice one who would become a psychoanalyst. The stakes in the psychoanalytic profession are high; the risks great; superficial friendliness may be of no avail in this difficult task. In addition to profound and genuine friendliness and compassion, the psychoanalyst must be able to perceive subtle feelings of the patient even when the patient does not verbalize them.

The ability to perceive nonverbal communication, called empathy, is indispensable in psychoanalytic treatment of mental disorders. It calls for an easy access to one's own unconscious, and a special talent for the feeling of other people's feelings. When the psychoanalyst faces the patients and listens to their voices and grasps their communications, he must be capable of joining the patients in the regressive journey to their infantile experiences. The analyst's ego, as it were, submerges into the unconscious state of increased sensibility. However, the analyst's ego must be strong enough to re-emerge. The ego of a neurotic is enmeshed in inner struggle; it is partly submerged in neurotic conflicts and partly involved in anticathexes. The psychotic ego is flooded by unconscious impulses. A normal ego rules over the unconscious impulses, but the ego of the analyst must have more than average mastery. To be able to cope with the emotional life of his patients, the analyst must exercise more than adequate control over his own emotions. He must have a pretty strong ego to be able to stay sane while exposed to continuous emotional onslaught, hour after hour, day after day. This is one of the reasons that psychoanalysts must themselves undergo psychoanalysis before they are able to analyze others.

The ego of a psychoanalyst must be not only strong but *flexible,* capable of entering the unconscious of the patients without succumbing to the morbidity therein (Wolman, 1956). This strength, combined with flexibility, is acquired through life experience and deepened and entrenched by the practice of psychoanalysis. While the psychoanalyst is capable of perceiving unconscious hints and irrational processes, his own judgment must be wholly rational. The neurotic ego mixes rational and irrational elements; the psychotic ego succumbs to irrationality; the psychoanalyst's ego *grasps* irrationality but stays rational.

Friendliness, sympathy, and empathy are fundamental personality traits, prerequisites for becoming a good analyst. Several research workers (Betz and Whitehorn, 1952; Holt and Luborski, 1958; Thompson, 1956, and many others) have studied the problems of therapists' personalities. Although there is no definite agreement, it seems that, in addition to the abovementioned traits, high intelligence, perceptiveness, self-control, a realistic approach to life, and broadmindedness are required for successful psychoanalytic practice.

TRAINING PROGRAMS

One cannot learn psychoanalysis merely by studying its principles, just as one cannot learn medicine by studying pathology alone. Psychoanalysis is both a theory and a technique, like physics and engineering combined; and to become a psychoanalyst one must master psychoanalytic knowledge and psychoanalytic skill. Of course, one acquires knowledge through studies.

At the present time in the United States there are two main avenues for becoming a psychoanalyst. The first leads through an M.D. degree and the study of psychiatry; the second through a Ph.D. degree and the study of clinical psychology. Some psychoanalysts, also, have gone through schools of social work and other training programs.

To use the first channel involves the usual four-year undergraduate programs, during which time the future psychoanalyst takes the premedical major. Then he goes to a medical school with the customary four years of training in all branches of medicine. Medical schools prepare for a general practice of medicine. The young doctor of medicine who wishes to specialize must apply, after one year of internship, for a postdoctoral program in his chosen field of specialty. In psychiatry these programs entail two to four years of residence, that is practicing, in a hospital and its clinics; and intense course work in psychopathology and a variety of methods of treating mental disorders.

Curricula vary from one school to another, with preponderance of physico-chemical methods in one place, and preference for psychoanalytic or other psychological methods in another.

To become a bona fide psychiatrist, the young physician must pass the State Board examination. From then on he is entitled to offer his psychiatric services to the public, and to open his office for the practice of psychiatry that involves treatment of mental disorders with whatever method the psychiatrist chooses. He is not, however, a psychoanalyst, though many psychiatrists like to call themselves analysts. Psychiatry is a legal term: no one who is not duly licensed has the right to use this title of psychiatrist. Psychoanalysis, however, is not a name of a profession but of a theory and a method. To become a psychoanalyst one must undergo psychoanalytic training in one of the psychoanalytic institutes.

Psychoanalytic Institutes

The requirements for admission to such an institute, whether it is Freudian, neo-Freudian, or non-Freudian (for instance, Sullivanian or Horneyan) vary. Most psychoanalytic institutes admit duly licensed physicians who have completed or are completing their postdoctoral training in psychiatry. The training program, administered on a part-time basis, takes from four to ten years. The programs, as a rule, include psychoanalytic theory and practice, case seminars, clinical conferences, study groups, and so on.

In addition to course work and seminars, students of a psychoanalytic institute are required to receive practical training in psychoanalysis in a treatment center or a clinic run by the institute. This psychoanalytic practice is done under close supervision by the institute's faculty, and forms an indispensable part of the training.

Of course every student of a psychoanalytic institute must undergo psychoanalysis. Such an analysis, usually called a "didactic" or "training" analysis is first of all a thorough and detailed personal psychoanalysis. Men and women who will analyze other people must gain a thorough knowledge of their own mental resources, and a mastery over their own emotional lives.

Didactic analysis helps in the final screening of candidates. Psychoanalytic institutes do not want to waste their time on training people who may not be able to function well as psychoanalysts. No human being is perfect and, indeed, psychoanalysis aims at the strengthening of weak egos. However, disturbed individuals represent a risk, and psychoanalytic institutes apply a variety of screening methods aimed at initial selection of the best human material (Holt and Luborski, 1958; Lewin and Ross, 1960).

Needless to say, students start supervised psychoanalytic practice after they have met a substantial part of the course and seminar requirements, and have completed their own analysis, or become sufficiently advanced in it.

Upon graduation from a psychoanalytic institute, psychoanalysts receive diplomas and are admitted as regular professional members to the psychoanalytic association that runs the institute. There are several psychoanalytic associations, Freudian and neo-Freudian. Membership in one of these associations means professional recognition, but it does not confer legal status; the law controls the licensing of physicians and psychologists, but does not regulate postdoctoral training programs.

Nonmedical Psychoanalysts

Psychoanalysts with Ph.D. degrees receive their early training on different lines, while their actual psychoanalytic training is almost the same as that of their medical colleagues. A nonmedical psychoanalyst starts his undergraduate studies in a school of liberal arts and probably majors in psychology. He cannot, at this level, choose any special area of psychology. If he is an outstanding student, he has a chance of being admitted to one of the doctoral programs in clinical psychology approved by the American Psychological Association.

These doctoral programs require a minimum of four to five years, but usually they take more time. The training is geared toward a deepening of psychological knowledge with emphasis on personality development, psychopathology, and diagnostic and treatment methods. Some programs emphasize preparation for research, while others combine research issues with training for practice. Doctoral programs in clinical psychology usually offer one year of clinical practicum in diagnostic and therapeutic methods. On completion of course and practicum requirements and submission of a dissertation based on research, a Ph.D. degree is granted. To become certified or licensed, a clinical psychologist needs two additional years of supervised practicum and must pass a State Board examination. (For a detailed description see the *Handbook of Clinical Psychology,* Wolman, 1965c).

A certified clinical psychologist may become a psychoanalyst in the same way that a licensed psychiatrist follows—training in theory, supervised practice, and didactic analysis in a psychoanalytic institute.

THE M.D. VERSUS PH.D. CONTROVERSY

Two terms require classification in the discussion concerning what degree a psychoanalyst should earn. In German, doctor means physician; in the English language, however, the word can also refer to a dentist, a veterinarian, an optometrist, a doctor of divinity, a psychologist, or anyone who has obtained a doctoral degree in any area of human science. Thus it must be kept in mind that, whenever Freud wrote about "doctors," he had in mind physicians, or doctors of medicine. (The terms "layman" and "lay analysis" are poorly chosen, also, for someone is either a layman or he is a professional. In this country many medical psychoanalysts object to the practice of psychoanalysis by nonmedical professionals.)

The fact that psychoanalysis was invented by a physician is not coincidental. Pinel declared the inmates of mental asylums to be mentally "sick." This "sick role" saved them from brutality and delivered them into the hands of the healing profession. As explained in Chapter Eleven, this was a major humanitarian revolution, for it turned the care of mental disorder over to people whose attitude and knowledge prepared them best for this difficult task. Since Pinel, the treatment of mental disorders has become the domain of medicine, with emphasis on organic factors.

Freud came to mental disorders *via* research in neurology and general office practice. Though Freud's start was medical, his interests led him beyond the limits of the medical science and, to some extent, against it. Freud was opposed to the idea that psychoanalysis might ever be submerged in psychiatry; indeed, he counted several nonphysicians among his most gifted disciples.

In "Notes on the History of Lay Analysis," Eissler mentioned that in July 1910, seven among the twenty-two members of the Viennese Psychoanalytic Society were not physicians. Although it is not known how many of the seven practiced psychoanalysis, any one of them "could have analyzed if he had chosen [to do] so" (Eissler, 1965, p. 33). Moreover, at that time "there was no objection or mental reservation or doubt."

The event, however, that led to Freud's booklet, *The Question of Lay Analysis* (1926-1927) and thus to a public discussion of the whole issue, was the threat of court action by a patient against a most promising member of the Viennese Psychoanalytic Society, a prominent non-medical analyst, an outstanding scholar and a pupil of Freud's, the writer of psychoanalytic texts of great merit. The analyst was exonerated; no trial took place (*Ibid.*, pp. 33-34).

Freud was strongly opposed to viewing psychoanalysis as a medical specialty and, till the end of his life, he was against "the obvious American tendency to turn psychoanalysis into a mere housemaid of psychiatry" (Jones, 1953-1957, Vol. 3, p. 300).

Freud suggested an entirely different solution to the problem of training of psychoanalysts. He wrote:

If—which may sound fantastic today—one had to found a college of psychoanalysis, much would have to be taught in it which is also taught by the medical faculty: alongside of depth-psychology, which would always remain the principal subject, there would be an introduction to biology, as much as possible of the science of sexual life, and familiarity with the symptomatology of psychiatry. On the other hand, analytic instruction would include branches of knowledge which are remote from medicine and which the doctor does not come across in his practice: the history of civilization, mythology, the psychology of religion, and the science of literature. Unless he is well at home in these subjects, an analyst can make nothing of a large amount of his material. By way of compensation, the great mass of what is taught in medical schools is of no use to him for his purposes. A knowledge of the anatomy of the tarsal bones, of the constitution of the carbohydrates, of the course of the cranial nerves, a grasp of all that medicine has brought to light on bacilli as exciting causes of disease and the means of combating them, on serum reactions and on neoplasms—all this knowledge, which is undoubtedly of the highest value in itself, is nevertheless of no consequence to him; it does not concern him; it neither helps him directly to understand a neurosis and to cure it nor does it contribute to a sharpening of those intellectual capacities on which his occupation makes the greatest demands. It cannot be objected that the case is much the same when a doctor takes up some other special branch of medicine—dentistry, for instance; in that case, too, he may not need some of what he has to pass examinations in, and he will have to learn much in addition for which his schooling has not prepared him. But the two cases cannot be put on a par. In dentistry the great principles of pathology—the theories of inflammation, suppuration, necrosis, and the metabolism of the bodily organs—still retain their importance. But the experience of an analyst lies in another world, with other phenomena and other laws. However much philosophy may ignore the gulf between the physical and the mental, it still exists for our immediate experience and still more for our practical endeavors (1926-27, pp. 93-95).

And this is, perhaps, the road to the future.

References

ABRAHAM, K. Notes on the psycho-analytical investigation and treatment of manic-depressive insanity and allied conditions (1911). In K. Abraham, *Selected Papers on Psycho-analysis*. London: The Hogarth Press, 1949. Pp. 137-156.

ABRAHAM, K. A short study of the development of the libido, viewed in light of the mental disorders (1924). In *Ibid*. Pp. 418-501.

AICHHORN, A. *Wayward Youth*. New York: The Viking Press Inc., 1935.

ALEXANDER, F. *Fundamentals of Psychoanalysis*. New York: W. W. Norton & Company, Inc., 1948.

ALEXANDER, F. *Psychoanalysis and Psychotherapy*. New York: W. W. Norton & Company, Inc., 1956.

ALEXANDER, F. *The Scope of Psychoanalysis* (1921-1961). New York: Basic Books, Inc., Publishers, 1961.

ALEXANDER, F. and French, T. *Psychoanalytic Psychotherapy*. New York: The Ronald Press, 1946.

ARIETI, S. *Interpretation of Schizophrenia*. New York: Robert Bruner, 1955.

ARLOW, J., and Brenner, C. *Psychological Concepts and the Structural Theory*. New York: International Universities Press, Inc., 1964.

BALINT, M. Sandor Ferenczi's technical experiments. In B. B. Wolman, ed., *Psychoanalytic Techniques: A Handbook for the Practicing Psychoanalyst*. New York: Basic Books, Inc., Publishers, 1967.

BELLAK, L., and Benedict, P. K., eds. *Schizophrenia: A Review of the Syndrome*. New York: Logos Press, 1958. Pp. 7-8.

BERNSTEIN, A. The psychoanalytic technique. In B. B. Wolman ed., *Hand-*

book of Clinical Psychology. New York: McGraw-Hill Book Company, 1965. Pp. 1168-1199.

BETZ, BARBARA, and Whitehorn, J. C. The relationship of the therapist to the outcome of therapy in schizophrenia. *Psychiat. Res. Rep.*, 1956, 5, 89-105.

BREUER, J., and Freud, S. Studies on hysteria (1893-1895). In *The Standard Edition of the Complete Psychological Works of Sigmund Freud*. Vol. 2. London: The Hogarth Press and the Institute of Psycho-Analysis, 1962.

BRODY, E. B., and Redlich, F. C., eds. *Psychotherapy with Schizophrenics*. New York: International Universities Press, Inc., 1952.

BYCHOWSKI, G. *Psychotherapy of Psychosis*. New York: Grune & Stratton, Inc., 1952.

BYCHOWSKI, G. The problem of latent psychoses. *J. Amer. Psychoanal. Ass.*, 1953, 1, 484-503.

BYCHOWSKI, G. On the handling of some schizophrenic defense mechanisms and reaction patterns. *Int. J. Psychoanal.*, 1954, 35, 147-153.

BYKOV, K. M. *The Cerebral Cortex and the Internal Organs*. New York: Chemical Publishing Company, Inc., 1957.

CHARCOT, J. M. *Leçons sur les maladies sur le système nerveux*. Paris: 1887-1888.

EISSLER, K. R. *Medical Orthodoxy and the Future of Psychoanalysis*. New York: International Universities Press, Inc., 1965.

ERIKSON, E. *Childhood and Society*. (2nd ed.) New York: W. W. Norton & Company, Inc., 1963.

FEDERN, P. *Ego Psychology and the Psychoses*. New York: Basic Books, Publishers, Inc., 1952.

FENICHEL, O. *The Psychoanalytic Theory of Neurosis*. New York: W. W. Norton & Company, Inc., 1945.

FERENCZI, S. Stages in the development of the sense of reality (1913). In *The selected papers of Sandor Ferenczi*. Vol. 1. (*Sex in Psychoanalysis*.) New York: Basic Books, Publishers, Inc., 1950. Pp. 213-239.

FERENCZI, S. *Final Contributions to the Theory and Technique of Psychoanalysis*. New York: Basic Books, Publishers, Inc., 1955.

FRENCH, T. M. Introduction. In F. Alexander, *The Scope of Psychoanalysis*, 1921-1961. New York: Basic Books, Publishers, Inc., 1961.

FREUD, ANNA. *The Ego and the Mechanisms of Defense* (1936). London: The Hogarth Press, 1937.

FREUD, S. *The Origins of Psychoanalysis: Letters to Wilhelm Fliess, Drafts and Notes: 1887-1902.* (Marie Bonaparte, Anna Freud, and E. Kris, eds. Tr. by E. Mosbacher and J. Strachey.) New York: Basic Books, Publishers, Inc., 1954.

FREUD, S. The neuro-psychoses of defence (1894). In *The Standard Edition of the Complete Psychological Works of Sigmund Freud.* Vol. 3. London: The Hogarth Press and the Institute of Psycho-Analysis, 1962. Pp. 45-61.

FREUD, S. On the grounds for detaching a particular syndrome from neurasthenia under the description, "anxiety neurosis" (1895). In *Ibid.* Pp. 90-115.

FREUD, S. Further remarks on the neuropsychoses of defence (1896). In *Ibid.* Pp. 162-185.

FREUD, S. Sexuality in the aetiology of the neuroses (1898). In *Ibid.* Pp. 263-286.

FREUD, S. *The Interpretation of Dreams* (1900). In *Ibid.* Vol. 4. P. 337. Vol. 5. Pp. 339-627.

FREUD, S. *The Psychopathology of Everyday Life* (1901). In *Ibid.* Vol. 6. Pp. 1-279.

FREUD, S. *Freud's Psychoanalytic Procedure* (1904). In *Ibid.* Vol. 7. Pp. 249-256.

FREUD, S. *Jokes and Their Relation to the Unconscious* (1905a). In *Ibid.* Vol. 8. Pp. 9-238.

FREUD, S. *Three Essays on the Theory of Sexuality* (1905b). In *Ibid.* Vol. 7. Pp. 130-24.

FREUD, S. Fragment of an analysis of a case of hysteria (1905c). In *Ibid.* Vol. 7. Pp. 3-124.

FREUD, S. On psychotherapy (1905d). In *Ibid.* Vol. 7. Pp. 257-270.

FREUD, S. Character and anal erotism (1908). In *Ibid.* Vol. 9. Pp. 167-176.

FREUD, S. Analysis of a phobia in a five-year-old boy (1909). In *Ibid.* Vol. 10. Pp. 5-149.

FREUD, S. The future prospects of psychoanalytic therapy. (1910b). In *Ibid.* Vol. 11. Pp. 139-152.

FREUD, S. "Wild" psychoanalysis (1910c). In *Ibid.* Vol. 11. Pp. 219-230.

FREUD, S. The handling of dream-interpretation in psychoanalysis (1911). In *Ibid.* Vol. 12. Pp. 89-96.

FREUD, S. Recommendations to physicians practicing psychoanalysis (1912a). In *Ibid.* Vol. 12. Pp. 109-120.

FREUD, S. The dynamics of transference (1912b). In *Ibid*. Vol. 12. Pp. 109-120.

FREUD, S. *Totem and Taboo* (1913a). In *Ibid*. Vol. 13. Pp. 1-162.

FREUD, S. Further recommendations in the technique of psychoanalysis on beginning of treatment (1913b). In *Ibid*. Vol. 12. Pp. 121-144.

FREUD, S. The predisposition to obsessional neurosis (1913c). In *Ibid*. Vol. 13. Pp. 311-326.

FREUD, S. The history of the psychoanalytic movement (1914a). In *Ibid*. Vol. 14. Pp. 7-73.

FREUD, S. On narcissism: an introduction (1914b). In *Ibid*. Vol. 14. Pp. 73-102.

FREUD, S. Instincts and their vicissitudes (1915a). In *Ibid*. Pp. 117-145.

FREUD, S. The unconscious (1915b). In *Ibid*. Pp. 159-204.

FREUD, S. Observations of transference-love. (1915c). In *Ibid*. Vol. 12. Pp. 157-171.

FREUD, S. *A General Introduction to Psychoanalysis* (1915-1917). New York: Garden City, 1943.

FREUD, S. Some character types met with in psycho-analytic work (1916). In *The Standard Edition of the Complete Psychological Works of Sigmund Freud*. Vol. 14. London: The Hogarth Press and the Institute of Psycho-Analysis, 1962. Pp. 311-333.

FREUD, S. Mourning and melancholia (1917). In *Ibid*. Pp. 243-258.

FREUD, S. Turning in the ways of psychoanalytic therapy (1919a). In *Ibid*. Vol. 17. Pp. 157-168.

FREUD, S. Introduction to psychoanalysis and the war neuroses (1919b). In *Ibid*. Vol. 17. Pp. 205-210.

FREUD, S. *Beyond the Pleasure Principle* (1920a). In *Ibid*. Vol. 18. Pp. 7-64.

FREUD, S. The psychogenesis of a case of homosexuality in a woman (1920b). In *Ibid*. Vol. 18. Pp. 147-172.

FREUD, S. *Group Psychology and the Analysis of the Ego*. In *Ibid*. Vol. 18. Pp. 69-143.

FREUD, S. Remarks on the theory and practice of dream interpretation (1923a). In *Ibid*. Vol. 19. Pp. 109-124.

FREUD, S. *The Ego and the Id* (1923b). In *Ibid*. Vol. 19. Pp. 3-63.

FREUD, S. Neurosis and psychosis (1924). In *Ibid*. Vol. 19. Pp. 149-153.

FREUD, S. *Inhibitions, Symptoms and Anxiety* (1926). In *Ibid*. Vol. 20. Pp. 87-174.

FREUD, S. *The Future of an Illusion* (1927). In *Ibid*. Vol. 21. Pp. 5-56.

FREUD, S. *Civilization and Its Discontents* (1930). In *Ibid*. Vol. 21. Pp. 64-145.

FREUD, S. Female sexuality (1931). In *Ibid*. Vol. 21. Pp. 225-243.

FREUD, S. *New Introductory Lectures on Psychoanalysis* (1932). New York: W. W. Norton & Company, Inc., 1933.

FREUD, S. Construction in psychoanalysis (1937). In *Ibid*. Vol. 23. Pp. 257-269.

FREUD, S. *An Outline of Psychoanalysis* (1938). New York: W. W. Norton & Company, Inc., 1949.

FREUD, S. *Moses and Monotheism* (1939). New York: Alfred A. Knopf, Inc., 1939.

FREUD, S. *The Question of Lay Analysis* (1926-1927). New York: Doubleday & Company, Inc., 1964.

FROMM, E. and French, T. M. Formation and evaluation of hypotheses in dream interpretation. *J. Psychol.*, 1962, *54*, 271-283.

GILL, M. M. Topography and systems in psychoanalytic theory. *Psychol. Issues*, 1963, *3* (2).

GLOVER, E. *The Technique of Psychoanalysis*. New York: International Universities Press, Inc., 1955.

HARTMANN, H. *Ego Psychology and the Problem of Adaptation* (1939). New York: International Universities Press, Inc., 1958.

HARTMANN, H. Comments on the psychoanalytic theory of instinctual drives. *Psychoanal. Quart.*, 1948, *17*, 368-388.

HARTMANN, H. Comments on the psychoanalytic theory of the ego. In *The Psychoanalytic Study of the Child*. Vol. 5. New York: International Universities Press, Inc., 1950a. Pp. 74-96.

HARTMANN, H. Psychoanalysis and developmental psychology. In *Ibid*. Vol. 5. 1950b. Pp. 7-17.

HARTMANN, H., Kris, E. and Loewenstein, R. M. Comments on the formation of psychic structure. In *Ibid*. Vol. 2. 1946. Pp. 11-38.

HARTMANN, H., Kris, E., and Loewenstein, R. M. Notes on the theory of aggression. In *Ibid*. Vols. 3, 4. 1949. Pp. 9-36.

HARTMANN, H., and Loewenstein, R. M. Notes on the superego. In *Ibid*. Vol. 17. 1962. Pp. 42-81.

HOLT, R. R. and Luborski, L. *Personality Patterns of Psychiatrists.* 2 vols. New York: Basic Books, Publishers, Inc., 1958.

HOLT, R. R. A critical examination of Freud's concept of bound versus free cathexis. *J. Amer. Psychoanal. Ass.,* 1962, *10,* 475-525.

HOLT, R. R. Freud's cognitive style. *Amer. Imago,* 1965, 22, 163-179.

HORNEY, KAREN. *New Ways in Psychoanalysis.* New York: W. W. Norton, & Company, Inc., 1939.

JONES, E. *The Life and Works of Sigmund Freud.* Vol. 3. New York: Basic Books, Publishers, Inc., 1953.

JONES, E. *The Life and Works of Sigmund Freud.* Vol. 3. New York: Basic Books, Publishers, Inc., 1957.

KRIS, E. On preconscious mental processes. *Psychoanal. Quart.,* 1950, *19,* 540-560.

KRIS, E. *Psychoanalytic Explorations in Art.* New York: International Universities Press, Inc., 1952.

LEWIN, B. J. and Ross, Helen. *Psychoanalytic Education in the United States.* New York: W. W. Norton & Company, Inc., 1960.

LOEWENSTEIN, R. M. The problem of interpretation. *Psychoanal. Quart.,* 1951, 20, 1-14.

NUNBERG, H. and Federn, E. *Minutes of the Vienna Psychoanalytic Society.* New York: International Universities Press, Inc., 1962.

PANEL. Some theoretical aspects of early psychic functioning. *J. Amer. psychoanal. Ass.,* 1959, 7, 561-576.

PAVLOV, I. P. *Lectures on Condition Reflexes.* New York: Liveright, 1928.

PRIBRAM, K. H. The neuropsychology of Sigmund Freud. In A. J. Bachrach, ed., *Experimental Foundations of Clinical Psychology.* New York: Basic Books, Publishers, Inc., 1962.

RANK, O. *The Myth of the Birth of the Hero* (1913). New York: Robert Bruner, 1952.

RANK, O. *The Trauma of Birth* (1924). New York: Harcourt, Brace & World, Inc., 1929.

REICH, W. *Character Analysis.* New York: Orgone Press, 1945.

SELESNICK, S. The technique of psychoanalysis developed by Franz Alexander and Thomas. In B. B. Wolman, ed., *Psychoanalytic Techniques: A Handbook for the Practicing Psychoanalyst.* New York: Basic Books, Publishers, Inc., 1967a.

SNYDER, F. The organismic state associated with dreaming. In N. S. Greenfield and W. C. Lewis, eds., *Psychoanalysis and Current Biological Thought.* Madison: University of Wisconsin Press, 1965. Pp. 275-316.

SPITZ, R. A. Countertransference. *J. Amer. Psychoanal. Ass.,* 1956, *4,* 256-265.

STRACHEY, J. The nature of the therapeutic action of psychoanalysis. *Int. J. Psychoanal.,* 1934, *15,* 127-159.

SULLIVAN, H. S. Sociopsychiatric research. *Amer. J. Psychiat.,* 1931, *10,* 77-91.

SULLIVAN, H. S. *Conceptions of Modern Psychiatry.* Washington, D.C.: White, 1947.

TARACHOW, S. and Stein, A. Psychoanalytic psychotherapy. In B. B. Wolman, ed., *Psychoanalytic Techniques: A Handbook for the Practicing Psychoanalyst.* New York: Basic Books, Publishers, Inc., 1967a.

THOMPSON, CLARA. The role of the analyst's personality. *Amer. J. Psychother.* 1956, *10,* 356-362.

WHYTE, L. L. *The Unconscious before Freud.* New York: Basic Books, Publishers, Inc., 1960.

WOLMAN, B. B. Psychoanalysis without libido. *Amer. J. Psychother.,* 1954, *8,* 21-31.

WOLMAN, B. B. Remarks. *Amer. J. Psychother.,* 1956, *10,* 363-366.

WOLMAN, B. B. Evidence in psychoanalytic research. *J. Amer. Psychoanal.* 1957, 11, 560-588.

WOLMAN, B. B. *Contemporary Theories and Systems in Psychology.* New York: Harper & Row, Publishers, 1960.

WOLMAN, B. B. Evidence in psychoanalytic research. *J. Amer. Psychoanal. Ass.,* 1964, 12, 717-733. (a)

WOLMAN, B. B. Non-participant observation on a closed ward. *Acta Psychotherapeutica,* 1964, *12,* 61-71. (b)

WOLMAN, B. B. Toward a science of psychological science. In B. B. Wolman and E. Nagel, eds., *Scientific Psychology: Principles and Approaches.* New York: Basic Books, Publishers, Inc., 1965a.

WOLMAN, B. B. Principles of monistic transitionism. In *Ibid.* 1965b.

WOLMAN, B. B. Schizophrenia and related disorders. In B. B. Wolman, ed., *Handbook of Clinical Psychology.* New York: McGraw-Hill Book Company, 1965c.

WOLMAN, B. B. *Vectoriasis Praecox or the Group of Schizophrenias.* Springfield, Ill.: Charles C. Thomas, Publisher, 1966a.

WOLMAN, B. B. *Eros and Ares: A Study of Love and Hate.* New York: (In press.) 1967a.

WOLMAN, B. B. The historical role of Johann Friedrich Herbart. In B. B. Wolman, ed., *Historical Roots of Contemporary Psychology.* New York: Harper & Row, Publishers, 1967b.

WOLMAN, B. B., ed. *Psychoanalytic Techniques: A Handbook for the Practicing Psychoanalyst.* New York: Basic Books, Publishers, Inc., 1967c.

ZILBOORG, G. and Henry, G. *A History of Medical Psychology.* New York: W. W. Norton & Company, Inc., 1941.

Index

233

DATE DUE			
FEB 12 '73	DE 30 03		
NOV 8 '73	AP 26 05		
DEC 18 '73			
DEC 17 '76			
MAR 9 1981			
NO 15 '89			
NO 15 '89			
JA 22 '91			
FE 20 '91			
NO 1 '91			
JY 05 '92			
8-19-92			
SE 20 '92			
OCT 25 '94			
MAY 4 '96			
11/18/96			
GAYLORD			PRINTED IN U.S.A.